Making a Miracle

Making a Miracle

HUNTER TYLO

POCKET BOOKS

New York London Toronto Sydney Singapore

POCKET BOOKS, a division of Simon & Schuster Inc.
1230 Avenue of the Americas, New York, NY 10020

Library of Congress Cataloging-in-Publication Data

Tylo, Hunter.
   Making a miracle / Hunter Tylo.
      p.   cm.
   ISBN: 0-671-02778-6
   1. Tylo, Hunter.   2. Television actors and actresses—
United States—Biography.   I. Title.

   PN2287.T95 A3 2000
   791.43'028'092—dc21
   [B]   99-057477

First Pocket Books hardcover printing March 2000

10   9   8   7   6   5   4   3   2   1

POCKET and colophon are registered trademarks of
Simon & Schuster Inc.

Book design by Jessica Shatan

Printed in the U.S.A.

*To the beautiful woman who shared her body with me
for nine months and gave me life in this world . . .*

*. . . and the beautiful children God has blessed me with
for helping me learn to appreciate life.*

Acknowledgments

The task of writing about your own life in an honest and truthful way, in spite of shortcomings, mistakes and faux pas, is painstaking, at best. I want to thank Harold Fickett for the hours and days and months of helping me formulate my words and accurately portray what I call "my testimony." The victories are easy to remember, but where we fall short in our lives—well, I know too well how we all would rather blot that part out. Harold so gently and patiently treaded through much quicksand with me, wiping away many tears. Thank you for making it easier.

An extension of that thanks goes to another extremely talented writer, Philip Yancey who ever so kindly sent Harold to me. He is everything you said he would be, Philip.

So many people have believed in me when everyone else abandoned me. Some of those people are: Marv Dauer, Scott Harris, David Rose, Nevin Dolcefino, Gloria Allred, Dolores Leal, Nathan Goldberg and Jody Stein.

Special thanks goes to the entire Bell Family for their belief in me and support. Bradley Bell has shown integrity and enthusiasm for working mothers and their families in a way I will never forget (and no one should for that matter!).

I want to thank each and every one of my jury members during my trial. I was so aware of the time away from your work and away from your families during what was a special time of the year—yet each one of you stayed committed and focused on Justice. May God bless you and your families for that.

Jane Cavolina is to be greatly credited. Where she perceptively felt there were "gaps" or need for more detail to connect time frames, it truly added richness and honesty to the book. Her demand for perfection was a challenge at times, but she was a pleasure to work with. I wish her the best in her future endeavors.

During this year and a half trek of compiling information, tracking down photos and editing material, much of my time with family and friends has been usurped. To my best friend Carla, whom I adore, I am sorry for being late returning phone calls. All my friends in Las Vegas and my brothers Cliff and Jay, and sister Elizabeth, thank you for loving me even though you haven't heard from me for months!

The patience and love shown to me by Michael, Chris, Mickey, Izabella and Katya has meant more to me than they will ever know. Of course without them much of this book would never have been possible since much of it is *about* them. Michael especially has shown the true depth of his love by helping me recall difficult events and giving them clarity.

Since I believe that prayer is the most powerful weapon we have, I must thank my pastoral prayer partners Dr. Jack and Carole Hamilton, Dr. Jack and Anna Hayford, and Pastor Jim and Diane Nelson.

Last, but certainly first—I am most grateful to the most high Son of God: Jesus Christ. Even though I am not perfect, with Your grace, You love me perfectly. I thank You for being my strength and my shield, but most of all for being my salvation.

Part One

Part One

1

My husband, Michael, and I were asked by our friends Gigi and Bill Smith to present the annual award for best sleight-of-hand magician at the Magic Castle Awards in Los Angeles on Saturday, March 23, 1996. Bill Smith builds many of the magic props for David Copperfield, Lance Burton, and other international magic acts. So I flew into Los Angeles from our home in Las Vegas early on Friday to pick up a gown from CBS wardrobe. For the past six years, I had played a lead character, the psychiatrist Taylor Hayes, on the soap opera *The Bold and the Beautiful.* The producers were always kind enough to help out with dresses for public appearances.

I got up about 4:30 A.M. for my early flight and I remember feeling not quite right. The cup of coffee I had on the plane upset my stomach and the short flight seemed much longer.

I took a taxi to the one-bedroom apartment that Michael and I maintained close to the CBS studios for those weeks when our shooting schedules spanned several days, as they often did. When I entered the apartment, I couldn't help but notice the rank smell. I love reptiles and have kept everything from chameleons to snakes as pets. At the time, I had a tegu, which is a fantastic black-and-white speckled lizard that looks like a baby Komodo dragon or alligator. They are gorgeous and they need minimal attention—a reptile mostly takes care of itself. But I knew I had to clean this tegu's filthy cage pronto. His food—Japanese hooded rats—made for furry droppings with a smell that would turn up a skunk's nose. For years, I thought I was going to be a veterinarian, and when I was in high school I assisted at a clinic. I've cleaned up after a lot of animals and none of it has ever bothered me. But that day, the cage stunk worse than I could remember.

I went to get the pooper scooper and started shoveling, but before I knew it, I was running to the toilet to throw up.

At that moment, my only thought was, I've never had a tegu before and I didn't know they became that gross as they matured—he was about three feet long then. (I had raised this lizard from a baby.) In a little while, I started feeling better. I even went down to the pet shop to replenish the tegu's food supply.

I went to CBS studios soon after the building opened and picked out a green velvet gown with rhinestones across the bodice. The fabric was stretchy and clingy and flattering. The seamstress in wardrobe needed to make a few adjustments, and we agreed that I'd return that afternoon to pick it up.

Then I went over to the Beverly Center. One of the stores had in new waist-length necklaces with silver cross pendants. One had a long chain studded with rhinestones, which would go perfectly with my gown. I liked the thought of wearing the cross because it wasn't simply decorative to me; I believed in what it stood for.

When I came home, I changed my clothes again, and I noticed that my bra fit too tightly. My boobs were really big. The seamstress had even said something about it.

I was beginning to get the pregnant message but still resisting. It can't be, I thought. It can't.

I remembered that last night I had chosen not to have a glass of wine with dinner. I knew that my period might be late, but I hadn't really counted, and yet I had still chosen to be careful. But the possibility was so far-fetched—almost impossible, for reasons that had to do with my health history.

I retrieved my calendar and started counting. I'm a twenty-six-dayer. Practically on the hour, every month. I remembered that my last period coincided with Valentine's Day. We had scheduled our romantic time after that, because I had anticipated nature's interference. I looked at my calendar for the following weeks. How many days? More than twenty-six?

I also remembered that I had come down with the flu around the twenty-second of February, while Michael was out of town helping a college in Pennsylvania develop a new TV and film department. I was so sick—running a temperature of 105 degrees—that I had lost almost ten pounds and couldn't work that week. An illness like that should have scrambled my hormones, making pregnancy even less likely.

Still, Michael and I had managed a romantic weekend—a sexorama, in fact.

I remembered that when Michael returned from his business trip, he wanted to be romantic. I was still so weak from being sick that I didn't have his enthusiasm, but I thought, okay, this is the only weekend we're going to have together before I've got to go back to L.A. and make up for all the days I've missed at work, so let's take advantage of our time together.

I also thought, fat chance I'll ever get pregnant. Two years before, Michael had reversed his vasectomy, as our marriage was resurrected from near death and he became willing, once more, to have another child: perhaps the girl we had always wanted. Although we had tried basic procedures to overcome our temporary infertility—like taking my temperature and saving time for ourselves whenever I was ovulating—nothing had happened. At this point, we had practically given up hope for a new baby. Michael stopped getting his sperm count taken and we decided not to use techniques like in vitro fertilization or fertility drugs. These struck us as taking the gift of life too much into our own hands.

We had spent our Valentine's weekend together mostly in bed—

a beautiful bed that Michael bought us from Ethan Allen—a French-country canopy bed. It was very similar to the bedroom furniture from the Saint Regis Hotel we stayed at in Paris on one of our second honeymoons. It had very soft, cream-colored sheer drapery on top that flowed down in curtains at each corner. Our bedroom in Las Vegas—in the dream home we had nearly destroyed each other building—was just as romantic, with a fireplace surrounded by Kohler tiles that had bunnies on them. (Yes, the choice expressed how strongly I wanted a child.) The room's giant bay window had massive plantation-style shutters, which opened on a view of the Strip, flashing and twinkling in the distance. For mood music, Michael put on Dean Martin. His musical taste runs to early rock and fifties jazz and mine to Led Zeppelin and the Stones; but when we want to turn each other's fingers and toes into Roman candles, it's "That's Amore!" for us. I remembered that weekend very well indeed, the crackling fire overcoming the chill of those desert nights. Our bedroom, I reflected, might have proved a perfect love nest after all.

I started feverishly counting again. I couldn't seem to bring that calendar into exact focus. I was thinking that I had left out a Saturday or should the first week start on a Saturday or Sunday and did that make a difference? One way or another, my count kept adding up to *late*—four or five days late. I became more and more excited, although I didn't want to get my hopes up needlessly, as I had many times in the past. Yet every other concern in my life simply dissolved. I sat there and I realized I was living totally in hormone land—major motherhood hormone land. I felt the elation coming, the sheer joy. We'll have a baby in the house again. A baby! But then I told myself to calm down and find out if I had reason to hope or if I was just freaking out.

I went to the drugstore and bought an over-the-counter pregnancy test. From the start of the test, a faint second line began to cross a more prominent line. Was that line coming or going? Thirty minutes later, there was an X in the window. I couldn't believe it. I was in the apartment's small bathroom, which echoed, and I yelled loud enough to rattle the coffee cups of my neighbors.

Oh my gosh. Oh my gosh! *Oh my gosh!* I'm pregnant. I was ec-static and my mind flew off in a thousand happy directions.

How would I tell Michael? And my boys, Chris and Mickey? The boys wanted a new baby brother or sister, too, and they were going to flip out! I knew I had a new job on the nighttime show *Melrose Place,* but I would take care of myself and give the producers plenty of notice. A new baby and a new job, what could be better? Michael and I had been contemplating moving back to Los Angeles, and now we would have even more incentive for the move. We would get a bigger place, with a new nursery, and we'd hear the baby coo-ing in her crib in the mornings and bring her into bed with us—even the all-night feedings felt at that moment like a blessing. To bring a new life into the world and have her in our home! I couldn't contain myself. I had never felt happier.

I went back to the drugstore and bought pink and blue and some purple and yellow ribbon. I strung this through the little hole at the end of the pregnancy-test stick, gathered the ribbons and tied them into a bow, then curled the ends with scissors. I bought a bag with a little baby angel on it and a small porcelain plaque of Noah's ark with the legend, "Shh, baby's sleeping." I wrapped the test stick and the plaque in tissue and put it in the baby angel bag and considered how to keep from busting a seam before Michael and the boys arrived on a midday flight.

It was finally time to go to the Burbank airport. I picked up Michael and the boys, virtually humming with excitement. They could see I was keeping a big secret and asked me what was up. I wouldn't tell them until we arrived back at the apartment.

Once there, I assembled them all in the living room and sat them down on the couch. "Okay," I said. "What's the most exciting thing that could happen to this family?"

Our nine-year-old, Mickey, instantly asked, "Did you win Ed McMahon's sweepstakes?"

"You got a Steven Spielberg movie," his older brother, Chris, said, guessing.

"What have we all been waiting for—for a long time?" I asked.

They kept thinking I had won a car or landed a role or had

bought them a horse—something material. Finally, I held up the bag to Michael. "Go ahead, honey, this is your present. I want you to open it."

Michael kept looking at me as if I were nuts. He looked inside the bag and pulled out the plaque. "Shh, baby's sleeping." He looked back at me, squinting his eyes, getting the idea. He put the plaque aside. Then he pulled out the test stick. "It can't be," he said. "It can't!"

"Yes! Yes! Yes! We're going to have a baby!"

The boys' eyes got big and they kept saying "Oh, wow!" and they started jumping up and down in absolute glee.

"We're going to have a baby brother!" Mickey said.

"No, a sister," Chris said.

"*A brother.*"

"What do you want, Mom?" Chris asked.

Michael had pulled me into an embrace. I stopped kissing him long enough to say, "It's going to be a girl."

2

ichael, the boys, and I returned to Las Vegas early Sunday morning. Michael and I began discussing how we should tell people about the pregnancy and when. I was afraid, as all women are in the early stages of pregnancy, that I might miscarry and was inclined to guard our privacy for a while longer. But I knew I needed to call my manager, Marv Dauer, and discuss the situation with him, particularly in regard to my new job on *Melrose Place*. (I had informed *The Bold and the Beautiful* that I wouldn't be coming back for the next season, as I had taken the *Melrose* job, and the show's writers had disentangled my character from six years of story lines to the point that I was only working about one day a week. The pregnancy would have little impact on finishing out my run at *B&B* through the end of May.)

I called Marv to tell him the big news.

"So what do you think, Marv?" I asked. "Shall we tell the Spelling people at *Melrose Place* right away? I would like to make sure everything's okay first. I haven't even been to the doctor."

"I understand, Hunter," Marv said, "but I think we'd better give them a call. That way the writers can start figuring out what you're going to be doing for the next four years. Maybe even give your character a name."

I knew he was right. "Okay, Marv," I said, "but let's not tell anyone else."

"No, no. No one else."

"No press, Marv."

"Hunter, come on. Would I do that?"

I trust Marv, but sometimes I feel I have to emphasize certain things, to guard against misunderstandings. "Just don't get out on the golf course and start joking around about it."

"Look, Hunter, I'll call the Spelling people. No one else."

"Let me know what they say."

"Well, of course. I'll get back to you."

I didn't hear from Marv for a day or two, and then on Friday, he called back. "I talked to the producer, Frank South," Marv said, "and . . . I guess the only thing I can say is, he's not happy."

"He's not happy?"

"No."

"What do you mean? What's he not happy about?"

"He's not happy about the news."

"What did you say to him? *Exactly.*" As someone who's inevitably in the middle of adversarial parties, Marv tries to make everyone happy, but sometimes his gruff-voiced bonhomie can be annoying, if you don't love him as I do.

"Well," Marv said, going on, "I told Frank that he wasn't going to believe what I was about to tell him. And then I told him you were pregnant and he just—he goes—he just basically told me he's not happy."

"So what's the next step? He must want to talk to Aaron or somebody."

"He was on his car phone. He was on his way home from a meeting at Fox and he felt like this might throw a wrench in some of the network's plans. He was surprised—sort of in shock."

"In shock? About a woman getting pregnant?"

"He told me he didn't think this was going to work, but I think it was the shock of the thing—the surprise. I'm sure it will work out. It can't be that big a deal."

"Marv, are you hearing what you're saying?"

"Look, I'll call this other guy over at Spelling Entertainment, Steve Tan. He'll give me a better read on how they're going to figure this thing out. I'll call you back as soon as I reach him. He's a good guy."

"Okay," I said, but I started getting nervous.

I waited through the weekend without hearing anything more. Then a week went by with no word.

I called Marv again. "What's going on?"

"I don't know," he said. "Nobody's available. Nobody's returning my calls. It's weird."

"Did you talk to that Steve Tan guy?"

"Yeah, he was a little irritated about the situation. But he didn't say much, really. I'm sure they're just figuring how to work this out. I'm sure it's no big deal."

"Why don't you call Frank South and ask him to talk with me? I'm sure I can allay their fears, if they'll just talk."

Marv tried, but he called back shortly to tell me no one would call back. "I don't know what's going on," he admitted. "Something's a little strange, but they can work this out. They're probably rewriting some stuff and waiting until they get clearances from everybody—from the network as well as Spelling—before they talk to us. That's probably what's happening."

I had never heard of an actress's pregnancy causing a problem. In fact, I knew that television shows use camera angles and body doubles and write or rewrite scripts to deal with such situations. As far as I knew, the *Melrose Place* producers had a very sketchy idea of the role I would be playing, which should have given them maximum latitude in dealing with the pregnancy.

My new job on *Melrose Place* had come about as the result of two things: hard work and a calculated risk. As I said, for six years I had been playing Taylor Hayes on *The Bold and the Beautiful,* and for the last four of these I had been working with an acting coach, Ivana Chubbuck, to improve my acting skills. The additional work with my coach had already paid off. Both the writers on *B&B* and the show's viewers took a new interest in my character once I stopped, under Ivana's tutelage, depending on certain crutches— mostly stock responses and gestures—and expanded my emo- tional range. I learned how to use my life experiences—through what's generally known as method acting—to bring genuine reac- tions to staged situations. Not only did our audience notice the dif- ference, but I began to find acting a far more fulfilling profession.

After six years, I began to feel that I had played Taylor Hayes in- side and out, and wanted a chance to explore new characters. I was also looking toward prime-time television, because the shooting schedule would allow more time with my family. In daytime, we shoot fifty weeks out of the year—there are no such things as re- runs or a hiatus for that matter. A prime-time show would also boost my earning potential and be a way into other venues, like movies of the week and maybe films. I wanted to see what I could do—how good I could become—as an actress. As to fame, I had already known enough celebrity to understand it's a mixed bless- ing—that wasn't my motivation. In Hollywood, as in most in- dustries, it happens that the spotlight shines brightest on those with the best working conditions.

In soap opera circles, making a move from daytime to prime time is called "catching the big-time bus"—a tongue-in-cheek way to joke about our hidden aspirations. A lot of actors have done it, including Demi Moore, Meg Ryan, Lauren Holly, and *NYPD Blue*'s Kim Delaney. Of course, a lot of soap opera actors have also taken their turn reaching for the brass ring only to find themselves nowhere. It was a scary thing I was attempting, as it involved re- signing a secure and financially rewarding job in favor of a venue in which I had only done a few guest spots.

Still, I wanted to try. In the late fall of 1995, I started working with my new manager, Marv Dauer, who promised to arrange a series of "go-sees"—getting-to-know-you meetings—with casting directors. Right away, Marv proved his worth. For several months, he and I were running all over town. We were hoping that I'd be cast in a TV pilot during the early spring and that the show would then be picked up by a major network. From the beginning, we were concerned that I not only land a part but the right part. I hoped to be in a show in which I could play a talented woman with strong convictions and a sense of humor.

In January of 1996, Marv and I had a one o'clock appointment with Pam Shae, the casting director for Spelling Entertainment, Inc. Spelling's list of hits goes back to *Mission: Impossible* and *Charlie's Angels,* and continues through *Beverly Hills 90210* and *Melrose Place.* The head of the company, Aaron Spelling, is famous for many things, including owning a home that is frequently likened to an exclusive hotel. His office building on Wilshire Boulevard was just as luxurious and impressive.

Most casting directors are located away from the production studios, in linoleum offices that look like those of insurance agents except for the production posters on the walls. But Pam Shae was in-house, in the big glass house with manicured grounds and highly visible guards. This was heavy-duty. I was already nervous.

When Marv and I had talked about where we might find work, I mentioned that I had worked for Spelling in the past. I had done a guest spot on a *Burke's Law* episode that Aaron must have particularly liked, because he had sent me a bottle of champagne—expensive Cristal champagne—and then hired me back for another spot on the same show within the same season—something the show's director told me Spelling never did. He sent a handwritten letter saying, "I would love to work with you," and that I should let him know when I was available. Marv thought that was great, and called Pam Shae and told her that indeed my contract with *The Bold and the Beautiful* would be up in less than five months.

Earlier that day, as I prepared for the appointment, my anxiety started to build. For most other appointments, I would dress down, with very little makeup, trying to break the soap opera image. But Spelling's shows often relied to a high degree on glamour—he wouldn't mind the upscale look so much. But I didn't want to leave the casting director with the idea that soap opera was all I could do. I had to present myself as glamorous and something more—I couldn't let her think of me as another pretty piece of set design.

I felt safest wearing some leggings, with a short skirt over that, and a jacket for the professional touch. All in all, a cute, trendy little outfit. And sexy. I put on more makeup than usual.

Still, I was a little self-conscious because I was slightly overweight. I hadn't been exercising as I should have. It was just after Christmas and the holidays, and though I usually weigh 107 pounds, I was about 118 then. The weight didn't look that bad, because the first extra ten pounds or so usually goes right into my boobs and I get a little shapelier in my arms and legs, which are—to non-Hollywood observers—quite thin. In fact, at my "ideal weight" most people ask me that "Are you eating enough?" question. Still, I wished I had been exercising more.

Marv and I stepped off the elevator onto this beautiful cream plush carpet in a giant hallway. Before us were thick glass doors with long brass handles. Everything was flattered by soft, recessed lighting.

Going through the doors, we reached a humongous reception desk with a beautiful gal sitting back there catching phone calls. She was busy, dreadfully busy. She was so busy she had to put up her hand like a traffic cop to halt us. Who are you? the receptionist's look said. I'll be with you in a moment—if you're lucky.

The office's wood-paneled walls had niches that held pictures spotlighted by discreet brass fixtures. The place reminded me of a Wall Street law firm. There were comfy, designer-upholstered couches and armchairs with wooden armrests—all with matching throw pillows—in impromptu seating areas, and everywhere, everywhere, the trained lenses of security cameras.

The receptionist said, "Why don't you just have a seat and Ms. Shae will be with you in a minute."

We sat down and I was so nervous that I thought I'd better run to the rest room. Somebody came out of an inner door to the left and through the door I caught a glimpse of a large, stainless-steel kitchen. Someone in a chef's hat was cooking in there!

Out of another door walked a man who was partially balding and wore wire-rimmed glasses. He appeared to be headed somewhere else, but then he noticed Marv.

"Hey, Marv! How are you doing?"

Marv stood up and they shook hands and gave each other a pat on the shoulder. "This is Jonathan Levin, Hunter. Jonathan is president here."

Marv looked at me like, get the message? Hello? Perk up.

Jonathan extended his hand to me and said, "You're right, Marv. She's absolutely beautiful, even in person."

I thought, Okay, good, it's going great.

Jonathan Levin was wearing an expensive, hand-tailored suit and had the aura of someone not only worldly but trendy. Even though he was a little older, he was a happening thing. He had an air of complete confidence. I knew that Marv and he had done a bit of skirt chasing together in their bachelor days.

I tried to respond to all the chumminess in kind as the chitchat went on. I said things like, "Marv tells me you two have had some wild times together." What I was really thinking was, don't do anything stupid. Push your hair back now, but *jeez*, don't poke yourself in the eye or anything! I could hardly move.

Jonathan said, "You know, Hunter, Aaron loves you. It's hard to find someone who is beautiful and funny and who can actually act. Your work is great. Especially that spot you did on *Burke's Law.*"

I was beside myself with excitement, my heart flew like a hummingbird's, and now I really did have to go to the bathroom.

"Do you know where the bathroom is?" I asked oh-so-daintily. I wanted to get out of there. I needed to get out of there.

"You'll have to ask the receptionist," Jonathan said. "She'll have to unlock the doors for you. Very nice to meet you, Hunter. I do hope we'll be working together."

The trip to the bathroom was bizarre. The receptionist gave me directions that seemed more complicated than trying to get from one place to another in Rome. A left, a right, another left, another, another, another.

I trailed my way through the maze. The hallways were full of large, ominous doors with no nameplates or other designations. I was thinking, gosh, what's going on behind all these doors? They're talking about working with so and so and writing this script and oh, they're probably producing something really huge right now. Maybe I should pretend that I've walked in the wrong room by accident. Just walk right in and go, "Whoops! Sorry!" But better judgment saved me—plus my nerves wouldn't have allowed me to pull it off.

Somehow I found the outside bathroom door. I had to stand there, push a buzzer, let the camera register me for the receptionist's video screen, and then have her push the buzzer to open the door. (There was a James Bond–style hand-recognition scanner there, too, but it only worked for Spelling's people.)

I heard the buzzing and opened the door. I had to make another turn or two before finally seeing "Ladies."

I went into this luxurious bathroom with marble sinks and recessed lighting and I remember standing in the privacy of a stall, my arms folded, taking more than a few deep breaths. Here I am, I thought. Something in my life is changing. My career is going to take off!

Okay, I told myself, calm down.

I washed my hands. I checked my lipstick. My makeup. I was fixing everything now. I tried to give myself a makeover by recessed lighting. I put my face right up to the glass, making sure my eyes weren't red, my eyeliner didn't look stupid, my lip liner was straight, and that I didn't have anything between my teeth.

Finally, I was ready to go out and through the maze back to the offices. When I arrived, Pam Shae was standing there with Marv. She looked at me like, Hello? You okay?

I pleaded getting lost in the maze. "I'm so sorry. It's a big place here."

"Oh, yes," she said. "I needed a map for a month."

Then she took us back to her office.

I picked up the small, thin briefcase I carry for such appointments—mainly, just to look professional—and we went into the inner offices, which were much more like the standard offices and half-walled cubicles of corporate America.

Pam Shae's corner office, where the fourth wall was glass, allowed a view of the interior, forest-like atrium of the building. Piles of trade publications and magazines and even *Soap Opera Digest* were scattered around—it was her job to check everybody out. I tried to think of an interview or photo shoot lately that might be in one of these publications. Something I could make a fast, casual reference to. Then I remembered all the articles about my past marital difficulties with Michael and I forgot about making coy allusions. Pam's office was also stocked with photographs of beautiful models, which made me mindful of the competition—the thousand and one women who wanted to be seated where I was at that moment.

Pam Shae had blond hair, cut shoulder-length, with a soft wave to it in a casual style. She wore slacks and was nicely turned out, with expertly matched accessories.

She didn't conduct the interview as an interrogation, but proceeded as if we were friends having a chat. Marv and she spoke of their mutual acquaintances. Then, without sounding too formal or as if she were prying, she turned to me and asked, "Now tell me, Hunter, when is your contract with *The Bold and the Beautiful* over?"

"In June. But you know, Pam, I have an 'out,' for pilots or a movie of the week." My "out" meant that I could take three to six weeks off from *B&B* before the contract expired.

Pam had a notepad and she scribbled this down.

"So I can do a pilot," I said, "and then if the show gets picked up, I'll be available in July for the start of production."

This was going so well, I asked, "What type of things do you have coming up?"

"Well, you know, I was just thinking there's a movie of the week you'd be perfect for. But I don't know if they've already selected somebody. It shoots in North Carolina and you probably can't go away that far while you're still working on *The Bold and the Beautiful.* But don't worry. There's a lot of product coming along. And Aaron loves you. He absolutely loves you."

I kept hearing this.

"He's here today, you know," Pam said. "Does he know you're here today, Hunter?"

Search me, I thought.

"I'll let him know you're here. We'll have him step in or we'll step over to his office and just say hi. That would be great if he could just say hi, because he really admires your work. That *Burke's Law* episode. He keeps talking about it. How fast you nailed that part. How funny you were."

We chatted some more and then she said, "Let me go get Aaron."

She stepped out and was gone for about ten minutes.

Marv and I looked at one another, our eyes wide. I knew we were both thinking, *Isn't this a trip?*

"This place is unbelievable," Marv said.

"What's the deal with all the surveillance cameras?" Then I thought, uh-oh, they could have taped that last statement. I glanced up and smiled for whoever might be watching.

"Look at that atrium, Hunter. What an office this is! Didn't I tell you Pam Shae was a powerful person? This is going to change things, I'm telling you. Your life won't be the same after today. They really love you here."

The big-time bus: Would it arrive in the person of Aaron Spelling? Right then, I certainly thought so.

"And I know Jonathan Levin," Marv went on. "He'll do everything he can to help you. He was just telling me while you went off to the rest room that he just thought you were out of this world. This is amazing. This is *it!*"

I began thinking of how I should appear when Aaron Spelling walked into the room. Should I be standing? Should I be casual, strike a pose with my hand on my knee? Should I act as if I met Steven Spielberg every other day?

Then Pam came back in alone. "I'm sorry, Hunter, Marv. Aaron must have just stepped out for a late lunch. He's going to be mad that he missed you, I know. I tried to find him, but he could be anywhere in this place."

I could believe that.

"I'm going to leave him a note. I'm going to tell him that we had a great meeting and that you are available. He's going to be ecstatic, believe me. I'm sure we'll be able to find something for you. Don't worry."

3

One week before our meeting with Pam Shae, I had auditioned for a new show for Disney and NBC that was being launched by the *Baywatch* production company. Their Santa Monica casting offices were located in a building indistinguishable from an apartment complex, which was normal for Hollywood, but a far cry from Spelling Entertainment's atrium-cored skyscraper. I remember stepping into the offices and staring up at a huge poster of Pamela Lee in an extremely tight black leather suit that showed off her bodacious cleavage. When I looked around the office, I saw it was filled with Pamela Lee wanna-bes, all in spandex and frosty pink lipstick. There were also pictures of Yasmine Bleethe, whom I had known casually in New York, and I reminded myself that her career had taken off as a result of *Baywatch*.

The part I was auditioning for actually had more to it than posing in swimsuits. I would be playing a brainy and beautiful astronaut, a woman who was still something of a tomboy, who had a terrific sense of humor. As I memorized my "sides" (the auditioning script) for the role, I came to like the character more and more.

The first audition went well and the *Baywatch* folks called me back for a second audition, which came after the meeting Marv and I had with Pam Shae. This time, the room had a lot more people in it, and I made sure that I had worked out some new "business"—actions that go along with the dialogue—that the producers suggested. The new people in the room were all from Disney or the network—they were "suits," power brokers.

The network people expressed appreciation for my reading, but they were far more interested in talking to me personally. In their formal way, they asked me about my life. I knew this was a routine part of interviews and that, for the network, casting came down to the actor's TVQ—how likable the actor might be and to what segment of the viewing audience.

"You have a child in high school?" they asked, incredulous.

"A fourteen-year-old. And I also have a son in grammar school."

"Really. You look so great. Like you've never even had a kid."

My looks, acting ability, and family life apparently made an attractive package. I saw myself through the eyes of the execs—the sexy homeroom teacher with the hunky husband in the background: an image akin to the brainy astronaut they wanted me to play. As our meeting concluded, the executives continued to be lavish in their praise, and I began thinking the *Daytona Beach* gig might work out.

Because of my heavy shooting schedule and the "go-sees" Marv was sending me on, I lived, mostly alone, in our Los Angeles apartment during January of 1996. In contrast to our substantial home in Las Vegas, where I felt secure and established, the one-bedroom apartment encouraged me to concentrate on all I had yet to accomplish.

On Feburary 5, I was at the apartment, working once more on the audition script for *Daytona Beach.* The week before, Marv had called to let me know that the producers wanted me to screen test. They would make a videotape of my performance to show around the network for final approval. Marv had given me the notes from one of the producers and I knew I really needed to nail the scene. He had already begun negotiating with the *Daytona Beach* producers and he wanted them to boost their offer of nine thousand dollars per episode. Shooting the pilot in Florida would take four weeks, and we had already informed *The Bold and the Beautiful* that I would probably be exercising my "out" in March. Marv had been told informally that I was already cast in the producers' minds and they just needed full network approval. The deal was more than halfway done.

"You get a good night's sleep," Marv said on the phone. "I don't want you going anywhere. Don't do anything but work on that script."

I was set to do exactly as he instructed. I thought I might go over to my acting coach's house in the early evening and go through the part one last time with her. Then straight to bed.

About noon, Marv called back. "You're not going to believe this."

"What?"

"Never in a million years are you going to believe this."

"What, Marv? Will you just tell me?"

"Pam Shae's office just called. They don't want you to screen test tomorrow for *Daytona Beach.* They want to offer you a part on *Melrose Place.*"

In my confusion, I said, "What's that?" As my head started to clear, I realized *Melrose* was Heather Locklear's show—a show college kids watched, a nighttime soap. I knew that much, but that's about all I knew.

"*Melrose Place?*" Marv said. "It's like one of the biggest shows on television."

"Okay, okay, Marv, but what do they want me to do?"

"I don't think they have a role yet. But they've put an offer on the table anyway. Fifteen thousand dollars per episode. And I think I can get them to go higher."

"No way!" I said. This wasn't for a pilot, either, but an established series. "So what do we want to do?"

"I'm going to see how serious they are. If you are interested, let's go for this."

"Well, of course I'm interested. But find out about the character."

Within minutes, Marv called back. "Hunter, they've taken my counteroffer. They're up to seventeen-five, and it's a four-year deal. They don't want you to screen test tomorrow. They're adamant that you don't test for Disney. We have to come to terms by the end of the business day."

I looked up at the wall clock I bought especially for this apartment, a campy, glittery rendering of the Statue of Liberty—as her arms went around, she seemed to be cheerleading for America. It was almost one o'clock in the afternoon.

"Marv, wait a minute. Let's just slow down. I've made stupid decisions in the past and I don't want to do something stupid today." I could already feel the weight of this decision, the importance of choosing one path or another at this crossroads. "I've got to think, Marv. Actually, Marv—you may think I'm nuts—but I've got to pray."

"Well, I know this is happening fast, Hunter, but . . ."

"I'll call you back, Marv."

I sat down at the kitchen table and tried to think. Preparing to play *Daytona Beach*'s brainy astronaut, I had grown to like the notion of how good that part would be for my career. I needed to play somebody tough and tomboyish—I like to think those are major aspects of my character and they'd never been seen in my work. So I had to ask myself whether I wanted to do an interesting part or whether I just wanted to make a good living for my family.

The phone rang again. It was Marv. "Hunter, can't you just give them a yes?"

"I'm thinking, Marv. I'm thinking. I'll call you back."

I tried to pray and I opened the Bible and read a few passages. I felt prompted to ask for a tape of the show. Shouldn't I see this production—at least one episode—before I signed on for four years?

I called Marv back. "Can you ask the *Melrose* people, Marv, to send . . ."

"What, Hunter? I can't hear you. What's making that noise?"

In its terrarium, my tegu chose that moment to attack its lunch, a live mouse. The mouse's shrill screams were interfering with what I was trying to tell Marv. You cannot tell a tegu to stop once it begins engorging its prey. "Is that that alligator thing you've got?" Marv asked. "Is it attacking *you?*"

"No, Marv, it's eating its dinner. Its once-a-week dinner. It *likes* its dinner, believe me."

"Sounds like it."

"I was trying to say that I need to see a tape of *Melrose Place.* I mean, this is four years of my life we're talking about."

"Okay, that's reasonable. I'll see what I can do."

Perhaps because my tegu took that moment to go on the feed, I began to think of everyone in my life who depended on me for their care—my children first and foremost, of course, not to mention my animals, including the zoo that I had accumulated at our home in Las Vegas. I even had custom terrariums built in the family-room walls for them, with shutters on the outside for squeamish guests. Who would care for the beasts and children? Michael and I had almost blown our marriage and destroyed our family by moving out to Vegas and seeing each other only in transit. Michael and my boys, Chris and Mickey, needed me more than ever. Which choice—*Daytona Beach* or *Melrose*—would be better for them?

I called Michael and explained. "I don't know, Hunter," Michael said. "You know how I feel about L.A. Why don't you just go ahead and shoot the pilot? If it becomes a regular gig, and you're filming in Florida, we can move back to New York or even to North Carolina and have the farm we've wanted. *Melrose* is bound to take us all back to L.A."

"You may want to work again out here, too," I said.

Michael kept his own counsel on that score.

"They're going to get me a tape," I said. "I want to look at an episode before I decide. Marv's all hot about this. He's acting like it's the end of the world."

"It is a big hit show, I guess," Michael said, his tone softening. "And I know you have to think about it. Whatever you decide is okay. I mean, really, it's okay."

"You mean that?"

"Of course I mean that. Maybe it'll take you on to other things, too. It's prime time. That counts. If we have to go back to L.A., we have to go back."

"Okay, I'll call you after I see the tape. I love you."

"Love you, too."

One of my agents at Innovative Artists, David Rose, called to say they were having trouble locating a *Melrose Place* tape. (I work with a talent agency as well as with a manager: a manager sends his clients out on auditions and the agents do all the deal-making, including working out the contractual details.) He told me another in-house agent, Nevin Dolcefino, would be calling. Nevin was an avid *Melrose Place* fan and could give me a better idea of what the show was like.

When he came on the line, Nevin said, "It's like the rage. Especially for young girls."

"Oh, yeah?"

"You'd fit in great there, Hunter. You'd be working opposite Heather Locklear. People will really be able to see what you can do. The show's funny, it's campy."

"Why can't you guys find me a tape?"

"You don't need to see a tape, Hunter. I'm telling you. It's a great show. It has great production values. They pour a ton of money into that thing and it all ends up on film. You'll look fantastic."

"I'm not worried about it being some crummy, low-budget thing, Nevin. I'm worried what people will take away from it. Particularly if young girls are so heavily influenced by it. What's the show about? Do people sleep around? Do they get away with doing a lot of immoral stuff?"

"*Hunter,* it's not meant to be *reality.* It's this campy, trendy thing. It's just meant to be fun and it is fun. I wouldn't miss an episode. You think I have lousy taste or something?"

"Is it like the *Dynasty* stab-you-in-the-back kind of thing?"

"There's some of that in everything. Don't get crazy on us, Hunter. This is a big opportunity. A big, big opportunity. It'll take you where you ultimately want to go."

"Let me think about it, Nevin."

So I called my best friend, Carla, a woman I had known for fifteen years and someone whose sensibilities were much like mine. I didn't mistrust Nevin's taste, but I thought I might get a more accurate reading from my girlfriend on the show's tone. The Statue of Liberty showed 2:30 now, and I realized that if I decided against taking the *Melrose Place* offer, I was going to have much less time to work on my *Daytona Beach* audition. The clock was ticking, ticking, ticking.

After explaining the situation to Carla, I asked, "So what's the show like? Have you watched it?"

"A few times. It's kind of racy."

"Racy?"

"It's cute, for the most part. I wouldn't let Abby watch it, though." (Abby is her pre-school daughter.)

"No?"

"A lot of times, they show people starting to have sex. Somebody throws somebody else on a couch or bed and they start kissing passionately. That kind of thing. It's not any worse than the daytime soaps."

That was bad enough, I knew. I thanked Carla and prepared to call Marv back. It was now past three in the afternoon. Lady Liberty seemed to be waving her arms ever more frantically.

During my conversation with Carla, several things began to come together in my mind. I knew now that the show depended in part on creating sexual situations and steamy romances. Few shows don't. I know what my business writes about. But I was intrigued to learn that young girls watched it. And, as far as things had been described to me thus far, my role remained undefined. I started wondering whether it might be possible for me to help the writers create the character in such a way that she offered a slightly different spin—a redemptive one—for those young girls who were such fans. After all, if I was going to play this character for four years, I'd better like the character myself.

It also occurred to me that I had to confess to the show's producer why I was having such misgivings; the deep commitment to God I had made almost a year before that wouldn't let me "just say yes" and never look back.

I called Marv. "Listen, nobody can get me a tape. If I'm going to take their offer, I'm going to have to talk to the executive producer. Can I talk to him? Will you arrange it?"

"I don't know, Hunter. What are you going to say?"

"This is a major career change. I need some questions answered. I need to know their ideas for the character. What if I go on the show and I have to play a character that I hate? What if it permanently typecasts me because everybody thinks I'm the new Joan Collins witch-bitch of the century? I don't want to get pegged like that."

"Okay," Marv said. "I understand. Let me see what I can do."

Marv called back faster than I could ever have imagined. "He wants to talk with you. The executive producer. His name's Frank South. You call his secretary and she'll put you right through."

Except in an unusual situation like this—less than two hours remaining to make a life-changing decision—I would be reluctant to bug a producer. I not only had to be fair to Spelling Entertainment, I had to be fair to Disney and the *Baywatch* people. I couldn't call them in the morning, when the crew and other actors were already on their way into the studio to shoot the screen test. So Frank South and I were going to have a serious talk. I was glad that I didn't know him or know of him: that reduced the pressure somewhat.

His voice when it came on the line made me feel at ease as well. From the first, he spoke to me as a friend, as if he already assumed we'd be working together. "Hey, Hunter," he said, "glad you called. We're all excited about this. We're going to make a lot of great shows together, I'm sure."

I said, "Listen, the reason I wanted to talk is just to get a better idea of the character. Is it somebody that—can you just tell what she's going to be doing? What do you have in mind?"

"Nothing's written in stone at this point."

"I understand that. But what are your ideas?"

"We don't really know that much. Aaron just loves you and said he'd like to have you on the show. We think your character's probably going to be from Kansas, and . . . she's had a rough life or lost her fortune. Maybe she drives an old Mercedes."

"So she's going to come to town and just get involved in the mix?"

"Basically."

"What's her name?"

"We don't have a name yet for her. You can help with that. We'll try to make it fun for you."

"I'd like to bring my own creativity to the character, sure. I want to like her, if I'm going to play her for four years."

"You can be part of the whole process of creating the character. An actor is, anyway—one way or another. That's just inevitable."

"Still, I know you must have had meetings about this. Isn't there anything more you can tell me?"

"Well, uh, we do know that you are going to be a rival for Heather Locklear. We need somebody strong, someone with confidence; someone strong, confident, and beautiful enough to make trouble for Heather Locklear's character, Amanda. We think you'll be perfect. You know Aaron—I can't tell you how much Aaron loves you."

Frank South went on to talk about my acting skills, and I felt that all the work I had put in with my acting coach, Ivana, had truly paid off. I could also tell that Frank South knew his business and I began to like him and hope the arrangement would work.

I took a couple of deep breaths and broached the subject of my convictions. "Don't get freaked out," I said, "but I'm a Christian . . ."

"Oh."

Because of his nonchalant response, I wondered how many times he'd heard people say that who didn't really mean it—who didn't "walk the walk." "Yes, and I don't really like the idea of running around in a bra and panties. I've done that on *Bold and Beau-*

tiful—the sexy, racy stuff—and I want to do something different.
I'd like to play a character that's more of a role model."

"On *Melrose?*"

"Well, maybe someone who gets in trouble, but tries to do the
right thing. Of course, the character has to make mistakes or she's
not interesting to watch. But she's not going to sleep with
everybody, is she?"

"Oh, no, not everybody."

"I mean, I don't want to be the Joan Collins character on *Dynasty,* either—the raving bitch. That's not what you have in mind,
is it?"

"It's pretty early, Hunter. I can't possibly give you a detailed description of everything the character's going to do. We don't know
that yet."

"Sure, I understand that. All I was saying . . ."

"We know your character's married," Frank said, cutting me off.
"Her marriage is troubled and about to break up. We want to see
the problems of a breakup play themselves out."

After my own marital problems, I could absolutely relate to that.
"What if she's married," I said, making a suggestion, "and having
problems with her husband, but she's trying to work it out? She
could be attracted to someone else but resisting. That's something
we haven't seen."

"Look, Hunter, we thought . . . while she's married, she might
end up getting involved with Heather Locklear's love interest. The
character's name is Peter. He's played by Jack Wagner."

Jack Wagner came from daytime, too. I liked him and I liked
Heather Locklear and I began to be intrigued by the notion of
acting with them. I thought the three of us could work well together.

"So your character," Frank said, "she's probably going to cheat
on her husband because he had an affair in the past, and she wants
revenge. She'll seduce one of the other characters to get it."

That put a stop to my hopeful thoughts. "That's tough," I said. "I
have a problem with that. What if her husband has been beating

her and he's squandered away their money? Otherwise, you're making her mean-spirited from the beginning and that's something I don't want to do. In fact, I won't do it."

"Hunter, with all due respect, you can't dictate to us what the character is going to be like."

"I don't mean to do that. Really. I'm only making suggestions for the way the character might be played. After all, you don't have the character written yet."

"Well, no, not written."

"The thing that matters most to me, Frank, is that the character *pays* for her mistakes. The Joan Collins raving-bitch type just goes on being that way, without ever suffering any consequences."

"That's not what happens on our show."

"I think it's a matter of motivation. I don't want her to be the initiator of her marriage problems. What if, like I was saying, her husband's a gambler or abusive and she comes to town to put her life back together and someone is there who reaches out to her and things just happen?"

"I don't mean to be rude or anything, Hunter, and it's not that we don't appreciate input from all our actors, but we are going to write the show the way we want to."

"But I'm not . . ."

"Look, it's all meant to be fun. It's not reality. It's totally tongue-in-cheek. But it's just—well, our characters sleep around. That's the way it is."

Without being sure why we couldn't agree, I felt enough resistance in what Frank said—and what he wouldn't say—to feel we were at an impasse. "I've got to tell you, I'm not sure this is going to work. I can't tell you how flattered I am by the offer. I would love to work on a Spelling show. But I don't think this is going to be the role for me. It's not for me."

4

Seconds later, Marv called. "What are you doing, Hunter? What is *wrong* with you? Isn't this what we started working for back in October or whenever? I mean . . . *what's* the deal? I mean, *no deal?* Is that what you are telling me. No deal?"

I explained to Marv how I felt.

"I'll . . . but you said . . . maybe I'll call . . . or talk," Marv said, in his classic way of sputtering. His voice finally collapsed with, "Oh, Hunter."

Nevin Dolcefino called next. "Hunter, one question: Have you flipped your everlasting bird?"

"Listen," I said somewhat impatiently, "I don't know why I'm in this position. But it has something to do with the fact that I've got to stand up for what I believe in for a change."

When my conversation with Nevin ended, I hung up knowing that I had done the right thing. That didn't keep me from feeling sad, of course, or clear away every confusion. Even though I had turned the *Melrose Place* job down, I was happy it had been offered. At the same time, a small, craven part of me couldn't help feeling, "Why couldn't I have become a serious Christian a couple of years from now?" But I kept reminding myself that if I had said, "Sure, send me the contract and I'll do whatever," I would have betrayed my essential commitments. I couldn't have lived with myself. Plus, I still had the *Daytona Beach* screen test in hand.

I went back to studying my *Daytona Beach* part—it was after four o'clock and I only had so much concentration left to nail the filmed audition. Even as I worked, I kept telling myself, I'm going to be okay. I did the right thing.

Then Marv called once more. "Frank wants to talk to you again," Marv said. "He feels you two just weren't connecting. He's really a terrific guy, Hunter. He wants this to work out. I want you to talk to him. I think it would be good if you talked one more time. I think this can still work out."

It surprised me that he wanted to talk again. I didn't know what to expect, but I was willing. I had already gone to the mat with the guy. Maybe he would be willing to accommodate my feelings after all.

I called. "Hi, Frank."

"Hello, Hunter, thanks for calling again. I guess we just got off on the wrong foot."

"I appreciate your willingness to talk about it."

We went over some of the earlier ground we covered, and as we talked, I felt like we were getting to know each other pretty well.

The conversation turned in an important direction when Frank said: "You have to understand. There's no show if we have people who are all good. Who wants to see that? Who wants to see a bunch of people who always do the right thing?"

"I'm not asking you to do that. That's not what this is about. I know I have to play a character who makes mistakes. My only request is that she pays for them. If she makes a mistake, I would like the audience to see the consequences of her doing something wrong."

"Our characters generally do—except they also have a tendency to live and let live. That's not a bad thing, is it?"

"Well, let's say she does have an affair. I don't mind playing that she has an affair or that she makes a mistake, but I don't want her to get away with it and not get caught. Young girls identify with actresses in these situations, and they have to know problems—real problems—come with the territory."

"Let's be more specific," he said. "As I said, we don't have it written yet, but we know this young woman is going to become involved somehow with Heather Locklear's husband, which will cause Heather to fight to get him back. You see, Heather's character has gotten too stable. There's no conflict for her. All the other actresses are already in their own story lines. There's no one to challenge Heather's Amanda. We need someone new to become a threat. But we don't know exactly how the story is going to unfold. We don't know. We wanted to know who the actress was and then go from there, because it's easier to write it once we know who the actress is."

I knew this was true in television. Not films, where scripts are more set. But in the soap operas I had done, the first few scenes would often be written first, then the writers would compose additional scenes after observing the speech, behavior, and reactions of individual actors and actresses. Whatever dynamics and skills they saw were incorporated into the story line.

"Look, Hunter," Frank said, "all I can tell you is that this character is probably from Kansas. She's had money in the past. She wears nice business suits and drives an old Mercedes. Like you, she's funny, she's sexy. She's very intelligent. She has great business savvy. All of these qualities make her a perfect rival for Amanda. Because your character has lost her fortune, she wants it back, and she might do whatever it takes."

I could understand someone being greedy—I had certainly been that at one time. "Okay," I said, "okay. But if I come across something in a script that I have a problem with, a bed scene, for example, are we going to be able to work out how it's staged until I'm comfortable with it? Are we going to understand the character's motivation—why she's there?"

"Hunter, all of my actors and I have a great relationship. Whenever there's something in a script, a speech or something that they don't really jibe with or it's not happening for them or they think it needs to be beefed up, they come into my office and we talk. We work it out, Hunter. Anything that comes up, my door is always open. You can come in here and we'll work it out until you're comfortable."

That's exactly what I needed to hear. "Your door is always open and we can always work it out until I'm comfortable?"

"Right."

"Okay, then. Super. I guess we've got a deal after all."

I was really excited and at the same time still apprehensive. *We would always be able to work it out.* I clutched that statement of Frank South's like a big, fluffy pillow. As long as I was willing to stand up for what I believed, I could remain true to my faith. Perhaps I could comment on the story line in interviews, providing insight for the young women who loved the show so much.

I called Marv. "It's a deal," I said.

"It's a deal?"

"Deal."

"Hunter, sweetie, your life is never going to be the same!"

By the end of the next day, we had a verbal contract that specified the major negotiating items. Spelling Entertainment messengered the contract itself the day after—February 7, 1996.

In the next few days, my excitement over my new role on *Melrose Place* grew. Had I caught the "big-time bus?" An avenue toward acting at the highest levels was opening up, and that meant more than I can say. It was hardly my only dream in life, but it was an important one, and it was coming true. With this new prospect before me, I was glad that I had taken a chance on leaving *B&B*, even though I would miss employers and peers who had always been exceptionally good to me. Most of all, though, I looked forward to having more time with my family.

Within a couple of days of agreeing to terms with *Melrose Place*, Michael and I received an offer on our Las Vegas home, which seemed wonderfully timed, if low. A week later, the house deal was done. Not too long before, I thought we'd have to install a chairlift on the banisters to get me upstairs when I was an old lady; I didn't think I'd ever leave the place. But now, even though we were selling on less than favorable terms, I was ready to give the place up, especially since I'd need to be in Los Angeles full-time starting July 1. Our true home resided in the love we shared as a family, not in a building.

I would be working on *The Bold and the Beautiful* through the end of May, as we set about finding a new home in Los Angeles and schools for the boys. Until that past fall, Michael had been working on *The Young and the Restless*. When the last option in his contract came up, the show chose not to renew, ending Michael's run there. Both *The Young and the Restless* and *The Bold and the Beautiful* are owned by the same parent company—in fact, the shows tape at CBS studios in adjacent spaces. In 1994, when Michael's and my battles were at their worst, we had staged some real-life knock-down-drag-outs in front of everyone, and I have to say that the worst of it was my fault. These episodes shadowed Michael's time on *The Young and the Restless,* and I have to wonder whether the fights I provoked didn't eventually result in the producers deciding that one Tylo was enough—with Michael getting the short end of the stick. Michael began working with the college in Pennsylvania and adapting himself to the role of househusband.

Once I landed the role on *Melrose,* Michael temporarily stopped looking for new work. He was going to take care of everything related to the move until we felt secure in our new place and my work life on *Melrose* became established. Michael, as much as any man, has a tendency to judge his own worth in terms of his work. For him to accept a nontraditional role and do so with good grace was a sacrifice and one that I appreciated—I knew how much it cost him.

Word filtered out that I would be leaving *The Bold and the Beautiful* for *Melrose* and speculation began in the soap magazines as to how the writers would dispense with my character, Taylor Hayes. I asked Marv to call the Spelling people periodically to check whether my new character had a name yet. Soon, not only the soap magazines but more general publications wanted to know who the character would be. *TV Guide* wanted to talk to me.

Marv put in a call to several people at Spelling Entertainment to inquire how we should handle this. What would *they* like us to say? He was directed to somebody in charge of public relations. The woman there only knew that my character would be a rival for Heather Locklear's Amanda and cause problems in her relationship with Jack Wagner's Peter. That was all the information we could get. It seemed odd that Marv would be directed to someone in public relations. Why wasn't Frank South or one of the writers helping us out? I kept receiving mixed signals about how much they knew about my new character.

I went ahead and accepted the *TV Guide* interview with a writer named Michael Logan. Michael Logan and I have history. He's done some favorable pieces on me—especially when I was on *TV Guide*'s cover with Antonio Sabato, Jr. (who became Calvin Klein's male underwear model) as one of the year's "ten sexiest stars." Then, during my quarrels with Michael, he decided I was a flake and a troublemaker and called me the "Roseanne Barr of daytime." After that, I criticized his work in another publication and a minifeud was on. I wondered how he would approach me this time.

Mr. Logan behaved himself at the beginning of the interview. "So you're leaving the show?" he asked. "You've been there how long?" He continued with questions to which he already knew the answers. I kept wondering what he had up his sleeve.

I tried to reach out to him by expressing a sentiment I knew he shared. "It's great to be working on an Aaron Spelling show," I said, knowing he was a Spelling fan. "I've loved doing guest spots for them, especially that appearance on *Burke's Law*. I know that factored into their decision."

Finally, he said, "Now, Hunter . . ." and I thought, *Here we go*. When his voice rose to a squeak at the end of his phrases, the stumpers always followed. "How can you go to *Melrose Place* and be a Christian?" he asked.

He was saying, *You don't walk the walk, baby*.

I wondered for a few moments how to respond without getting pegged as a religious fanatic, then decided I'd just tell the truth. "I talked with Frank South before I accepted the job," I answered, "and basically I told him that I didn't want to play a character who was mean-spirited or ruthless. That I would like the character to be a role model."

Dead silence on the other end of the phone. "On *Melrose Place?*" he finally asked.

"Yes," I said. "I told Frank that I understood my character has to make mistakes, or it's not interesting to watch, and that I had no problem with the character making mistakes. But I wasn't going to be doing anything dicey.

"Frank was very accepting," I said, going on. "He told me he had an open-door policy and we could talk about anything I felt uncomfortable with."

"Oh. Okay," Michael Logan said, for once stumped himself. And that ended the interview.

I still hadn't received any more details about my *Melrose Place* character when the *TV Guide* article came out in the February 28 issue. I was proud of it. Mr. Logan quoted me saying I was a Christian and wouldn't be doing anything dicey. He reported my conversation with Frank, and Frank's statement that he had an open-door policy and we could work out any conflicts that arose. He was fair to me and I appreciated that.

Within twenty-four hours of *TV Guide*'s publication, Marv called me. "Hunter, Hunter, Hunter," he said. "We've got to talk about this thing you did in *TV Guide*."

"What about it?" I asked.

"Frank South doesn't like it," Marv told me.

"What?" I was surprised. "It's promoting the show. What are you talking about?"

"He doesn't like what you said in there," Marv said.

"Said what in there? What did I say? I didn't say anything overly personal about our conversation. I gave a general description."

"That's what he doesn't like," Marv said.

"Marv, what are you talking about?"

"Well . . . you talked about the Christian thing. You said that you wouldn't be doing some things . . ."

I could tell Marv was between a rock and a hard place. He wanted to please me, but he wanted to mollify Frank South and whoever else was upset at Spelling. He was having a hard time finding the right words. Marv always stutters and stammers when he can't figure out what to say. He became all breathy and I could just picture him waving a cigarette around and freaking out while trying to sound calm. He probably smoked three cigarettes during this five-minute conversation.

"Hunter, Frank didn't like that Christian comment," Marv said, repeating himself. "He didn't like that open-door comment, either. He says that was a private conversation between the two of you. He doesn't like that being made public."

"Marv, it's the truth!" I said. "You want me to lie?"

"He feels like you've put him in a corner. By making the conversation public, he feels that you're trying to put something on the record that you can use to twist his arm. He feels . . ." He didn't quite know how to put the rest of it into words. Not yet. He hemmed and hawed for a while longer, trying to get me to understand why Frank South was unhappy.

Then he got to the point. "He wants you to make a retraction, Hunter."

"What?" I didn't get it. "A retraction on what?"

"I think the whole thing."

"Well, I'm not going to say that I'm not a Christian," I said. "And I'm not going to say he doesn't have an open-door policy. He told me I wouldn't have to do anything I was uncomfortable with. If Frank wants to renege on the promises he made me, he'd better tell me now—himself. This is all stuff he and I talked about. There shouldn't be a problem with it being printed."

"Hunter," Marv said, "he probably feels that it's going to make the other actresses wonder why you get this privilege and they don't. Why do you get to decide whether or not you'll be running around in your bra and panties or doing anything dicey? Why do you get that privilege and they don't?"

"But Marv," I said, "he told me he has an open-door policy with *all* his actors. I wasn't saying he was prepared to give me special treatment. That's not going to be the way it is. Not unless he's lying to me."

Somehow, Marv played the diplomat with Frank and the other Spelling people and calmed them down. I learned later that Marv was told, "We don't want people thinking the show's going to turn boring now because of the Christian thing. We can't make our audience worry that the show isn't going to be exciting." Spelling Entertainment wanted the reputation of *Melrose Place* to remain as racy as possible.

By this point, I had tuned into the show a couple of times to check it out for myself. I saw one episode in which Daphne Zuniga's character realizes that a little girl is being abused by someone she knows and stands up for the girl. I thought that was great—a show exposing the reality of child abuse and presenting a character who puts her own neck on the line by confronting an abusive friend. Then I saw another more vampy episode in which one of the actresses hit on Jack Wagner's character. She ripped back her shirt and ripped his shirt off and they fell on a sofa together. The way it was shot made the scene highly suggestive but not explicit. It disturbed me, I'll admit, but it didn't put me off totally. I'll deal with my story line as it comes up, I thought. I'll look at each scene in the context of the larger story.

My difficult conversations with Frank South, coupled with his request for a retraction, kept bothering me. There's usually a period in any new arrangement in which the kinks have to be worked out, especially among creative people. I wasn't worried, exactly, but I wondered what implications this might have down the line.

Before I ever heard that Spelling Entertainment took my pregnancy to be a problem—before I even knew I was pregnant—I felt compelled to review the situation. Was Frank South uncomfortable because he did not intend to live up to his promises? Was I attributing more to Frank's "open-door policy" than I should? Had I been so caught up in my own desire for the *Melrose Place* job that I prompted Frank to offer up the sop my conscience needed? Did that mean that at some level I knew this deal was a bad one? Had I screwed up? Had I not listened closely enough to my own conscience and God's prompting?

I went into the walk-in closet off the master bedroom, and shut the door to keep anyone from finding me there. I carried the Bible I kept on my side table—a thick one with Moses before the burning bush on the cover. For the past nine months, I had been seeking God's direction in every aspect of my life. Most often, I found the answers I needed by opening the Bible and reading passages I felt directed to. Many, many times, the passages I read spoke directly to my most urgent concerns.

I bent down on my knees and prayed. Have I made a mistake here? God, are you upset with me? Did I mess up? If I acted on my own human desires—if I let my own dreams get in the way of your will—please don't be mad. Don't be angry. I'm just human. If I screwed up, if I made a mistake, Lord, please get me out of it.

I cried as I prayed those words because, with all my heart, I sincerely did not want to grieve God. My questions kept pounding away at me: Had I clung to a conversation hoping for one thing when Frank meant another? Had I somehow misled him, which caused him to be offended by the article? I had been so proud of standing up as a Christian in the *TV Guide* article, but that had upset Frank South. That couldn't be good.

I opened my Bible with an expectant attitude. My past experiences had taught me to count on answers through Scripture. But what I read—the passage that took hold of my imagination—didn't make sense. The passage came from Psalm 127: "Children are a heritage from the Lord. They are like arrows in the hand of a warrior."

I didn't understand it, but I knew this was the truth I needed to hear. It resonated in a way that told me this Scripture contained my answer. But I didn't know how or why. I must have reread that verse twenty times trying to make sense of it, as I pored over the surrounding Scriptures for context. Somehow I knew that verse was for me.

What does that mean? I wondered. Is that really an answer? If it is, I'm afraid I don't get it.

I remembered reading this passage before. It was as though I were being brought back to it. "Children are a heritage from the Lord. They're like arrows in the hand of a warrior."

Could I become pregnant again? I wondered. Would my child be an arrow? An arrow in God's hand? How? I had given up on trying to become pregnant. Still, I underlined the verse and dated it, March 17, 1996. In another six days, I would find out I was pregnant and yet the verse would retain much of its mystery for a long time to come.

I didn't know what any of this meant, but I knew it was significant. God seemed to be warning me somehow. I didn't feel afraid, though. I definitely felt the peace that God always gives, the settledness of receiving my answer, but *what* had been settled I couldn't fathom.

5

*A*fter Marv told Frank South about my pregnancy and learned he wasn't happy, I didn't hear anything from Spelling Entertainment for more than a week. I wasn't terribly worried. I had a sense of these matters being left in God's hands. Maybe the arrow passage from the Psalms meant that my pregnancy would be written into the *Melrose Place* scripts in a manner that would make my new character truly worthwhile. I was confident the writers at *Melrose* were creative enough to meet this challenge. They must be taking the time to figure out how. The happiness of having a new baby and a new job returned.

On April 10, in the afternoon, I was in my Las Vegas kitchen, trying out a new recipe. Chris and Mickey were watching television in the adjoining hearth room and Michael was working in our home office. The aroma of what I was preparing—orange-glazed duck to top a salad of baby greens—filled the house. I felt a little sad that I would soon be leaving this kitchen, with its leaded-glass cabinets of my own design, wrought-iron hanging racks for my copper pans, and long, inlaid Corian counters. Earlier that day, I found out that our closing date for the new house was scheduled for June 1. We'd have to be out by then, which meant that we'd have to

make all the arrangements for a new place as I finished out my
B&B contract. I had already gone to the Los Angeles suburb of
Valencia, where *Melrose Place* is shot, and found possible rental
homes.

Then Michael came into the kitchen looking as if he'd just been
told about a death in the family.

"What's wrong with you?" I asked, alarmed.

"Honey . . . hey, guys," he turned to the boys. "Turn off the TV.
Go upstairs. I want to talk to your mother for a minute."

I don't like this, I thought. It's never good news when he clears
everyone out.

"Honey, I have to talk to you about something," he said. He was
holding a rolled-up piece of thermal fax paper. "But I want to
know first if you are feeling okay. Are you?"

"Yeah, fine," I said. "What is it?"

"I need to talk to you," he said, repeating himself. "I don't want
you to be in a weird frame of mind or upset. We're just going to
talk for a minute."

"What is it, Michael?" I said. "Don't play games like this. You're
getting me scared. Tell me what's going on."

"This fax just came to Marv," he said, handing it to me. "He sent
it right on to us."

I had to uncurl the page to read it. I noticed the Spelling Entertainment logo at the top.

STI [Spelling Television, Inc.] has been advised by our representatives that you are pregnant. Although we wish you much joy in
this event, your pregnancy will result in a material change in
your appearance during producing of a substantial portion of
the 1996/7 season of the Series. Your material change does not
conform with the character you have been engaged to portray.
This character is by necessity not pregnant and your material
changes would not meet the requirements for the portrayal of
the character. Accordingly, STI is hereby exercising its right to
terminate the Agreement pursuant to Paragraph 10(a) of the
Standard Terms and Conditions of the Agreement.

I sat there, disbelieving. It didn't seem real. I kept looking for a paragraph further on: P.S. We'll call you tomorrow to discuss ways of more satisfactorily resolving this conflict. But there was no P.S.

I must have looked at that letter and reread it ten times before I looked up at Michael. The contradictory statements were so confusing. *We wish you much joy . . . Your pregnancy will result in a material change in your appearance.* They were firing me, I finally realized. They were firing me because I was pregnant. But they also wished me much *joy?*

I looked again at the letter, at the name of the person who had signed it. "Who's Cortez Smith?" I asked.

"I don't know," Michael said. "It doesn't really make sense. The point is, they fired you. I'm so sorry, Hunter."

"They can't do that!" I said. "Isn't it against the law to fire someone who's pregnant?"

"I guess not."

"Who is Cortez Smith?" I asked again. "I've never spoken to anybody named Cortez Smith."

"It looks like he's an attorney," Michael said, already wary of antagonizing me further.

I called Marv immediately. Michael moved over to the phone with me, staying near.

As soon as I got Marv on the phone, I asked, "What is this? Are they firing me? Where's Frank South?" I *could not* believe it.

Marv was very apologetic. "Honey, I'm sorry. I'm so sorry."

"No," I said. "No, wait a minute. This is not right. There's nothing in my contract that says that I'm not supposed to be pregnant. Send me the contract. I want to see paragraph 10(a)."

"Okay, okay, I'll do that. I can certainly do that. Just as soon as we hang up." He was trying to calm me down—everyone would keep trying to calm me down for the rest of that day. I was insulted. I was indignant. I didn't even know who Cortez Smith was. Why didn't the letter come from Frank South? Why didn't it come from Aaron Spelling? Why didn't it at least say, "Give us a call if you want to talk about it"? But it said nothing like that, just legal jargon from somebody named Cortez Smith. Legal jargon terminating me after wishing me much joy!

Nobody from Spelling had been willing to talk to us for more than a week now. Then they saw fit to send me a one-page note that instantly turned my family's life upside down. I had not only re-signed from *The Bold and the Beautiful* but even announced in print that I would be going to *Melrose Place*. We had sold our home. My husband, in order to accommodate my career, had stopped looking for work outside the home. *And I was pregnant!* Had anyone stopped to think for two moments how this decision might affect the baby?

At least I'd better start thinking about it, I realized with a start. I took a couple of deep breaths.

"Honey, it's okay," Michael was saying. "Honey, don't get mad."

The killer was the sentence, "Although we wish you much joy in this event, your pregnancy will result . . ." I kept thinking, they're so overjoyed they're going to fire me?

Why hadn't we had a meeting in Frank South's office to go over the options? Why wasn't Marv saying, "Fly here right away! We're going to march into Frank's office and we're going to talk"? Why wasn't Michael mad as hell?

I was being deprived of having any say in a decision that would determine much of our future.

I was shaking with anger. I felt as if I had been kicked in the teeth, and I knew what that felt like: In elementary school, while playing volleyball, I didn't realize there was a stone wall behind me and when I turned to run I smacked into it, teeth first. I had never forgotten that pain and this one felt remarkably similar.

I kept realizing I had better calm down. Women have had mis-carriages over less. I had now lost my new job, sold my home, scut-tled my husband's working life, pulled my two boys from their schools and preregistered them in Valencia—I couldn't lose the baby as well.

I grabbed the phone once more. Michael was begging, "Stop it, stop it! Sit down! Sit down! Don't touch the phone!"

But I was already punching in numbers. I called my agent David Rose. Then I called my other agent Nevin Dolcefino. I called Marv again.

They all said the same thing, "I'm sorry. We're sorry."

Not only had I been fired, but now I was a charity case!

"This is not legal. This is wrong. This can't be happening."

"We'll get you something else, Hunter. Don't worry. We'll get you something else," they said, trying to placate me.

"No," I said. "No, it's too late. It's *April!* It's too late in pilot season to get anything else, and you damn well know that. I've got nowhere to go. I don't even know where we're going to live. I just pulled my kids out of school. This can't happen. You have got to call these people and set up a meeting. We have to talk."

That day was so bad I ended up with a blinding migraine headache, complete with the halo effect, shooting meteors, brain-cleaving pain, and an overwhelming nausea that made me vomit up all the orange-glazed duck I had tasted. I'm surprised I *didn't* lose the baby.

In recounting this, I'm embarrassed at my temper, but the fury—the rage—that came to me with that letter of termination took hold and wouldn't let go.

For the next two weeks, I tried to talk to somebody at Spelling Entertainment. Just about anybody would have suited me. A big, black thundercloud hung over my head. I couldn't even muster up the desire to talk to God—that's how oppressed I felt. Every single thing I had worked so hard to help redeem—my marriage, my family, my career—all of it was threatened. Everything was at risk. Especially the person I had felt myself on the way to becoming.

I'm aware now that some of the Spelling people thought I was looking for any reason to sue them simply because they have a lot of money. That thought never entered my head. I felt utterly trapped. I couldn't help fixating on the threat to everything in my life: my family, my children, my husband, my home, my career, the baby I was carrying. These concerns drove me through two weeks of hell, while I demanded that *somebody* talk to me.

I'm going to fire all of my agents, I said to myself. I'm going to fire Marv. The whole lot of them are going to get tossed if they cannot find someone who is willing to talk to me. I don't care if it has to be on the phone. If they don't want to see me face-to-face—fine. I want to talk to Frank South again. Where's his famous open-door policy now, huh? Somebody had better find the key to that particular door. I can't understand this—Aaron Spelling's always been so appreciative. Why won't he talk with me and work this out? What's the deal with the champagne and the special notes thanking me for the good work and now he won't take my phone calls? What did I do wrong that everybody hates me so much?

Finally, I did have a conversation with the head of my talent agency, Scott Harris. Innovative Artists has always been on the cutting edge of what's happening in the business, and so I felt confident I would get good advice from Scott.

Initially, Scott apologized like everyone else. Then he said candidly, "Now, listen to me, Hunter. I've got a whole agency full of people that need to work. I am not going to get adversarial with Mr. Spelling. I'm not going to take sides here. I know they're unhappy. I don't really know why. I've never seen this happen."

This was honest at least and I was listening.

"I have a relationship with Mr. Spelling," he said, continuing, "and I believe we have a close enough friendship that I should be able to call him and talk to him."

Immediately I felt somewhat calmer. "Are you going to call him, then? He doesn't want to talk to me. They won't talk to me. Will you talk to him?"

Scott assured me he would talk to Mr. Spelling. "I'll find out what's really going on. Tell me: How do you feel? What would you like to see happen?"

"I need to work," I answered bluntly. "This is not right. I've just sold my house. I've just walked away from the show I've been on for all this time. I thought we were going to work together."

"I'll talk to him and see what he can do," Scott said. "I'll just talk to him. Don't worry about it."

Everybody kept saying that.

More time went by, and I heard nothing further. Everyone remained unavailable. I was hardly working anymore, since my character, Taylor, on *The Bold and the Beautiful* had nearly been written out. I had time to brood, sitting around in my soon-to-be-sold Las Vegas house, wondering what was going on. I couldn't decide on whether to call a storage company or to investigate the possibilities of backing out of the house deal.

As I thought about what recourse I had, I felt increasingly uncertain. If I fought this, Innovative Artists might drop me. Marv too. Who in the industry would want to touch an actress who challenged Spelling Entertainment?

I began wondering what I could have done. Were they right? Had I broken the contract?

I remember sitting on the edge of our canopy bed beset by another severe migraine, trying to sort it all out. Spelling Entertainment believed that I had violated or breached my contract. Had I? I wanted to take a reality check. If someone breaches a contract, then he or she *should* be fired. I believed that to be true. If I had done something wrong, then I wanted to be honest with myself and figure out what that could be.

Paragraph 10(a) specified that I wasn't allowed to change my appearance. They were saying pregnancy automatically means I've changed the way I look. But I didn't look any different. What did that appearance clause mean, anyway? In the entertainment business, usually it means deliberately changing one's appearance—that's what most actresses understand it to mean. If I decided to change my hair, shave my head Sinead O'Connor–style or crop it short and dye it blond, or if I put an earring in my nose and I did that in the middle of a season and it didn't make sense for the character, then I would be materially changing my appearance. If I had wanted a nose job and went down and had it done without telling the show and they couldn't account for it in the script, then I would have screwed up. That's how that clause usually applies.

Then I thought, okay, what are the ways to resolve something like that? If I had started wearing an earring, I would take the earring out. If I cut my hair short or dyed it, I'd put on a wig for a while. If I had gotten a bad nose job, I'd have more surgery to correct the problem. If I'm having a baby, I can have surgery to take it out . . .

The moment that thought entered my head, I immediately hated myself. I hated that they had even caused me to think such a thought. Truly, how dare they? I felt ashamed for having considered the possibility—even hypothetically.

Then I grasped that, however repugnant the notion, it was logical. Sitting on the edge of the very bed in which my child had been conceived, I saw that an abortion was a logical solution—a way out—in a situation where pregnancy breached a contract. Where pregnancy caused other people problems. Solve the problem. Take the child out.

At that moment, after not talking to God or listening to him for quite a while, I heard God speak to me very clearly: *Do you think you are the first one who ever felt like this or faced that thought?*

Everything came down to that moment. The whole course of events seemed to gather above my head in a furiously condensing thundercloud that whipped around the room before settling before me as my own Pandora's box.

There it is, God told me. *You think you're the first? This is a problem much bigger than just you. This is your battle. This is your work.*

"Oh, my gosh," I said out loud.

I could hear the rationalizations I once was tempted by. It's just tissue at this point. Nothing more. I've worked for this my whole life. I could call and say I had a miscarriage. That would be true, in a way. No one gets that upset over a miscarriage. You don't have funerals for miscarriages. In time, I could have convinced myself.

You're not the first, God said to me, *you won't be the last.*

Immediately, I was frightened. If I fight this, they're going to kill me. My career will be over.

But if I didn't fight it, then the problem might never be addressed. People in Spelling Entertainment's position would have the power to influence working women not to bear children.

They must be assuming I'll go away, I thought. Most women would. That or actually have the abortion. How many already have? No one will ever know that. Why would a woman in that position ever tell anyone? The shame would be too much. Who would ever come forward and confess to this act, or even its temptation? Who?

Only a woman willing to make one of her first truly unselfish choices. I had already made enough selfish ones for a lifetime, many of which were still haunting me.

Part Two

6

The first time I went through a "problem pregnancy," my experience matched millions of other young women who are in too much of a hurry to grow up.

In the spring of 1980, the year I graduated from high school, I was working at the cosmetics counter of a Striplings Department Store. This slick guy came up in a suit and tie, a Rolex at his wrist. "Hi, what's your name?" His voice didn't have a trace of Texas accent. He claimed to be a golf pro.

He wondered if I'd like to go out some time.

He looked like a terrific guy to me, but I knew he came straight out of my mother's worst nightmare. Even I thought he might be too old for me.

So I said, "Maybe. But how old are you? The reason I'm asking is, my mom doesn't want me to go out with guys who are a lot older."

"How old can they be?"

"Twenty-two. No more than that."

"Well, that's exactly how old I am. Twenty-two."

At the time, Tom was actually twenty-five, but I was in no hurry to find out the truth.

He drove the twenty miles from downtown Fort Worth, where he lived, to Springtown to pick me up—a sure sign he liked me. I kept telling my parents he was only twenty-two. They noticed his all-too-smooth manner. My mother knew he couldn't be twenty-two.

To all her objections, I kept repeating, he's twenty-two, he's twenty-two. Isn't he cute? He's a nice guy. He's already a pro golfer! And he's only twenty-two!

Tom kept up the ruse by his willingness to enter into my teenage activities: We went to the senior prom together.

After we had dated for a while, he called me while my parents were twenty-five miles away from home, visiting my grandmother. There was a bad thunderstorm. He said he was driving out and wanted to know if I'd go play tennis.

"It's raining here," I said. I wasn't supposed to leave the house when my parents were gone.

"It's fine in Fort Worth," he said. "I'll pick you up and bring you out of the rain."

"But my mom and dad aren't here, and if I leave, I'll get in trouble."

"Leave a note, then. They know we're dating. Look, you can blame it on me. If they're angry I'll come right over and talk to them about it, just like I've talked to them every other time I've come over. I want to see you. Besides, you're going to be eighteen this summer!"

I left the note and he picked me up. We did go to play tennis. Then we went to his apartment and slept together for the first time. I thought, he's older, we can handle this. But afterward, I didn't feel right about it at all and insisted we stop having sex until we were married—if we ever would be.

One month later, I graduated from high school, and my older sister, who was a stewardess, took me to Acapulco. The first night there, although I was still only seventeen, I drank a margarita. We didn't drink in our house and this was a new experience. The next day, I was horribly sick—presumably from the margarita. But every day of that week I woke up sick to my stomach and felt nauseated until exactly ten o'clock each morning, when the feeling mysteriously disappeared.

I kept telling myself that the unusual food or the water was making me sick, but I suspected I was pregnant. I couldn't be pregnant, though, could I? How can a girl get pregnant the *first* and *only* time she sleeps with a guy? (I'm here to tell you, it *does* happen.)

I went back with my sister to her home in Nashville. The morning sickness kept up. My sister noticed that my breasts were now bigger than hers. Even her boyfriend, noticing how blue in the face I was one morning, asked whether I might be pregnant.

Covering madly, I asked them to take me down to the drugstore—I wanted to buy some tampons. All the way down I kept thinking of a girl I knew in high school who had had five abortions before graduation. I remembered all the trouble she had been through—her sadness, her grief. That would never be me, I decided.

Instead of buying tampons, I bought a pregnancy test. When I found out that, sure enough, I was pregnant, I thought, I'm not going to freak out. It'll be okay. It'll be all right. Fine. Good. I wanted to leave Springtown anyway. This is my ticket outta there. I'm out of high school, it's time to grow up, it's going to be fine.

When I returned to the Dallas–Forth Worth airport, Tom picked me up. I knew I had to tell him and tried to make a game of it. "Remember you were talking about getting married soon?"

"Yeah, sure." His expression fell and his face turned white.

"Maybe we should do it really soon. Would you like that?"

He was too scared now to reply.

"I'm pregnant."

A long moment passed.

"What do you want to do?" Tom asked.

"I guess I need to see a doctor."

"A doctor? What kind of doctor?"

"An obstetrician," I said. "What other kind of doctor would I see?"

He let that be the final word on the matter. I began my prenatal care visits, which Tom drove me to, helping to conceal the pregnancy from my parents.

Tom bought me an engagement ring. He went to my mom and dad and sat down with them one evening, asking for my hand.

My mother protested that I was too young. I needed to go to college. I had been awarded a four-year scholarship to Texas Woman's University.

"She's *going* to go to school," Tom said. "I make a decent living as a golf pro. I only want to make her happy. We'll buy a nice house—maybe on the golf course at Colonial—and we'll settle into a real life. She won't be far away, either. You'll probably see her more than you do now."

My parents doubted the wisdom of this, but what could they say? They saw how determined we were.

I asked my mother to buy tampons for me and in other ways misled her about my pregnancy.

Not long after Tom and I were married, on July 18, my parents visited me in our apartment. I had left my prenatal vitamins out on the bathroom sink, and my mother found them.

She came out of the bathroom with the vitamin bottle in her hand. "What is this?"

I was thinking, I'm married now, she can't ground me! Then I noticed her expression. I saw how deeply my betrayal had hurt her. Without saying another word, she ran out the door. "You've really done it this time," my father said sadly and followed her.

My mother wouldn't talk to me for several months after that. I expected as much. Many times as I grew up, she'd turn red at dinner over a family fracas and begin to combust. Like Laura Petrie from *The Dick Van Dyke Show,* she'd blow up with an "Oh, Rob!" and storm off to her bedroom, where she'd remain for the rest of the evening.

This time, my dad served as a reconciling go-between, visiting me from time to time at work or stopping by the apartment. My dad and I always had an unusually close relationship. While I was growing up, my father represented Hunt-Wesson Foods to grocery stores in central Texas. I was Daddy's girl and loved to go with him on overnight trips to Wichita Falls or Waco, where I could swim in the motel pools. In the grocery stores, he'd get down on his knees rearranging the displayed cans, dust the shelf off with Windex, and fix the price cards. His elegant handwriting made the "Sale" signs look like calligraphy. In the smaller stores, where my dad often had long-standing friendships with the owners, he'd say, "Got anything for my little girl here?" The owner would reach behind the counter and present me with a bag of candy. When my dad and I watched TV together in the evenings, he would stroke my hair. I adored him.

One day he brought the cutest pair of booties, a baby hairbrush, and a little toothbrush set. He told me Mom had picked them out, but that she just needed more time. Then he asked me when the baby was due. I told him.

"Well, when your mom cools down," my dad said, "I want you to come back and visit us. Are you going to come visit us?"

I could only nod yes, because I was crying.

"You have to understand," my father said, "your mom got married when she was fifteen. She had your older sister, Elizabeth, when she was younger than you are right now. She just wants you to have . . . she just wanted you to have the kind of life she never had. She wanted you to grow up free of so many responsibilities."

"I know, Dad," I said, "I know Mom wants the best for me."

He kissed me and kept visiting until Mom was ready to see me again.

Tom's grand plans for our future seemed to evaporate the moment we were married. Right after my son Chris was born, we learned that our apartment complex didn't allow children. Worse, Tom's income couldn't provide for another apartment. We had to move back in with my parents.

I'll never forget holding little Christopher, nursing him as an infant in the bed I'd slept in through my own childhood, thinking: What is going to happen to my life? Is this ever going to get better?

Like many new mothers, I was suffering from postpartum blues, and my sweet little son's suckling had produced a very large, very sore blood blister.

In that terrible situation, my own childhood dreams came back to me as a torment. When I was little and couldn't sleep, I would crawl or tiptoe down the hall and lie down outside my parents' bedroom door. They kept the door closed and the kids out as much as possible during the night. Lying there close to them helped me feel secure. I would begin to dream of being beautiful like my older sister, Elizabeth, or even a fairy princess like Cinderella—not the ugly duckling I felt I was. My brother Jay called me Chili Lips— "Looks like you ate a big old chili pepper," he'd say, and I'd bite my full lips.

I guess I thought someone loving me would turn me into the beautiful woman I had always wanted to be, but that hadn't happened—far from it.

Tom worked sporadically selling cars and as an assistant pro in Grapevine. Our life improved for a while. After we had lived with my parents for six months, we moved into our own apartment in Fort Worth.

Tom depended on me to make life better as well. On the one hand, he wanted his clothes washed and ironed and dinner on the table every night at five o'clock. On the other, he expected me to put Chris in day care and find a job—or two jobs.

I began serving drinks at Billy Bob's, in the VIP room. I wore the requisite denim skirt, tuxedo shirt with a tie, and heels. Very hillbilly. I used to bring lemonade to Donny and Marie and drinks to a variety of country music stars. My life was hell, but my customers were doling out twenty-, fifty-, hundred-dollar tips.

I also worked happy hour at a strip club that was owned by Spencer Taylor, who also owned Billy Bob's. I think he offered me the job because he felt sorry for me, as I was having such a hard time making ends meet. At the strip club, I wore a long-sleeved black bodysuit and a long black Danskin wraparound skirt down to my ankles. The other girls wore much skimpier outfits and received better tips, but the place terrified me. Men would ask me to dance. Waitresses can't do that, I'd say in the harshest language I could muster. I began getting a tough edge, putting those characters down.

For many young women, the trip from serving drinks to stripping to hooking can be as fast as a few straight shots of tequila, and my kinder customers didn't want to see it happen to me. I had already watched girls sleep with managers and patrons for "shopping sprees" or weekends in Vegas. I was learning what could happen.

I began thinking of other ways to make money. It was becoming clear that Tom couldn't hold on to a job. He had now bounced back and forth from the life of a golf pro to that of a car salesman four or five times in the two years of our marriage. I was becoming convinced I'd have to be the family's chief means of support—that meant both paying the rent and saving for a college education, because my scholarship had expired. I was already preparing myself to leave the marriage, because I didn't know how much longer I could stand living a nightmare.

Like many people trying to cope with a problem-riddled existence, I reached into my past for two "alternate selves"—two different people I had once been—in order to overcome my present circumstances.

I hadn't always been the boy-crazy girl at the cosmetics counter. In fact, I had been a tomboy through most of my girlhood. When I was eleven, my family moved to Springtown, where we had a countrified house on five acres—the dream house my father spent his life saving for. I was an animal lover and promptly turned the backyard into a zoo, with two alligators, snakes, a red-tailed fox, a ring-tailed cat, a raccoon, and an assortment of cows, kittens, dogs, and guinea pigs.

My tomboy years included participating in the Future Farmers of America. I was the only girl, so the boys made me an honorary guy by calling me by my last name, Hunter. (That's part of the reason why, when I was choosing a screen name later in life, I found it natural to drop my original first name, Deborah, and combine my maiden name with my married last name.) Besides learning about raising livestock, I learned to ride well enough to participate in rodeo barrel races. That's where many of my first boyfriends came from—those young cowboys at the rodeos. I always looked to see if they had a snuff can (good ol' Skoal) in their back pockets. If I saw a telltale ring, that zeroed them out for me. Not that I wasn't down-home myself. I liked to run around barefoot, in frayed cutoff jeans and men's shirts.

As I came to face the difficulties of my marriage, I knew I would have to toughen up. The animal-doctoring, barrel-racing Hunter could do that, and I needed to rediscover the realism and courage those experiences had ingrained in me.

The tomboy needed to be complemented by another personality. My mother actually encouraged me to find the second "alternate self" that I now laid claim to once more.

When I was fifteen, she grew tired of my tomboy phase. She came to me one day and said, "You know, instead of using the money we've saved for a down payment on a car, I'd like to spend it on something else."

"What?"

"I think you need to go to charm school. You're too much of a tomboy. You sit with your legs open. You walk funny. You're slumping your shoulders."

"*Mom,* a charm school?"

"It's not really a charm school—I shouldn't have said that. It's more a modeling school. You can learn about modeling."

That's how I ended up at John Robert Powers in Fort Worth, Texas, right across from Texas Christian University. A woman there named Mrs. Bates took me under her wing. I learned how to introduce myself, how to greet people. I learned how to dress and apply makeup so that it didn't look like I had taken blue billiards chalk and smeared it above my eyes. We also learned a little about modeling; how to pose for photographs, how to make turns on a runway.

The school offered its students a chance to have a professional photographer do head shots of us. This cost two hundred dollars, and my family didn't have money for such things. But Mrs. Bates convinced my mother to have the pictures taken—I think the kind woman worked out some discount for us.

When the pictures came back, even I was impressed. I'm very conscious of two little bumps at either side of the bridge of my nose, but with makeup and lighting, they went right away. Look what they can do! I thought.

The pictures resulted in a couple of modeling jobs. The first was a photo shoot for *Hawg Jaws* magazine. In the photograph, I'm wearing a sporty, two-piece swimsuit and holding a big, jumbo bass dangling from the end of a fishing line. "Hey, look what I caught!" my expression says.

Soon thereafter, I began to realize how competitive modeling would be and lost interest, but I remembered these experiences now when I most needed to. I dug out my John Robert Powers book. Maybe I can make some commercials, I thought. But I'd have to lose my Texas accent. Didn't my old charm school teach diction classes?

Even if I did lose the accent, I'd have to learn to read aloud—an old bugaboo. Up until this time, my acting experience had been limited to participating in the Texas Junior Miss pageant and 4-H Club productions. I liked being up on the stage—I felt excited and comfortable there. But I knew I couldn't read out loud; in fact, I was terrified of having to do so after years in school stumbling through passages under a teacher's reproving eye. (My 4-H Club stage roles had been limited to virtually nonspeaking parts, in which I relied on physical actions to get laughs.)

My acting career may well have started with the decision I made right then—and the determination with which I followed up on that decision—to learn to read aloud. Every day for three months, I sat in our apartment—either while Chris was taking a nap or watching his favorite TV program, *The Price Is Right*—and read aloud from newspapers, or novels, or anything else that came to hand. I taught myself how to make the sentences sound as if they were making sense, how to use phrasing. Too embarrassed to admit to anyone else that I couldn't read aloud, I worked and worked at it until the sentences no longer ended in midair but ran along meaningfully to their conclusions.

Then I began making calls—to the photographer who had taken my head shots and others I knew in the modeling business. The man who did the *Hawg Jaws* layout was doing a new commercial. When I read the commercial's copy for him, he said, "You're just saying the words. You're not putting anything behind it. There's an acting coach in Dallas you should go see. Don Shook."

That's how I met the man who saved my life. Don Shook became my Svengali.

Don accepted me into his acting class. In exchange for classes, which I couldn't afford, I did office work a few hours a week for the theater company. Don also convinced me to perform a monologue. He asked me to memorize one of Sofie's long speeches from *Star-Spangled Girl.* I looked at it and thought, This is pages and pages of material, how am I ever going to memorize all this?

By tackling Don's challenge, I learned that I actually had a talent for memorizing dramatic speeches. I worked on the monologue for two or three days, trying to think how I would say the speech if I were talking to one of my friends. At the same time, I worried about others' reactions. I could see the girls in the class saying, "Yeah, yeah, watch her, she's awful." In the scene, Sofie's supposed to get so worked up she nearly bursts into tears; my terror of the audience's opinion got me halfway there before I started.

I rehearsed the scene beforehand with Don. He kept telling me, "Everybody wants to see you succeed. They want to enjoy your performance. Don't think that they want to see you fall on your face. That's not fun for anyone." He was tremendously encouraging—like a father figure.

I did the scene and when I was done, everybody said, "You almost made me cry. Oh, you were so good." I didn't much believe them, but I didn't forget my lines and I had gotten through it.

That alone was enough to give me a tremendous amount of satisfaction.

I entered into all the standard acting exercises of mimicking a cat, pretending to be an armchair, and improvising scenes with other actors without a script.

Don started teaching me about culture. He took me to my first play, *Sweeney Todd,* and I was blown away by it. It inspired me.

Don put me in a ballet class over at Brookhaven Community College, which is in North Dallas. He got me running two miles every other day. He would tell me, "Your legs are flabby. You have a potbelly. What are you, twenty-one, twenty-two? How can you be in such awful shape? And you've got to get rid of that accent!"

He actually taught me five or six accents to make me aware of my own and cure me of it. He often invited me over to his house, where he had toys in the backyard that Chris could play with. He worked me relentlessly.

Don had a performing group called The Actors Company. Every weekend, he loaded up a van full of actors and took them to perform plays at country clubs, playhouses, dinner theaters, and community groups. He was booked every weekend, all year long.

He called me over one day during class. "I've got to talk to you about something very serious."

"Okay."

"Marla, who's supposed to play JoAnne in *Vanities,* is sick. She can't do the play next Saturday. I want you to do the role. I'll pay you three hundred dollars for the weekend's shows."

Vanities is about three girls who are cheerleaders in high school. The three acts follow these young women through the different phases of their lives. It's a funny play based on Texas society, so my accent didn't present a problem.

The two other young women in the show were made to rehearse more than usual because I was just learning how to listen for my cues and know where to move at what time. Fortunately, the play is simple to perform physically—the set consists mostly of three chairs that are configured the same way during the whole piece. I actually learned the play's movements in the first rehearsal. We devoted the following rehearsals to working out business (physical actions) and ways our personalities could exploit the play's comic potential.

The first time we performed, we received a standing ovation. I couldn't believe Don had brought me so far so fast.

In fact, I had already achieved my goal: making extra money through local performances. I had no plans to go further in acting. I believed that additional modeling jobs were out of the question. The dominant modeling agency in the Dallas area, the Kim Dawson Agency, wouldn't represent me because I wasn't tall enough. I did find a small agency to represent me as a model and actress, but they never sent me on any interviews. I thought I had come as far in entertainment as I was likely to go.

In the meantime, my relationship with Tom was becoming ever more strained. He spent many weekends away, either working or playing golf. He became more and more abusive. He would push me down on the bed, again and again, demonstrating I was powerless against his strength. He wanted to make me feel totally dependent upon him.

One night in bed, I cried and told him I couldn't live this way.

He said, "You'll never leave me. You can't. You couldn't possibly cope with the world without me. You don't know how to take care of yourself."

He was so smug that I knew he believed that about me—that I couldn't handle life on my own.

Like many people, I used to be someone who "went along." I found myself in various situations rather than choosing to participate—that was the way it felt, at least. That night in bed, lying beside a man who had married me because he felt I would remain dependent upon him, no matter how badly he treated me, I made perhaps the first clear-cut decision of my life, and a momentous one at that.

The next day, after Tom left to look for work, I recruited my friends and we cleaned out everything that belonged to Chris or me in the apartment. We left the place practically bare. Tom came home to nothing but his clothes hanging in the closet.

Chris and I went to live with one of Don's close friends, Carol, in Prestonwood, an exclusive North Dallas suburb. I felt more relieved than I could say.

At the same time, I had been raised to believe that divorce was wrong. Chris loved his father. For these reasons, I debated getting back together with Tom. After six months of separation, we began seeing each other again.

While Tom and I were dating once more, a movie company came to Dallas to shoot a teenage horror flick. They were hiring local actors for non-principal roles because Dallas actors came cheaper. I was offered a part. When I read the script, I noted that there was a group shower scene in a high school girls' locker room. I asked the producers how the scene would be shot and was told the camera would take a long shot down a corridor toward a steam-enshrouded group. No one would ever be able to make out what the other actresses and I looked like naked. I had my doubts about the movie, but Tom urged me to take it, thinking it might pave the way to much bigger things.

When we were actually setting up for the shower scene, I saw that the director meant to bring the camera "up close and personal." It was still a group scene, but there would be no doubt what any of us looked like undressed. I walked off the set, refusing to do the scene.

Everyone pounced on me. Not only the producers and director but the local head of the Screen Actors Guild of Dallas as well. They told me I was acting like a prima donna. "Take off your clothes and get on with it!" they all but ordered. "These are Hollywood people!"

What was really upsetting was that even Tom didn't defend me in this situation. I saw he was so intent on exploiting my value as an actress (and wage earner) that his love for me as his wife meant little. I went back and did the scene, but I felt doubly used.

I had landed a weekday job at an advertising agency and was trying to build up a college fund. One day, I wrote a check on my college fund account and it bounced. I thought there must be some mistake and went straight to the bank. They showed me the series of withdrawals Tom had made that completely drained the account.

The instant I returned to our apartment, I called him at the country club where he worked.

The woman who answered told me that Tom hadn't worked there for several months.

When Tom arrived home, he explained that he had been let go in circumstances that were beyond his control. I had heard that one before. He did his best to make it all very confusing. The long and the short of it was, my college fund had gone to pay for day-to-day expenses.

In the spring of 1984, I was acting in another Don Shook production in Dallas and was spotted by Joan D'Inchecco, a casting director associated with the soap opera *All My Children*. She was giving workshops at Weist-Barron in North Dallas—a studio that helps actors prepare for commercials. Would I like to tape an audition for *All My Children*? The show was looking for a new actress to fill a contract role.

The day of the audition, I had one of the worst migraines of my life. I called my talent agency to beg off, but they told me that I ought to go in and do the audition, however badly it might go. An actor who gets a reputation for blowing off auditions . . . well, it's not good.

I had received the auditioning script earlier and worked through it, so I was ready to perform the part, as long as I could bear the pain and stand up. The migraine had the paradoxical effect of relaxing me. I was in so much pain I didn't much care how the audition went. Joan stood to one side of the camera and asked me to act the part as if I were speaking to her. She seemed to like what I was doing. "You'll probably hear from us in a few days."

I called my mother and I told her of the casting director's encouragement. She told me to take the audition as a compliment and keep on doing my plays but not to expect anything.

That was always my mother's way, and her negativity haunted me for many years. It also went back into my early adolescence. The first time anyone noticed that I was growing up was the Christmas I was fifteen. My mother finally took me out of plaid and polka dots and let me wear a stylish shirtdress with a slit up the side and the slip-on shoes called Candie's. My sister was already working as a stewardess for American Airlines and she showed me how to do my hair and put on makeup. We went visiting my parents' friends, and they noticed the transformation. "Your daughter is so beautiful," they said. "Oh, she's so pretty."

"Don't tell her that now," my mother said, making light of their comments. "Pretty is as pretty does."

My mother's comments to her friends were chitchat, but her instructions to me afterward carried a far more serious tone. "Don't you dare go getting a big head. Don't you dare think that you're beautiful, because you're not. You're not. What matters is if you're beautiful inside."

I understand what my mother was trying to do now—the trouble she meant to spare me—but the way she expressed her fears blasted my confidence. I felt ever hungrier for affection and approval. Mothers have to find ways of warning their daughters against presuming their looks will get them where they want to go without making them feel unloved, as my mother and I both now know.

Anyway, three days later, despite my mother's nay-saying, *All My Children* called my talent agent. They were sending me a first-class ticket and putting me up at the St. Moritz on the Park Hotel in New York City. They wanted me to do a screen test with the show's star, Larry Lau. They were seriously considering me for the contract role. If I was offered the part, I would have to move to New York.

My mother kept saying, it's never going to happen. Enjoy New York. This will be a wonderful memory.

I flew to New York sitting beside another young woman who would also be auditioning for the part, someone I had met at the Junior Miss pageant. We liked each other and calmed each other down. Her being there made the whole experience less frightening.

When we arrived in New York, we enjoyed seeing the city together. We went to Greenwich Village and SoHo in a cab and then had to walk back most of the way because we ran out of money. Like most newcomers to the Big Apple, we couldn't believe how big and energetic and expensive the place was.

We went to tape our auditions and another actress was there to audition as well. We would all be doing a scene as Robin—a street kid who steals a guy's camera on the subway. The man chases and catches her, and as a result of their encounter, in which he finds out her sad story, he befriends her. These scenes were meant to set up a long story line.

The other actress from Texas and I watched a New York native go through her paces. She was good. Too good. She nailed that character. Oh, well, we thought, it's been a nice stay in New York.

I played the part, as did the other actresses, with Don Scardino, who was subbing for the star, Larry Lau. I might have been overwhelmed in Larry Lau's presence, since I was a longtime *All My Children* fan. Don made me feel much more comfortable and I enjoyed the audition. I played the part like the character Libby in *I Ought to Be in Pictures,* one of the plays Don Shook mounted. I enjoyed the audition and thought I had done well, but remained convinced that I would be living in Dallas for the foreseeable future.

I flew back home on Tuesday. I told my mom the trip went great, but I was certain that this other girl was going to get the part because she was a terrific actress and she had that New York attitude they wanted. That talented girl's name was Lori Petty, who later starred in *A League of Their Own.*

On Friday, three days later, *All My Children* called again. They called to say "Yes!" They wanted me in New York by Monday. The part was mine, for the next three years.

7

My new life in New York in the spring of 1985 quickly worked itself out in ways that were more wonderful than I ever could have imagined. By the end of that Friday, when *All My Children* called to offer me the part, my father came to my apartment in Dallas and helped me put my furniture in storage. We parked my car in my parents' driveway. They agreed to take care of Chris for me until I could get established in New York.

It just so happened that a girl in my acting class had recently broken up with her New York boyfriend. He lived in a penthouse on Sixty-second Street and First Avenue. When she found out I was going to New York for an interview, she let me know that her old boyfriend was looking to let out a room. As it turned out, he was leaving New York for three months to go yachting in an international competition. He was willing to rent the whole place to me for the price of one room if I would walk his dog while he was away.

I began making $666.13 per show. At the time, that seemed like fabulous wealth. It gave me the means to find my own studio apartment once the penthouse's owner returned. More important, it helped me take care of Chris and put some money in savings. I was still thinking that my time as an actress would soon come to an end. Then I could go back to school to pursue my childhood dream of becoming a veterinarian.

The first two or three months, I flew back every weekend to be with Chris. These weekends sometimes stretched to four and five days because I was new on the show, still learning how to act on TV, and the writers kept my story line "light"—I was only taping a couple of shows per week.

I learned as soon as possible what I needed to know in order to bring Chris to New York. A longtime soap opera actress, Mary Fickett, who played Ruth Martin on *All My Children* for years, suggested home-care nurses that I could absolutely depend on, even if I had to pay as much as seven dollars an hour. (I was paying seventy-five cents back home in Texas.) That was good advice, and when Chris came to New York he was well taken care of by registered nurses.

Others gave me invaluable advice as well. I remember Mark LaMura taking me aside one day—he played Erica Kane's brother Mark Dalton. He told me, "Don't be stupid. Save every cent you make on this show. Don't drink it away. Don't snort it up your nose. Save it."

My three-and-a-half-year-old Chris adapted to New York far faster than I did. Sometimes he would come with me to work. He'd sit up on the makeup chair and watch me on the cameras. He knew that when I went off camera, I'd soon be by his side once more.

Chris even learned to handle the fans. When we'd come out of the studio, people would be waiting for the actors to sign autographs. I liked to oblige. I felt I owed the people that much. Chris would wait for me in the cold—his little cheeks red—only so long. He'd get really mad and he'd frown and start saying, "No, no, no. She's done. She's done working. She's my mommy now and we're going home!"

The fans would ooh and ahh at the little man sticking up for his mommy, and we'd go home.

I took Chris all over New York with me, and we enjoyed ourselves, whether we were eating at the Russian Tea Room or having a pretzel from a street vendor.

I had been part of *All My Children* for two years when Michael Tylo joined the cast as Susan Lucci's new love interest, Matt Connolly. The buzz on the set had it that Michael had been a big deal on *Guiding Light* and was sure to attract even more attention in Susan's company. He seemed to have a chip on his shoulder, though, with a particularly nasty attitude toward women. I could see he was cute, but I wanted nothing to do with him.

If there's a fine line between love and hate, Michael's and my relationship started well south of the border. He made me sick—or threatened to. In one of our first scenes together, my character, Robin, was supposed to be using Matt Connolly to make my boyfriend jealous. Robin's boyfriend was to walk in the door just as Robin and Matt began to kiss.

The day we shot the scene, Michael looked green about the gills during rehearsal. As we ran our lines together, he told me that he had spoken to the producer and recommended drastic cuts. "This line's out, that line's out," he said. He argued that his character would never be interested in a "high-school Harriet" like my character and so the scene had to be cut drastically—mutilated, in my opinion. We ended up with about four lines together, hardly worth doing.

This guy's really got some nerve, I thought. Who does he think he is?

When Michael came back on the set to shoot the scene, he suddenly turned from green to pale gray to white, and then he fainted. They had to take him away in an ambulance.

The producers asked me to stick around. They said Michael would come back after being checked out, and we could shoot our scenes at the end of the day. I waited around, thinking, This guy is truly weird.

But when he came back, I felt sorry for him because he looked so ill. As we were about to do our kissing scene, I joked, "This isn't something I'm going to catch, is it?"

"Just do the scene," he said flatly.

When he walked off, I turned to a friend of mine and said, "That's got to be the biggest ass I've ever met in my life."

Before too long, though, Michael's attitude toward me started to change. He invited me to a movie several times "just as friends."

What's this guy doing? I wondered. What was this about?

Michael's approaches continued and became more serious. One day during rehearsal, when I still had rollers in my hair and no makeup, he came up to me and asked, "Has this ever happened to you? When you've known someone for a while and then you look at them for the first time and realize how beautiful they are?"

"Is that a line or what?" I shot back, my face getting red with embarrassment. "Listen," I told him, "I made this rule. I don't date people I work with. I don't date actors. Period. You got that?"

He went away looking so stricken that I felt guilty for being so hard on him.

He also took an interest in my personal affairs and even my morality. That season on *All My Children,* my character came under the influence of an evil guy and was working in a sleazy bar as a waitress. I had to wear fishnet hose with a skimpy little bodysuit.

Michael came up to me one day and said, "You know, you've got suntan lines on your butt and it really looks kind of cheap. You should do something about that."

This angered me plenty, but I would have been even more disturbed if I hadn't recognized a hidden kindness in the remark that keyed my own memories of Billy Bob's and the strip joint. Only five years had passed since I had worked as a cocktail waitress. I knew far more about how women come to regard themselves as "cheap" than Michael could possibly have guessed. I remembered my old customers telling me to get out of that life, and how glad I was I took their advice!

When Thanksgiving rolled around, Michael invited Chris and

me to the Macy's Thanksgiving Day Parade. He had tickets. It would be nice for Chris to see the big cartoon-character balloons, he said. He tried to assume a casual attitude. "No pressure," he said. He gave me his phone number on a piece of paper. "Give me a call if you'd like to go."

I took the phone number with every intention of calling him to turn him down. I was going to tell him I couldn't do it because I had made reservations with Chris at a hotel buffet. We were perfectly happy eating Thanksgiving dinner by ourselves. Chris, as an extraordinarily worldly-wise five-year-old who liked to dress up in suits and eat oysters, loved having me all to himself. But then I lost Michael's phone number. I really did. Michael tells me to this day how he sat by the telephone all day, eating a turkey sandwich and cranberries out of a can, waiting for me to call for dinner. He blew off the parade tickets, waiting.

Perhaps I lost Michael's number because I was involved in another romantic intrigue. I had been dating a New York doctor for more than a year, a dermatologist whom I met after the heavy, wax-based show makeup started ruining my complexion. We were becoming more serious all the while, even as a soap opera–like conflict pursued us.

This doctor—I'll call him Seymour—had an old girlfriend who would not go away. She would show up during our dates, knowing all the places Seymour hung out. She would even leave threatening messages on my answering machine.

In turn, I would leave messages on Seymour's machine, complaining about her messages. I'd make sure to leave my clothes behind in his apartment for her to find if she came over. During her visits, she left out photographs of their time together. He always claimed she was an uninvited guest, but now I'm sure he was playing us off against one another the whole time.

During this particular Thanksgiving, it dawned on me that Seymour wasn't at a medical symposium at all, as he claimed, but was probably with his old girlfriend at her parents' house.

Then, strangely, the next week, he invited me to go with him to upstate New York for a conference on hair implants. He wanted me to stay with him in a nice bed-and-breakfast with a beautiful fireplace. Chris left right after Thanksgiving to stay with my parents for the month; I was very busy on the show and didn't want him sitting at the studio all day. Everything seemed to work out for me to go, and Seymour and I had a wonderful time.

Upstate New York was beautiful, with all the trees covered in ice and snow. I thought our relationship must be getting serious, especially when he told me, "I'm buying a beautiful apartment on Seventy-second Street and I want you to help me decorate it."

On the way back from our weekend, we stopped to look in several bathroom-supply and fixture stores. I helped him pick out pedestal sinks, tile—stuff that I had always wanted. We were shopping like a young married couple.

Wow, I thought, he's asking me to decorate the house. He's wants me to furnish it so that I'll be happy. *Here comes the proposal!*

A few days later, I thought I would surprise Seymour with a Christmas gift. Who but the wicked "ex-girlfriend" answered the phone that night. She proceeded to tell me that they had just made love, that they were working everything out.

"What are you talking about?" I asked. "We picked out bathroom fixtures. We picked out toilets, for God's sake. You can't be back together."

Pure soap opera dialogue.

"Yes, we are," she said, insisting. "We're more in love than ever. He wants to have children and we're going to have *our* children. His mother hates your guts, you know. And if his mother doesn't approve of you, you might as well not waste your time."

"Put Seymour on!" I demanded.

When he got on the phone, he said, "I'm sorry. I'm really sorry. You know how she is."

"What is she doing there?" I screamed. "Why would you even let her in?"

"She had a Christmas gift for me," he said. "How can I turn away somebody who's bringing me a gift?"

"And I'm sure we both know what that gift was."

"No, no, it's not like that."

"You know what?" I asked. "That's it. I've had it with you. I'm sick of you playing these games. I've wasted my time with you long enough."

I spent Christmas and New Year's with my family in Texas. Michael was with his family as well.

Both of our families were asking similar questions. Michael's family pressed him: "Mickey [as they called him], what do you think about that younger girl who plays Robin McCall? She's really interesting. We like her story."

Michael told them, "Oh, she's a spoiled little fast-laner. She's only interested in herself."

My parents and family wanted to know, "What's that new guy like who plays Matt Connolly? He's really good. You know, he was on *General Hospital* or *Guiding Light*, wasn't he? We think he's great. Is he a nice guy?"

"No, he's the biggest jerk that ever walked the face of the earth," I told them.

By the end of January, though, I started seeing what my family already had.

After the holidays, Michael found a successful way of disguising another invitation. He had our friend Mark LaMura stand in the corridor with him as they chatted about the bet they were making on the upcoming Redskins-Giants NFC championship football game. "You want in on this action?" Mark asked me as I walked by. "This stiff from Detroit thinks the Redskins are going to get over on our Giants."

"Sure," I said, thinking I would help LaMura antagonize him.

"Loser takes the winners out to dinner."

"Sure," I said.

I don't think I really got the point until I arrived at the restaurant, Wilson's, and saw Mark LaMura sitting by his date and

Michael sitting by an empty chair. Win or lose, I would be going out with him. I prepared myself to spend the evening fuming.

That night, though, I met the real Michael. His marriage of eight years was in serious trouble. His wife and he had actually been separated for three years. He had wanted children. Now he didn't even have a relationship and he resented that and felt cheated. After a few drinks, he poured out his heart.

Through the course of that evening, I realized there was a lot more to this person than I had first seen and that his whole macho, tough act was nothing more than a show.

After the other couple left, Michael offered to walk me home. We stopped at another bar; we just wanted to extend the evening and get to know more about each other. As he told me more about his life, I kept saying, "I can't believe—why didn't you just tell me you were going through all that stuff? I wouldn't have been mean to you. I just thought you were a jerk!"

At that point, we both knew I was going to break my rule about not dating actors.

When we arrived at my doorstep, I still felt I should not make anything too easy.

I could tell he wanted to kiss me. He asked to come up for a cup of coffee.

"I don't have any coffee. I don't drink coffee."

"It's just a cup of coffee," he said.

"You're not coming upstairs, Michael. I'm going to bed—alone."

Michael leaned forward to give me a small kiss, which turned into a humongous kiss. When I didn't back away, he took me in his arms and the longing for him I'd been trying to suppress tightened my own arms around him. Our passion was instantly stronger than anything I'd ever felt—just in that one kiss. Fifteen days ago, I hated this guy's guts, but that night I cared for him and suspected I always would.

8

ichael and I began dating, and within a matter of two or three weeks we could hardly get enough of one another—that's how quickly we bonded. The intensity of our romance expressed itself in small attentions that led to agreements that were the first pledges of our affection and fidelity.

As we got to know each other better, I began to know how to make his day by doing things as simple as carefully choosing what I wore on dates. I usually wore flesh-colored panty hose for my work on the show, and pretty much every other time. One particular evening early in our dating relationship, I decided to dress up in a very dramatic black outfit, and go all out on the hair and makeup. I probably took the most time I've ever taken to get ready to meet him over at what became one of our favorite New York restaurants, Il Vagabondo. I sensed that we were at that stage where Michael might confess to falling in love with me and I wanted to encourage him to the max.

I chose to wear a pair of off-black panty hose with seams up the back. He says he's never forgotten watching me get out of the cab when it pulled up in front of the restaurant. Il Vagabondo has big wood-framed doors with glass panels, and I remember looking through the glass as the cab driver made change. I had a direct line of sight to Michael in the midst of the crowd at this dimly lit, old-fashioned Italian restaurant. I put one leg out of the cab just as Michael looked, and at that moment, he says he just about died because he knew he was totally in love with me when he saw the panty hose with seams up the back. It just drove him nuts. He knew immediately I had done that especially for him.

When I went into the bar, the crowd parted for us to meet, almost as though in slow motion. It was a moment out of a movie. As we moved toward each other, I could hear *"Ooohhhh . . . how cute"* from the crowd. We kissed each other right there in the bar.

After cocktails, we had a wonderful dinner and a couple of bottles of wine. Michael was trying to tell me that he loved me, but we were both feeling shy. His confession kept coming out "I luh-luh-luh . . ." The drinks and wine hindered us as much as they helped. When he did finally say that he loved me, I wasn't sure if I'd heard him right. I worried he'd simply had too much to drink. This confusion kept me from saying I loved him back. If I said it then, I knew we'd both be wondering the next day whether the alcohol had been doing the talking.

Later, Michael told me he was worried that I thought him stupid or that he had bungled the job. We shouldn't have drunk as much as we did, but we were still nervous around each other. Even in the midst of the drinking and our anxieties, a surer bond came about because of that night. In describing that evening's perfect happiness, he uses a line from Shakespeare's *Othello*, "If it were now to die, 'twere now to be most happy."

One day, early on in our dating, we arrived back at my apartment to find a phone message from my old boyfriend Seymour. He was calling to tell me he realized he really loved me and wanted to get back together. "I'm so sorry about everything that happened," the message went. "I miss you and I love you." Seymour had never told me he loved me during the year and more we dated. *Now* he had finally said it.

"Who is that? Michael asked.

"It's my old boyfriend," I said. "The one with the old girlfriend from hell. He should have left me this message six months ago."

"Okay then," Michael said. "So . . . are you going to tell him to forget it?"

"Yeah, I'm going to," I answered. I called Seymour and told him he was too late, that I was in love with someone else. He was distraught and bugged me for a few more days, but finally went away. I truly enjoyed showing Michael how much I loved him by calling the guy back in front of him and saying it was over.

Our increasing passion for each other also resulted in terrible fights. We had our first shortly after our dinner at Il Vagabondo, and it was occasioned by those same black-seamed stockings.

It was April and Michael had just about moved into my apartment, although he kept his own place as well. I was living at Columbus Avenue and Seventy-sixth Street, only about four blocks from the studio. By that time, Michael and I already knew we were going to get married—we just didn't know when—and we couldn't stand to be apart.

I had an audition for a commercial. The casting description called for someone "sexy, fun, spunky, young, and pretty." One of the unwritten rules about auditions is that an actress goes in looking right for the part, and yet not too well defined, in case the concept changes. I wanted to look long and tall, elegant and sexy. So I chose a plain black tank dress I could dress up or down, with ankle-strapped black-heeled shoes and the black panty hose with the seams up the backs.

When Michael saw what I was wearing, he started questioning me. "You're wearing that? In the middle of the day?"

"What's the big deal?"

"You're really going to an audition looking like that?"

"I put it on, didn't I?"

"You're not wearing that," he said, and he was dead serious. He was downright impassioned about it.

What? I thought in disbelief. I've never, ever had a boyfriend say

I'm not wearing something. If anything, men were usually proud of the way I looked and encouraged me to dress even sexier. But Michael was enraged.

I was shocked and extremely upset and I remembered I couldn't be either if I was to do well at the audition. Any actor knows you don't upset somebody before a major audition. Michael was not only trying to control me out of possessiveness, he was even being unprofessional! I was so mad I was shaking.

"I can't believe you're doing this to me!" I cried. "I'm upset and I've got this audition. I can't do it when you're treating me this way. Don't you care about how well I do?"

"But," he finally blurted out, "those seamed stockings are only for me!"

I could see this meant the world to him. He didn't want me to wear them for anybody else. This guy is nuts, I thought, but I was also deeply touched. He had attached so much meaning to those stockings. I knew he really did love me. We ended up striking a lot of deals with each other over things like this. Which shoes were his, which skirts. He didn't like me wearing short leather skirts unless I was with him. And all shoes with ankle straps were strictly his. When the panty hose thing happened, he wanted to define other things that "belonged" to him. By this point, he also had given me some jewelry, which I wore only for him.

For my part, I was very clear about him carrying a picture of me at all times in his wallet to show people who his girlfriend was. We both agreed not to go to any parties without the other one—ever. We still hold to that today. Appearing alone at social events has a way of starting rumors, so we simply don't. I also wanted him to agree not to run lines with other actors or actresses in the dressing room with the door closed. He was working with a beautiful girl on the show, whom he had asked out before we started dating.

During most of that spring, Chris was living with my mother and father in Texas. This gave him a much more stable home life than he would have had with baby-sitters and me in New York. I was only working two or three days a week and commuted weekly back to Texas for long, free weekends with my son. For Michael and me, this meant a lot of long good-byes and passionate reunions. After we had been apart, we practically smashed back into each other.

Some of Michael's and my subsequent agreements—like not drinking in bars without the other person—came out of incidents of almost blinding jealousy.

One evening, Michael and I went out to a Mexican restaurant called Comacho's on Broadway. The food was good and the margaritas were, too. Other actors frequented this restaurant as well and part of the fun of going there came from spotting people we admired. I had only been in New York about two years then and I was still impressed by the whole acting world.

We were seated up on a platform, about four or five steps up from the rest of the dining room, overlooking the other tables— right up with the "important people." At the time, Michael and I thought no one knew we were dating. We thought we were being real sneaky. (Our friend Mark LaMura had dated a woman on the show, only to see her fired because of the relationship. Most producers of daytime television are adamantly against in-house romances, because the inevitable breakups cause too many problems.)

As we sat there in the back of the restaurant, who should come in but Steven Bauer, an actor from the movie *Scarface.* I loved the movie, partly because I love Al Pacino. He's a great actor and so handsome, tough but good—for me, the ultimate combination. Bauer, who played Pacino's friend from Cuba, has a similarly attractive look.

Steven Bauer was with a date or friend. We couldn't really tell and were trying to guess. Then he looked up and smiled at me a couple of times.

"Look! He's smiling," I told Michael. I wasn't interested in the guy; I was stupidly starstruck.

Their table was situated so that I could look past Michael and right at Steven Bauer, which I did more than a few times.

Michael didn't like this. "You know, I want to see if we can get another table," he finally said.

"Oh, stop it," I said. "He's not flirting. He smiled because I'm looking over there like an idiot. He's just acknowledging he saw me and now I can quit. It's no big deal."

After we finished our dinner, Michael went to the men's room. While he was gone, Steven Bauer got up and came over. His date was also in the rest room. He politely introduced himself, but didn't ask for a date or my phone number or anything. He just said hello, and I said, "I loved you in *Scarface*. You're really a great actor. And I saw you in that movie of the week not too long ago. What are you doing now?" I was so starstruck, I couldn't get beyond typical fan questions.

Then I saw Michael coming back across the room, smoke practically coming out of his ears. We were going to have a problem.

"Oh, here's my date," I said hastily, gathering up my things. "It was nice meeting you. Good-bye."

I wasn't even going to let Michael make it back to the table. I got up to meet him halfway.

"What was that about?" he asked. "What the hell was that?"

"I just told him that . . . that I liked him in *Scarface*."

"What else?" Michael wanted to know.

"Nothing. He's with a girl. Look, he's got a girlfriend."

"What did he say? Did he hand you his phone number?"

"No. No he didn't."

"I saw him put something in your hand," Michael said, insisting.

"No, we were shaking hands. I said good-bye."

"Let me see your hand," and Michael grabbed my hand to see if Steven Bauer had slipped me a note or something.

"*Michael.* I was just meeting him. I was just telling him that I really liked his work."

Michael wanted to go back over to their table. He wanted to know if the woman was his girlfriend or his sister.

"I think it's his girlfriend. It's his girlfriend, all *right*? Don't worry about it."

Once again, we had had a few drinks—in fact, we were blasted—

and this made the situation particularly volatile. I literally dragged Michael out of the restaurant and halfway down the block. "Don't act like this, Michael," I said. "Do not act like this. You're being so stupid. I can't believe you're acting this way. It was nothing."

But Michael was beside himself. We hailed a taxi, and as we were heading back to Columbus Avenue we kept fighting. The cab driver kept looking in his rearview mirror at us.

"This guy doesn't want to hear your crap, Michael. Would you just shut up?"

We were getting so angry that I finally threatened to hop out of the cab. "I'm going to walk the rest of the way home. To hell with this. I don't need it," I said, tapping the driver. "Pull over."

"Don't you dare," Michael said, trying to stop me.

"Pull over, driver! I want out. I want out of this car." I opened the door.

Michael tried to pull me back in. That's when the sloppy fisticuffs began. When I get into a fight, especially with Michael, it's knock-down-drag-out time. I was hitting, slapping, clawing.

"What are you *doing?* You scratched me," Michael said. In his look, I read, What am I going to do with her? How am I ever going to control this person? How am I going to deal with her? I love her so much, but what am I going to do with her?

I got out of the car and stormed right off. I was going to show him he couldn't control me. We were on Central Park West. I crossed the street and intended to walk into the park, hoping to freak Michael out at the thought of me alone in the park past midnight. I got up on a park bench and acted like I was going to climb over the wall.

"Don't you do that! Don't you do that!" Michael was screaming. "Come back here!"

The cab driver drove away, tires screeching.

Michael kept trying to grab me, to get me down off the bench, away from the wall. I was acting like a total brat, giving him a hard time. I hopped up on the wall and as he went to grab me, I went over. It turned out to be a ten-foot drop.

Just at that moment, two doctors pulled up to the stoplight, saw us fighting, and witnessed me go over the wall. They flew out of their car. Michael jumped over the wall to get me. The doctors and Michael lifted me back over the wall and sat me down on the park bench.

When I fell, I hit my head on a rock, making a giant, open cut on my eyebrow.

One of the doctors said I needed stitches.

"No, I don't," I said. "Just get this guy away from me."

"I'll take you to the hospital," Michael said.

"Take me to the hospital? I don't want to ever *see* you again. I hate your guts," I told him. "I hate you. I hate you. I *hate* you. You're a jealous jerk. You're never going to let me have my life and I don't want to ever see you again."

One of the doctors asked if we were married.

"No, we're not," I answered. "And we're never going to be."

Then the other doctor offered to take me to an emergency room, showing his identification and assuring me that he was legitimate. "You don't have to go with this guy," he said.

I agreed to go with the doctors. On the way, they asked me what had happened. I was still angry. I told them my boyfriend pushed me. Did I want to file charges? they asked.

That began to calm me down. I admitted I didn't know exactly what had happened—how I had fallen. Secretly, I knew I was still madly in love with Michael.

I was given a couple of stitches and sent home. Michael retreated to his own apartment. He tried to reach me for several days. He wanted to know if I was okay, to tell me he was sorry. He was devastated.

When he finally got me on the phone, he told me he wanted to see me. Of course, I wanted to see him, too.

Still, when we met at a restaurant, I made sure to show him the stitches. I wanted him to feel nice and guilty.

But in truth, I forgave him within about five minutes. I already knew he was contrite, guilty and sorrowful, asking for my forgiveness and telling me things would work out. "Please, I promise I'll never let that happen again," he said. "I won't get jealous. Never again."

That was hardly true, but it was more the right thing to say than not.

I had my own moments of intense jealousy, too.

Michael liked to go dancing down in a club in Greenwich Village that played 1950s music. One night, just after we got there, I went to the rest room right away. When I came back, I found some girl slinkily close to Michael at the bar.

I was instantly furious. As I walked up to Michael, I made sure to bump the girl out of the way, basically pushing her. "Excuse me," I said, sort of punching her out of the way with my shoulder, and giving her a haughty, catty look as if to say, "He's mine."

Then I started in on Michael. "What were you doing that made her think that she could come over here and do that? Why would she feel that that was okay?"

No sooner had I turned to the bartender to ask for a drink than she was back on the other side of Michael, edging her way in once more. I overheard her say something about how she loved him on the show with Susan Lucci.

"Excuse me," I said, "excuse me, we were talking."

"Well, he was talking to me," she shot back.

"Well, he's not anymore. Do you mind getting out of here?"

A catfight was imminent and I could tell that Michael had no intention of stopping it. I don't think he'd ever had women fight over him like that and he was loving it.

The slinky interloper went away once more. Michael and I danced a couple of numbers, with him swinging me around on the floor. I hate fifties music, but I had to admit I enjoyed dancing with him that night, showing everyone he belonged to me.

When we got back to the bar, the woman came around again. She had decided to give me a run for my money.

She was real cute and I didn't like it. I didn't like it at all. I turned around and said, "You touch him again and I'm going to twist your tits off. Now get out of my face!"

That's the maddest I've ever gotten. I've never been so close to a fight with a woman before. My next move probably would have been a drink or a slap in the face. I was so jealous, it was as if I had discovered that emotion for the first time.

The girl went away. She could see I was dead serious. If she hadn't, she might have lost both boobs. We had caused a big scene. Everyone around us was watching. They had seen this building up for a while and they were glad she backed off. Michael enjoyed the whole thing.

By May, Michael and I had taken a couple of trips together: promotional junkets at which we signed autographs and then stole away. We took a trip to Puerto Rico, where the casinos often host television personalities. It was very romantic, lounging on the beaches there, with people asking for our autographs. We were still hiding the fact that we were dating—at least in our minds. While we were at dinner one night in Puerto Rico, the maître d', with whom we'd become friends, commented in a conspiratorial fashion, "Oh, the two of you together again. You two are getting awfully close."

"Well, that's because we're getting married," Michael said.

That was the first time he said that. "Oh, really?" I asked.

"Really," he replied. The maître d' knew I was hearing this for the first time. His wife was there that night, and they brought out a bottle to toast us.

But I told them, "I haven't said yes yet, you know. We have to talk about this."

9

Michael's love soon went far beyond the formal proposal he eventually made; it reached into my relationship with Chris, the place where I needed to be most sure of Michael's love and his capacity to act wisely and unselfishly.

In April, after the trip to Puerto Rico, Michael and I were living together full-time. Chris would be leaving his weekday home with my parents to spend Easter week in New York. Michael and I knew this time with Chris would be a test of our relationship. My five-year-old needed to know that Michael and I were headed for marriage.

While I was working that week, Michael took Chris to Central Park to see the great children's zoo, with its huge, transparent seal tank and petting zoo. They ate pretzels together, slid down the long slides that are built into the side of a hill close by the zoo, and visited the famous statue of Alice in Wonderland.

Chris was, to say the least, an outspoken child. The time he spent with me in New York made him street-smart in a hurry. He copped a New York attitude. Remember, he knew how to steal me away from a crowd of autograph seekers.

One evening during Easter week, Michael and I took Chris to a favorite Mexican restaurant, a place right around the corner from our apartment on Columbus Avenue. I watched how Chris related to Michael, judging his reactions, trying to anticipate how he'd accept our engagement. I had dated Seymour for a year or more and never came close to allowing the doctor this close to my son. Admitting a new man into both of our lives proved harder than I expected.

At dinner that night, I tried to hint what all the playtime with Michael might ultimately lead to. "Did you enjoy playing with Michael today?" I asked Chris.

Chris looked up at me suspiciously, his little mouth twisting.

"Because if you liked it, you know, that might become a regular thing."

In a whining voice, Chris said, "Other people take care of me enough!"

Michael leaned over the table and said, "Be careful how you speak to your mother."

Chris looked at him with an expression that asked, Who are you to talk to me like that?

As dinner went on, Chris started squirming, and kept threatening to walk away from the table and wander around the restaurant.

"You have to stay in your seat," I said to him. "We won't be here that much longer."

He folded his little arms and went into a classic pout.

"Don't act that way, Chris," Michael said. "We've taken you here as a special treat."

Maybe it was the "we" that did it. All at once, the pieces fit together for Chris, and at the realization of our romantic conspiracy, he screamed out, as loud and long as he could, "I—THOUGHT—YOU—SAID—NO—MORE—MEN!" He pounded the table with his little hands as he said each word, rattling the plates, forks, and margarita glasses.

It was an E. F. Hutton moment: Everybody in that restaurant turned and stared in total silence. I could only think, *Did I say that?*

Michael sat there for two seconds, quite taken aback, then he looked at me as if to ask, *May I?*

I knew this moment could be decisive. If we were truly serious about becoming a new family, I had to let Michael be the dad. Right here. Right now.

"Okay," I said, getting up.

Chris was looking at us in total confusion. *What's going on?*

Michael reached over and took Chris's arm, pulled him out of the booth, and took him straight to the bathroom. Chris griped the whole way. "Get your hands off me, you big jerk! Stop it, you're not my dad!" He was screaming mad.

This was the hardest moment in my new relationship with Michael—far harder than any barstool encounter. I didn't know exactly what Michael would do. I just had to trust him to be the dad.

As I sat there waiting for them to come back, I realized how much was at stake: If Michael couldn't handle this, how could I marry him?

It seemed as if they were in the bathroom for twenty minutes. I was getting worried, knowing that Chris has a temper like mine. *He's probably in there telling the guy off and kicking his shins and Lord knows what else.*

But when they came out, they both looked calm. I could tell Chris had been crying, because his eyes were red. He sat back down and looked down at his food and bit his lip.

I looked at Michael. *What happened?* I wanted to ask.

Chris finally looked up and said, "I'm sorry."

"Thank you," I answered almost automatically, still not quite sure his regret could be real. It seemed real, though.

I didn't find out until later what had happened in that bathroom. Michael had gotten down on one knee and spoken directly into Chris's face. He told Chris to button it. From now on there would be two rules. The first and most important would be that Chris could never, ever show disrespect to his mother. "I'll take a lot of stuff," Michael said, "but *that* I will never, ever tolerate. You will never talk back to your mother. You will never speak down to her. You will never tell her no. Do you understand?"

And Chris responded, "Yes, sir. Okay."

Nobody had ever disciplined Chris like this before, especially not a man. My father might have given Chris a little swat here and there, but he loved Chris and babied him. Michael's discipline was of a totally different order.

Michael also told Chris he didn't have to have affection or care for him, but he did have to be honest. I was having trouble with Chris telling whoppers—as many five-year-olds are inclined to do—and this second rule told him we had both noticed and there was a real difference between playful pretending and trying to manipulate with lies. Michael stepped right in and pretty much cured Chris of his two worst habits in one never-to-be-forgotten talk.

During the next few days, I saw how Chris's attitude to Michael changed. He began looking up to Michael, respecting him. And the affection that Michael hadn't insisted on or even asked for sprouted up and flourished.

Not only could Michael be the dad, he was very, very good at it, which of course made me love him all the more.

A few more days went by, good days filled with kite flying and canoeing in Central Park and other favorite five-year-old activities. We went to the place in the park that New Yorkers have nicknamed The Yard—a large, open area where kites can go up in the sky forever. Michael also took Chris to his favorite store, The Last Wound-Up, a shop filled with windup toys. Michael showered Chris with new toys, showing him that the disciplinarian also had an ample heart.

Our next dinner out was at Tavern on the Green. We had decided that this would be the evening to tell Chris that we were going to get married. Chris already accepted us as a couple. We needed to tell him that we were going to become a family.

We picked Tavern on the Green because Chris had always wanted to go there after seeing the horse-drawn carriages in the front and the Christmas lights in the trees. New York made Chris an uptown kid from the beginning. From the earliest age, he insisted on wearing a suit and tie on important occasions. Shopping with Chris was what women dream of—having a little doll who loved dressing up. We would go to Macy's and he'd pick out suits and ties, matching them himself by age four. That night, Chris selected a cream-colored jacket, a white tuxedo shirt, red bow tie, and black slacks. He was wearing the same outfit Michael's character wore on *All My Children* as the bar owner. Chris's years of going out to dinner with me also prompted him to eat foods that other little children (and some adults) won't touch. The moment he saw a waiter with a tray of oysters, he wanted some—and he actually enjoyed them. He went on to develop a taste for clams, calamari, caviar, mussels, pâté de foie gras—every elegant food imaginable. Tavern on the Green was *his* kind of place.

As his attempted wanderings at the Mexican restaurant showed, however, Chris was still immature enough to get out of his chair frequently. Tavern has a very quiet, soft ambience and we didn't want to disturb other people. We hoped for a table in the corner, out of the way.

We ended up smack-dab in the middle of the place. As we sat down with Chris, I said, "Honey, please don't get up from your chair. This is a very nice restaurant. We have to sit in our chairs, okay?"

"Okay," he said.

Dinner got off to a good start. The three of us chatted happily, although after a while I could see that Chris sensed, once again, that something was up. After the first course came around, Chris got up out of his chair. He was breaking the rule. But he didn't look as if he meant to wander away, so I refrained from snatching him back into his chair. He straightened his tie and jacket like a Mafia wise guy, and then came right beside my chair and wrapped his arm around my shoulders, the little man protecting his mom. In his loudest voice he demanded of Michael, "So, you gonna marry my mom or what? What's the deal?"

Michael and I almost died laughing. We were conspiring away

about how to tell him and he had it all figured out—right down to one-upping us with his outfit.

Everybody in the entire restaurant couldn't help but share the moment—and there was a collective sigh. Everybody waited to hear Michael's answer. I was speechless. I couldn't believe Chris was doing this, but at the same time, I thought it was so cute.

"Yes," Michael said. "I'm going to marry your mother. Do you mind? Will that make you happy? Can we be a family?"

Chris was exuberant. "Yes! Yea! Yea!" Chris jumped up and down on his little feet.

And again the entire restaurant went, "Aaahhhhhh." I think they even gave us a hand.

We'll always remember that priceless moment. From that time on, we knew we were going to be a great family.

Michael took me home to meet his parents that same April. He warned me not to expect anything grand. His father worked as a plumbing contractor and, while plowing all his extra earnings back into his business, he had built the family home with his own hands on a corner lot in a modest Detroit suburb. His parents raised six kids there. Michael hadn't been home to Springtown with me yet, but from my description of our home on five country acres—for which my father had slaved for most of his life—he must have thought I was used to certain amenities, like air-conditioning. "My parents aren't rich," he said, explaining, "and it's hot there. They don't have air-conditioning, so don't wear heavy clothes. If it gets uncomfortable, just let me know and I'll open a window or whatever."

I assured him that my family had gone through a lot of months when an unexpected car repair bill reduced our evening meal to pork and beans on toast—or my dad's favorite, chipped beef and gravy. We were both children of the working class. "That's not important. I just want to meet them," I kept saying.

Meet them I did, in all their glorious honesty. Michael warned me that his mother, Margaret, could be particularly direct, and I experienced this sooner than I could have imagined.

In fact, as soon as his parents picked us up from the airport, I could sense Michael's mother sizing me up, watching my every move. His father, Ed, was much more openly welcoming and even affectionate. He patted me on the shoulder and said, "Wow, you're really beautiful. I saw you on the show the other day and you were so good." Margaret only asked me polite, brief questions like, "Did you have a nice flight?"

We arrived at their cute little house on the corner. I looked around at the neighborhood, which was indeed very modest and middle-income. I only thought, *Good, that means Michael is a real person.*

Everything in the house was strictly 1953—the year the house was built. It was a three-bedroom brick ranch, with avocado-colored appliances. Nothing surprised me, particularly, except I did wonder how they could have raised six children in such a small house. Photo collages of all six showing them at various ages hung on the walls, and I spotted Michael's immediately. He was a really cute baby. We're going to have great-looking kids, I thought.

"Where should I take my bags?" I asked. I had both a shoulder bag and a suitcase and probably way too many clothes, but I just wanted to make sure I had the right outfit for whatever came up.

Margaret directed me. "Go right down that hallway and take a right and the first left." Michael had already told me his old room was the middle bedroom, so I figured I was being directed there.

I went down the hallway, my shoes tapping on a wooden floor that sounded hollow. The sound reminded me that his dad had built the place. Then I heard another set of feet clacking along right behind me. Somebody seemed to be in a hurry and I slowed down to let the person by, but he or she didn't pass. I realized that there might not be enough room for passage in that hallway, so I speeded up and headed into the middle bedroom.

Just as I swung my suitcase up on the bed, I heard the door close. His mother stood before it.

"Isn't this the room I'm supposed to be in?" I asked, startled.

"Yes, this is the room," she said. She kept her hands on the door-knob behind her back. I wasn't getting out of there, I could see, until we had talked.

Michael must have been dying because he had seen his mother take off right behind me. He knows his mother and could have anticipated how she would introduce—or declare—herself to me.

She didn't waste any time getting around the end of the bed and right up into my face.

"Do you love my son?" she asked point-blank.

I didn't have a moment to think. There was no preliminary chitchat. She was looking me square in the eye. I couldn't move. I saw a mother's face intense with love and concern. Her expression said, *If you lie to me, I'll know it.*

"Yes. Yes, I do. I do love your son. I love Michael," I said.

"And you're going to make him happy?"

I was blown away by each question—questions as all-embracing and forthright as those in a catechism. But I knew my answers were absolutely truthful. "Yes, I'm going to make him happy."

"He just had a horrendous marriage that almost broke his heart," she told me. "It almost killed him. It made him sick. Above everything else, do not break his heart."

In trying to answer her last question, my voice must have risen five octaves. "I'm not, I'm not, I'm not, I'm not going to. I'm going to make him happy." I tried to think quickly of how I could convince her—what one thing I could say that would make all the difference. "I want to give him children," I said. "I want to have children with him."

When I told Margaret I wanted to give Michael children, her face brightened right up. That made her happy. We were making progress. She could tell I meant what I was saying. Michael was just then turning thirty-eight, and he had wanted children for many years. By telling Margaret that I wanted to have children with Michael, I was agreeing with her that he had been deprived of many good things—that I was aware of this, just as she was, and wanted to bring him the happiness he deserved.

Margaret may also have been worried that I was just another actress who wouldn't want to "ruin her body" by having kids. I knew I needed to tell her—right then—who I was and what I was hoping for in life.

"You have to understand, Margaret, I'm planning to go back to school—to Fordham—as a premed student. I want to be a veterinarian. I hope I'm not just another actress who cares only about her career. In fact, at the moment, there's not much to the career."

I went on to explain that my option wasn't being picked up for *All My Children.* (As it happened, Michael had been informed first of my possible termination. The producer called Michael into his office, before I was notified, and said, "I don't like this." Apparently, he told Michael to go ahead and sleep with me if that would help make me a better actress, but he said, "Don't marry her. We can't have both of you on the show married." He and Michael got into a fight that escalated to the point of Michael throwing a big bowl of matchbooks this guy had collected out his window. Nevertheless, when we insisted on marrying, I found myself without an acting job. I suppose I could have pursued this legally, but I didn't feel I could win in a situation like that—especially with my husband remaining on the show.)

"Not only am I going to give him children and pursue becoming a vet," I told Margaret, "I'm going to take his name. Even professionally. I'm going to use my maiden name as my first name—everyone called me Hunter when I was growing up, since I was a tomboy. And I'll take Tylo as my last name. From now on, it's Hunter Tylo. What do you think? Michael and I really like it."

Margaret gave me the biggest hug and a kiss. She even cried. I was too stunned by the whole thing to cry myself right then. I had never seen a mother care that much for her child, to the point of risking her future relationship with someone at their first encounter. But she didn't care. She loved her son that much. She's still like that today.

Soon I got to see another side of Margaret, a very sarcastic and funny side. On Sunday, we went to Mass, and we had pictures taken. Later that day, we were riding in the car, heading to a place called Miller's Bar, a hamburger hangout they liked to go to. It was their family's special place. It looked exactly like what it was—a neighborhood bar that had been turned into a hamburger joint. It was so "neighborhood" that they didn't give out checks; they relied on their customers' honesty to tell them what they had eaten. The burgers were to die for.

On the way, we were having a conversation. Ed and Margaret were up front and Michael and I were in the back. Margaret and Eddie sounded like a loving version of the Bickersons. Margaret made a wisecrack. Eddie made another and another. Margaret and Eddie went on for a while being wiseacres. Finally, Margaret blurted out, "Eddie, you're the perfect asshole."

I could tell it was playful, but I couldn't believe she talked like that to her husband. Nobody took it seriously or became offended. So I laughed, partially out of embarrassment, I'm sure.

"Don't laugh," Margaret said to me. "You're marrying the heir apparent." I almost died. I saw the family had an unexpected side—a very unexpected side.

When we got to Miller's, I met Michael's three brothers, Mark, Alan, and Sam. Alan looked much like Michael, only smaller in frame. He seemed to think he was a Native American. He wore his hair down past his waist, long, blond, straight hair, and he wore a lot of Indian jewelry. He was very laid-back and cool. We got into a conversation about the Cherokee Indian blood in my family.

I also met Michael's sisters. The first, Terry, lived not far from us in Brooklyn, but we hadn't gotten to know one another yet. She was a pistol, funny and pretty and very New York. Michael's little sister, Sarah, was there, too, and though she's known within the family as the "princess" she was far less prissy than I'd been led to believe. She's a Detroit girl, with a fun-loving nature. Both sisters embraced me immediately and said in their actions, Thank God we've got a new sister. In fact, right at that first lunch, they dubbed me Sister Woman and started showing me new ways to do my hair and caught me up in pleasurable girl talk.

During that lunch, I kept reflecting how much more expressive Michael's family was than mine. Their way of kidding one another was to say, "Hey, kiss my blankety-blank." They made me feel like part of the family immediately. They made me feel important, too.

Later, Margaret asked a few questions about Chris. How old was he? Was he going to live with Michael and me right away? I brought pictures to show her and she was excited. She was eager to extend her love to Chris.

Perhaps because she so thoroughly and completely blasted any notion of pretense between us, I grew close to Margaret right away. I sensed that she would complete my experience of being mothered. As an orphan, my own mom had trouble connecting emotionally with people, even, at times, with her own children. My mom loved me and she was there, but she wouldn't talk about things much. For example, when I was thirteen, she told me I was going to be starting my period. She handed me a book to read: *The Stork Is Dead.* That was it. We didn't have long mother-and-daughter conversations. She simply didn't know how. Fortunately for both of us, we have a much different relationship now.

At that time, though, Margaret became a "mommy" for me in an important and healing way. She treated me like one of her kids from the get-go. Before that first week was out, I asked permission to call her Mom. She took that as a compliment and agreed gladly.

Michael and I were married in New York at the First Church of Religious Science on July 7, 1987. A friend from *All My Children,* Chris Holder, introduced us to the minister of this congregation, a woman with famous children in the entertainment business. She seemed friendly enough, and I was so unsure of my religious commitments at that point that the First Church of Religious Science seemed fine to me. They talked about Jesus, if not in the way of my church at home.

At first, we wanted to have a big wedding, but we settled on a smaller ceremony for family in Juilliard Hall, and a big, blowout reception at Wilson's—the site of my first dinner date with Michael after the infamous football bet. It was also the place he gave me my engagement ring.

We invited all our friends from *Guiding Light* and *All My Children*. Michael's nephew Kaine, who is about Chris's age, was there, and the two of them became fast buddies. The wedding was fun. Chris stood up with us. In the video, he tries to close his eyes and pray, but he keeps looking up out of the corner of one eye to see if it's really happening. He was just beaming, he was so happy. He had a mommy and a daddy now.

I remember how right it felt, especially compared to my first wedding. Five seconds before I walked down the aisle on my dad's arm for my wedding to Tom, I recall thinking, Well, if it doesn't work out, I can always get a divorce. This time, I was thinking, There is nothing in the world that could possibly make me stop this wedding. I'm hanging onto this. I'm hanging onto *him*, my man, Michael.

The reception was as beautiful and fun as we had hoped it would be. Lauren Holly, who is a big movie star now, caught my bouquet. Even the diva of divas in soap opera, Susan Lucci, came. I was honored that so many people I looked up to and had been grateful to work with attended. Ruth Warrick, who has played the character Phoebe on *All My Children* forever, provided an extra special gift by collecting money from all my fellow cast members. They bought all our china, as well as our requested silver and crystal, and even supplied an envelope of money to spend on our honeymoon. They couldn't have been nicer or the day more filled with love.

Part Three

10

Michael and I spent our wedding night at the Plaza Hotel and then rushed to the airport for our honeymoon flight to Hawaii—so fast and in such a groggy state from staying up until 3:00 A.M. partying that I left my special wedding earrings on the nightstand. The earrings' loss—they were nowhere to be found when we inquired—was quickly forgotten, though, as we took our island-hopping honeymoon. We went first to the Royal Hawaiian Hotel on Oahu, which Frank Sinatra, Dean Martin, and the rest of the Rat Pack made famous. A big band played swing music there for a dance at sunset. Afterward, we would cozy up in bed and order room service. From the Royal Hawaiian, we went on to Kauai, visiting its dramatic waterfalls and rain forest. We also took a helicopter ride around the other islands as well.

After the luxuries of Hawaii, we went straight to Michigan for a rugged camping and fishing trip with Michael's family, and then, after a short stint back home, to Colorado for a golf outing at the Kissing Camels Golf Course with our friends Jerry and Caroline Barger. A celebrity golf tournament was being held there and Michael and Jerry would be hooking up with other buddies.

Michael and I wanted to start having children right away, and I had stopped taking birth control pills before the honeymoon. I could tell that my body responded quickly—I felt like a little kitty in heat. Somewhere in our travels, I must have conceived, because by Colorado I was feeling all the symptoms, especially an upset stomach in the mornings. I didn't tell Michael at first. I wanted to make sure.

One morning while Michael was out at the golf course, I turned on the television and caught *All My Children*. I'm actually not a big television watcher and prefer nature and science shows, but I was curious to see how the show was running, what plot lines were being developed. I happened to catch a big scene between Michael and Taylor Miller, the actress who played Nina. Nina had just found out that her husband had died in a plane crash and was being consoled by Michael's character.

Consolation quickly (and somewhat improbably) turned to passion. Michael started kissing her neck and then ripped open her blouse and buried his face between her breasts. I knew that soap operas were competing with each other to see how risqué they could be, urging their actors to appear in bubble baths, to be shot naked from behind, to be as suggestive as possible about what their bodies must be doing under the covers. But Michael had sworn to me that he wouldn't participate in "acting with his butt," as he sometimes called it. This was an important extension of the promises we had begun to make to one another after the black-seamed stockings episode. Now he had his face buried between his love interest's breasts! And he was kissing those breasts—the camera left no doubt about that. She was closing her eyes as if she was about to shudder with ecstasy. If this was acting, I was convinced. I was furious!

Actors often claim that seeing their spouses in love scenes with other actors doesn't bother them in the least, and that it's all technical. Well, it does have a technical side, with worries about lighting angles and things like that. But feeling another person's hands on your body, feeling his or her skin against yours, has an effect. The great director Alfred Hitchcock said that every love scene he ever directed on the set was finished in the dressing rooms. I don't know of any actor who is truly comfortable with a spouse's love scenes; not until the husband or wife gets to know his spouse's love interest and that love interest's home life. Michael and I even speak of "spraying our territory" like animals when it comes to warding off the attentions of costars. We will come on the set and meet a costar and have a friendly conversation, all the while letting the other person know that we are real and not to be messed with.

At Kissing Camels, I had just become convinced that I was pregnant and now my brand-new husband was showing, I felt, that he couldn't be trusted. I thought of Tom, of course. How could I not? Had I married someone else who would betray me? Had I gotten into this too soon and then gotten pregnant to boot, so there was no easy way out of it?

My emotions were still raging when Michael returned from an extra-long day on the course. It was clear that his buddies and he had more than a few drinks at the nineteenth hole. I was locked up in a hotel room, watching him make love to another woman, while he was drinking with his buddies. Everything about the situation added fuel to the fire. But I started our conversation as cool as I could be.

"Michael," I said, "hasn't it been nice to have all this time this first summer? I'll bet you'll be busy when we get back next week. They'll be working you a lot."

"Yeah, I suppose," he said.

"You think they'll be doing anything special with your character?"

He shrugged and went over to the room's dorm-sized mini refrigerator and pulled out a beer. His face was pink with sunburn.

"You know, my friend Carla called me. She said it looked like they're going to make Taylor Miller—the Nina character—your new love interest."

He was looking at me now. "It's got to be someone. It's a soap."

"I know, I know," I said, still cool. "You tried to date her once, right?"

"I didn't date her. She came along once or twice when everyone went out for margaritas." He went over and half reclined on the couch, looking out the window toward the golf course.

"Carla said they had already started developing that plot line. She said she saw a love scene with Taylor and you. A pretty hot one."

"Carla's got her head up her butt—as usual. I haven't done anything like that."

"Michael, Carla and I talked today. She said the scene was on today."

"She's crazy."

"She's crazy?"

"Crazy. Totally crazy."

"She isn't crazy, you piece of crap. *I* turned on the television today and saw it myself. You had your face buried in her tits!"

Michael's pink skin flashed crimson.

"We are married for a month and you are lying to me!" I yelled. "You not only did this, but you just lied about it. You must have enjoyed it plenty if you felt you had to lie. If this is the way our marriage is going to be, I don't want to be married."

"Hunter, wait."

"I mean it. In fact, I want you out of here. Right now. Get another room. I can't stand the sight of you."

"Hunter, please, I didn't tell you because I didn't want to upset you. I went to the producer and gave him all kinds of grief about it. But that's the way the director wanted it. He insisted. I kept begging off and he kept screaming at me. You just lost your job. I didn't want to lose mine. Then where would we be?"

Our friends Jerry and Caroline started knocking on our glass patio door. "Hey, hey, guys, what's going on? Let's work this out now. It's a vacation."

"Go the hell away!" I screamed.

They stared in a moment longer, then retreated.

"Hunter, they're our friends!"

"They're your friends, pal."

"Hunter . . ."

"Are you going to get out of here or not?"

"Hunter . . ."

"And the true bitch of it is, I'm pregnant with your baby, you tit-kissing weasel. What do you think of that?"

His mouth actually dropped.

"It's not that much of an accomplishment, you jackass. You are such a . . ."

And it went on and on and on. My hormones were raging with motherly protective fury and for a while I just couldn't stop screaming at him. He kept explaining that he hadn't wanted the news to mar the happiness of our marriage; he was trying to protect me; he had no choice; he had to keep his job. All of which made sense, although I didn't like it. Not at all.

After a long time, I calmed down.

"Are you really pregnant?" he asked.

"Yes. You're the liar. Not me."

He shook his head, warding that one off. "You're really pregnant."

"Yes," I said. "Really."

"Really?" he said, brightening.

"You can't get any more pregnant."

"Honey, I'm so happy. I mean, I want to be happy. Can't we be happy? We're going to have a baby. A baby. Really and truly. I'm a dad."

I nodded. "You're a dad."

"And we can be happy now?"

"If you won't do that again. I mean, *ever*. If you have to do a scene like that, *tell me*."

"I will. Of course I will."

"And just don't do any more scenes like that."

"Come here," Michael said. He came over and held me and stroked my hair. He kissed me lavishly, although I noticed he was reluctant to get anywhere near my neck or breasts. "My bride," he said. "And now there will be three of us. I'm going to be ecstatic once I see you smile again."

I looked up at him and the happiness of having a child with this man I had to admit I loved finally broke through.

•   •   •

In the fall, I started attending Fordham University as a premed major. I cruised my way through high school, but now I was totally motivated, both because I wanted to realize my long-held ambition of becoming a veterinarian and also because I was paying my own tuition—the money came from savings I had accumulated during my years on *All My Children*. I asked Michael for help editing my papers; I wanted every detail to be just right. He was enthusiastic about an essay I wrote on *Hamlet,* a high compliment, I felt, from a dedicated Shakespearean. I aced all my classes that semester.

Just before we married, Michael and I bought an apartment in New York in the West Eighties, two blocks from Broadway. There were cafes and new shops aplenty for us to walk to. Michael and I often went out for a coffee together or to satisfy my craving for goat cheese.

Our home was part of a building that had been converted from a senior-citizen residence. It only had two windows and would have been cave-like but for the halogen lamps we installed everywhere. All the rooms were tiny except for the living room, which was the size of a racquetball court. Our living room had once been the rest home's industrial-sized kitchen. JFK Jr. had lived there for a short period of time previously.

Michael and I bonded while shopping for furniture to fill up the cavernous living room. I had always wanted a green Italian-marble dining table—a long, rectangular one, with black lacquer chairs. Michael let me buy the most expensive version I could find. We also bought a sectional sofa together; a Chinese gray, black, and white wool rug that looked great underneath the dining-room table; a new TV; a sideboard; end tables; and plenty of knick-knacks. Michael has a wonderful visual sense and furnishing our home brought us that much closer. I felt that he was delivering on his promises to care for me, to care about me, in a way that contrasted sharply with my unhappy first marriage.

Michael's interest in Chris remained constant. Almost every day, he walked Chris to school, P.S. 87, on his way to the studio. He talked with him about the new baby brother or sister that was on the way and I could see that this blood tie increased Chris's sense of security.

I suppose I should simply have sworn off watching television, but the next time I turned on *All My Children* I saw Michael and Taylor in another love scene. They were in bed together. Taylor was lying on top of Michael. The camera caught her hand slide under the covers. Then she kissed his nipple. That detail made me totally crazy.

I remembered that I had picked up a recent script, offering to run lines with Michael. He had practically snatched it out of my hands. Then, two weeks before, I had gone to work to have lunch with him. I found him in his dressing room in a robe. Was that his wardrobe? Oh, no, he insisted, even though he should already have been in wardrobe for his upcoming scenes. He scrambled into a shirt and trousers and took me out for the world's quickest lunch. That had been precisely two weeks ago to the day, which meant that he must have been shooting this day's love scene. He must have had on body makeup underneath the robe. Everything came together—he had done it again!

When he came home, I gave him every chance again to tell the truth. "I was thinking of coming by the studio tomorrow. To have lunch. Would you like that?"

"Sure, that would be great," he said.

"You're not going to be too busy, are you?" I asked. "Like last time. I don't want to have to whisk in and out of some place. It's always great seeing you, but that wasn't really fun."

"No, I'll have time tomorrow. We can walk to Houlihans."

"Why were you so rushed last time? Did you have a lot of scenes that afternoon?"

"Yeah, we were pretty busy. We had all these technical assistants all over the place. Stunt people."

"So you were doing fight scenes?"

"Yeah, fight scenes."

If I hadn't been a mother-to-be on the warpath, I would have felt sorry for the guy. He just walked into it every single time. "Michael, I saw Taylor and you in bed together today. Our lunch was exactly two weeks ago, the day those scenes were shot. You lied to me that whole day and now today. Can't you ever tell the damn truth? What's wrong with you?"

"Hunter, look, don't get crazy on me again."

"You must really be getting off on this stuff. Why else would you feel so guilty about it?"

"It's called *acting,* Hunter."

"Oh, that's what it's called. I thought it was called having a pregnant wife at home and getting some on the side."

Once again, Michael told me he had spoken to the producers, made himself a pain, but he had to keep his job. All the soaps were pushing the sexual limits to the max. I knew that, didn't I?

"Well, why does Taylor call here, then? Why does she think it's okay to break into our private lives with her phone calls?"

"She wants to talk over scripts. She wants to talk over plot development."

"She's working, what does she care about plot development?"

"I don't know. I suppose she wants to *keep* working."

"She can't call anymore. The next time she calls, I'm telling her you don't work that way. Our time is our time."

"Fine. That's fine with me."

"You really have no idea how much this upsets me, Michael. I have to be able to trust you."

"You can. This time, really, I will, I'll show you all the scripts. I'll tell you about anything uncomfortable that might be coming up. I'm not totally in control of this situation, you know. But I will do my best. You're making this assumption that Taylor means something to me or is after me or something. She's not. That's *not* the way it is. I'm married to the most beautiful woman in the world. Even if I wanted to be interested in somebody else, I couldn't. You've spoiled me. You've taken a perfectly good womanizer and wrecked him for life."

I was still too angry to let his humor improve my mood. "I don't feel I can trust you. Not now.

That's where we left it, although I knew I had spoken the truth: I was so upset—or "obsessed"—about what I had seen that I knew I had to take action. I told Michael I'd like to take Chris down to Jamaica for a vacation. I had a fall semester break coming up. I'm sure the idea, under the circumstances, threw a scare into Michael, but he agreed. (Maybe he was even relieved to get rid of the pregnant harpy for a while.)

So Chris and I went down to Jamaica, went to turtle-races, and built sand castles. Michael's and my future started to come into clearer focus. Sitting on the beach, I could imagine our soon-to-be family of four taking vacations like this—the new baby toddling at his big brother's heels. The relaxation did wonders for my mood.

When I came back, Michael kept his promises to me. We had a couple more incidents in which I wasn't sure he had told the whole and absolute truth, but I did notice that he was wearing a pajama top in his next love scene. I knew that could have only been a result of his insisting. Taylor stopped calling the house to discuss scripts and Michael seemed as pleased as I was.

During the Christmas holidays, we had a scare. My maternal serum alpha-fetoprotein (MSAFP) screening test came back with a high count. This indicated that my baby might have spina bifida.

I now know that a high reading does not necessarily mean a baby has spina bifida. In fact, MSAFP cannot diagnose a birth defect. It only indicates increased risk. (Just ten percent of women with repeated high readings actually give birth to children with birth defects.) The test often says nothing more than that the baby is a few weeks older or younger than was thought. The best medical advice now says that the test should always be repeated if the first test shows abnormal results.

At the time, though, my female ob-gyn stated coldly and matter-of-factly that the high reading from my first test probably meant that my baby had spina bifida. She explained that spina bifida is a birth defect of the backbone, resulting in varying degrees of leg paralysis and bladder and bowel problems. She informed me that I had the option of terminating my pregnancy.

I asked her whether the test might be wrong. She didn't think so. But couldn't the problem be corrected?

There were corrective measures that could be taken, but my child's quality of life might be permanently impaired.

Shouldn't we have the test run again to make sure?

If I insisted.

I insisted.

And I'm glad I did, because the next time, the results were normal. I couldn't believe the cold and impersonal manner of my doctor, and I knew that if I had jumped at taking her implied advice to terminate the pregnancy I would have made one of the greatest mistakes of my life. I wanted this child and no one was going to take it away from me.

After the second test, Michael took me to Saks Fifth Avenue to buy a gown for New Year's Eve, and we celebrated once again at Wilson's. We were relieved to have the spina-bifida scare behind us and found comfort in having worked through our first marital conflicts. We were truly looking forward to the New Year.

As I continued on with my studies that next spring, I began to experience a lot of weariness in the last stages of pregnancy. I told the doctor that this was going to be a *huge* baby. She assured me every woman felt that way.

My parents arrived at our apartment near the due date in early April and the baby watch began. They were still there two weeks after my due date. "We're going home if this baby doesn't come soon," my mother teased me. I started feeling more and more overwhelmed by carrying around all that weight. On April 21, I took to my bed and stayed there for two days, depressed, unable and unwilling to get up.

My parents and Michael concocted a scheme to send me into labor. My mother insisted I get up. She helped me get dressed and did my hair. Michael then took me on a walk down to Lincoln Center, a good twenty blocks away. My mother thought a walk might kick labor into gear, but nothing happened.

When we got back, Michael and my parents ordered in barbe-
cued ribs and potato salad, the greasy, gooey food I like best. I had
felt so full from the baby pressing on my stomach that I had pretty
much stopped eating. But I went to the table and tasted a rib or
two.

Then I went over and sat back down on the couch. Chris came
bouncing out from his room after a long nap. "Mom's up!" he
cried. He ran to me and jumped into my lap with his knees pulled
up, crashing his head into my chest.

"Ow!" I couldn't think for a moment for the pain.

He scrambled off but stayed right before me. "Mom," he said, his
eyes huge. "You're *wet*. Your water broke. Mom's water broke!
Mom's water broke!" Now he was screaming it.

A distant "What?" came from the kitchen and then a "Yeeow!"
followed by a crash and heaving groans. Michael had been bending
over, putting something in the dishwasher, when he heard Chris's
screams. He raised up so fast that he threw his back out and then
fell flat on his backside. He was laid out on the floor, in terrific
pain. "My back!" he cried.

"My back!" I cried in turn, as the contractions came on.

Mom looked from the screaming man in the kitchen to the
screaming woman on the couch. "Which one should we take to the
hospital?"

If I hadn't just gone into labor, I'm sure Michael would have
been on his way to the emergency room himself. As it was, he accompanied *me*, although I could see from his white face how much
pain he was in. When we arrived, the first thing he asked the doctor was, "Do you have some Demerol?" For him, of course.

My water had broken at about 7:30 P.M. My contractions
stopped about 10:00 P.M. This had happened with Chris, too. My
labor progressed up to a point, then tapered off and quit. The doctors and nurses insisted that I walk to get the labor started again,
and my nearly crippled husband and I hobbled up and down the
corridors supporting one another. As I was passing one of the
rooms, I noticed that *Saturday Night Live* was ending. It was almost 1:00 A.M.

The doctor started administering pitosin, the drug that brings on labor, because once a woman's water has broken there's no going back. I asked to have an epidural right away. I had waited too long with Chris to have any help with the pain and didn't want to do that again. The needle went into my spine, the drugs began to flow from the IV bag, and I began to feel great. This was truly awesome. I could tell I was experiencing bad contractions as a result of the pitosin—my hands could feel my stomach gripping—but I didn't have any pain.

Michael and I played a few games of chess and then I took a nap.

When I woke up, the doctor told me that the contractions weren't getting us there quickly enough and he upped the pitosin dosage. Now, even with the epidural, I could feel how strong the contractions were. They would have torn me apart without the drugs. The activity around my bed became increasingly frantic. The baby had come a certain distance down the birth canal and was now stuck. The umbilical cord was wrapped around his neck and every time I had a contraction, his heartbeat went way down—he was being strangled.

All the nurses and doctors around me were urging me to push. Push! Push!

"You've got to get that baby out right now," instructed one of the nurses. "Otherwise we're going to have to break your hips! You hear me, girl? We're going to have to break your hips. Push that baby out now!"

They brought my back up from the bed toward my feet so that I could push more effectively. I heard a snap. Instantly, I knew what had happened. It had happened once before when my horse had kicked me. The baby had broken the tip off my lower rib. Cracked it clean through while I was trying to push. "He's broken my rib. He's broken my rib," I screamed.

"You've got to push anyway. You've got to!"

I pushed and pushed and my doctor must have used forceps to pull the baby the last few inches down the birth canal. Finally, Michael II (or Mickey, as we call him), came into the world. He had two black eyes, a flattened nose, and bruises everywhere. But he was alive, healthy, and, as I predicted, *huge:* He weighed 10 pounds. He was born at 8:30 A.M. on April 24.

I rested for half the day, and that evening Michael brought Dom Perignon and a pizza with goat cheese. I wasn't supposed to be eating like that so quickly, but those were "love foods"—signs of our intimacy. They kept mothers in the hospital for three days then, and Michael stayed with me full-time, even sleeping in my narrow bed against one of the side rails. He went to the studio each day and then came back to me at night. Mom and Dad brought him changes of clothes. Mickey became rosier by the day and because he was such a big boy, he slept through the night almost from the beginning and was always an easy baby.

11

A few weeks after the baby was born, Michael landed the role of Dee Boot in the outstanding television miniseries *Lonesome Dove*. He would be playing his principal scenes opposite the talented Glenne Headly and would be meeting one of our favorite actors, Robert Duvall. *Lonesome Dove* was being shot in Santa Fe and the chance of combining a vacation with the shoot was too good to miss. We went together first to Dallas, where we dropped off the kids at my mother's (I would only be away from the baby for four days), and then on to Santa Fe. We had a great time together and Michael did outstanding work.

With the *Lonesome Dove* part, Michael's career looked to be on the rise. His costar on *All My Children*, Taylor Miller, then decided she needed to move to Chicago to be with her boyfriend. Most soaps are structured around a central family. The actors who play the family parts are fairly secure. The "outsiders" who are causing the family problems or creating tangential story lines are less secure. Michael's contract came up for renewal at the same time that his love interest on the show decided to leave and his option wasn't picked up. Just why that happened would be something that would create ongoing tension between us.

We began living on our savings. For a time, Michael thought he might be asked to come back to *Guiding Light.* That's what we were hoping. But Michael's time out of work stretched on and we began having serious marital problems.

Most nights, after putting Chris and Mickey to sleep downstairs in their corner bedrooms, Michael and I would go up to our second-floor living room and settle into a game of chess and what all too often turned out to be heavy drinking. We are both incredibly competitive people and we played chess against each other so hard that I would sometimes get headaches from sheer concentration. Thirty minutes could pass between moves. We talked about our job situation, and the more we talked and the more we drank— wine, martinis, or Jack Daniel's—the darker our future appeared. We began blaming each other for our situation. If I hadn't been so jealous and allowed him to do the love scenes the way the show wanted, he'd still be there. If he weren't such a prima donna and knew how to talk to people without antagonizing them, he'd still be there. That was the real reason. No, it wasn't. He had heard . . . and on and on.

Michael wanted me to look for acting work as well. I resisted. I loved being in school. (So much so that three days after I gave birth to Mickey, I took my second-semester finals at Fordham and aced each one, even though I was still hemorrhaging slightly from the third-degree lacerations of Mickey's problematic delivery.) I remembered struggling with working and trying to raise Chris as an infant, and I didn't want to have to struggle that way again. Couldn't it be different this time?

Our conflicts came to a head on the night of our first anniversary. We went out to Wilson's again, the site of our first date and our wedding reception. By the time we came home, we were both more than a little drunk and starting to yell at one another. (We never cared who heard us. We thought any audience would chalk the matter up to our being "artistic.") Before we left, we had taken the top tier of our wedding cake out of the freezer to defrost. We would cap the evening off with a piece, as tradition dictates, for good luck. As our words became ever meaner, Michael took the cake and threw it onto the floor, burying the two figurines under a mess of rum cake. He stalked off into the building's lobby to have a smoke.

I was so angry that I locked him out. When he wanted back in, I wouldn't let him.

"Go away!" I screamed. "You're not coming back in here."

"Hunter, what the hell are you doing?"

"I hate you. I don't care if I ever see you again."

He began pounding on the door. "Let me back in, you stupid bitch."

"No."

"This is my house. I bought the damn thing." He started pounding again.

Whenever he'd stop, I'd throw another barb his way, he'd reply, then pound.

Before too long, I heard the jangle of utility belts and looked through the peephole to see that two young police officers had appeared. (Apparently, the neighbors didn't think that screaming at 2:00 A.M. was "artistic.")

"Is this your apartment, sir?" one of them asked.

"Of course it's my damn apartment. Why else would I be standing here?"

"Why are you standing here, then?"

"The bitch in there locked me out!" He was slurring his words.

I didn't care. In fact, I was enjoying his being hassled by the cops. I was that angry. I thought I'd take advantage of the situation while I had them there. "That's right, officers," I screamed through the closed and locked door. "I threw him out. He was cussing me, being mean to me. He pushed me! I don't want him in here."

The officers began to discuss with Michael whether he might go somewhere else for the night.

He told them he could stay with Mark LaMura, but he would be damned if he was going to wake his friend up at this hour. He was standing in front of his own apartment and it was none of their damned business what was going on between his wife and him.

"Sir," one of the cops said. "This is a situation that's it's just better to walk away from. It doesn't matter who's responsible for the problem. You've been drinking, but we want you to straighten up and walk away. That's the best solution at this point."

"Or what?" Michael asked. "Are you going to take me in?"

"Sir, you are disturbing the peace here. It's obvious your wife doesn't want you in the house tonight. Get your head together and do the smart thing: Walk away."

"Hey, buddy, you know what you can do? You can kiss my everloving ass, that's what you can do!"

"Okay, sir, now we are warning you, officially, that if you don't straighten up and walk away, we are going to arrest you. You aren't leaving us an option. We don't want to do that. But you have to walk away now. We'll give you a ride to your friend's."

"You're going to arrest me? You can't arrest me. You don't have a warrant. You don't have anything. I'm standing outside of my own damn house, for God's sakes. You're going to arrest me? I dare you. I dare . . ."

I heard two decisive clicks. I peeped out and saw Michael being led away in handcuffs.

Now I didn't think the cops coming was funny any longer. I wondered whether I should rush out and tell them I didn't mean it about Michael pushing me. (I didn't, actually.) I panicked at the thought of real trouble. I had sent my own husband away to jail.

At 6:00 A.M., after a sleepless night and the onset of a stomach-turning hangover, I received a call from Michael. "Hunter, baby, I'm in jail. I'm in jail *in midtown New York*. You have got to get me out. I need to post a five-thousand-dollar bond. You've got to help me. I've got cockroaches in my clothes. I'm being threatened. There's a guy in the cell who recognizes me and who's going to kick the shit out of me the first chance he gets. You've got to get me out of here. You've got to!" On the other end of the phone, he started to break down.

I was still so angry at him and confused that at first I wasn't inclined to grant him any mercy. "Five thousand dollars?" was all I could ask.

"Call John Giroux. You don't actually have to come up with five thousand. You pay a portion of it to a bail bondsman, which we get back as long as I don't get convicted or run away. Don't you understand anything about how this works?"

"I understand what an asshole you've been. And you're still being one."

"Hunter, please, really, I've never been this scared. I'm sorry. I'm sorry for the whole thing. I was smashed. I didn't know what I was doing. You've got to help me."

"All right. But this is the first and only time. I don't want anything to do with you after this. You *dared* that cop to arrest you. What did you think he was going to do?"

"Just call John."

"Okay."

I called our lawyer, John Giroux, and he promised to check the situation out immediately and get back to me about what we had to do.

I also received phone calls from Michael's sister Teri and his mother. We know Michael's been a creep, they said, but you've got to get him out of there. You're the only one who can.

An hour or two later, Michael called me back again. "Hunter, they transported me from the station lockup *to the city jail*. They put shackles on me and sat me down in one of those police vans next to about fifteen rapists and murderers. Are you getting me out of here?"

"We're getting you out. John's finding out what we need to do. Don't worry," I said, "you'll be home soon enough." My tone was softening, a little.

John Giroux called me back and said, "This isn't going to be easy. Michael took a swing at one of those cops. They don't like that. They are never terribly forgiving about resisting arrest and assaulting a police officer. We need a good criminal defense lawyer on this, and you're going to have to do your best to make the D.A. drop the matter."

The criminal lawyer and I went down to the D.A.'s office. I knew that Michael was no threat to me, but I had to swear up and down to make them believe it. I had to pay a fine and the attorneys. Our anniversary "celebration" cost us ten thousand dollars.

Then the writers' strike of 1987 came on and there wasn't even the possibility of work.

The experience made Michael and me face the fact that our marriage was clearly in jeopardy. We went to the woman minister at the First Church of Religious Science, who had married us, for advice. She told me behind Michael's back that she knew the marriage was never going to work in the first place. Michael had that macho-jerk attitude. In her opinion, I should divorce him.

"Why did you marry us in the first place?" I couldn't help asking.

"Somebody else would have if I hadn't. They're your lives."

Yeah, thanks for nothing. Whatever the woman believed now struck me as neither religious nor scientific.

Michael and I eventually found more conventional marriage counseling, and this provided a temporary fix to our problems. It was only a Band-aid, but we were grateful that we managed to make it through the rest of the summer and the fall of that year. This marriage still differed greatly from my first. Michael might have been out of work, but he didn't spend his time lying to me about it. In fact, he beat the bushes and also helped take care of the kids while I continued my education at Fordham. Our marriage counseling started opening me up to the possibility that going to college and working as an actress might not be mutually exclusive. When the writers' strike ended, I began to go on calls for commercials and landed quite a few. I wasn't known enough to command good rates, but the work brought in food money, at least. For all the big expenses, though, we were still dependent upon our savings.

The casting people at ABC kept me in mind and asked me to test for a part on *General Hospital* in December. They wanted someone for a short stint who would play a concert pianist. As they went through the casting process, they happened to find a terrific young actress who actually was a concert pianist, Edie Lehmann. The casting people promised to keep me in mind. They were interested to hear that Michael and I would be willing to move to Los Angeles.

They soon called back, wondering whether Michael would screen test for an upcoming part on *General Hospital*. Michael flew to Los Angeles, tested, and was told the same day that he had the part. He called me with the good news and asked me to pack the house. He had a two-year contract. Although Michael is no great fan of Los Angeles, he was willing to adapt—we needed the work.

I felt the same way, despite my reluctance to leave Fordham, and it just so happened that I was cast in three commercials about that time, one for Cover Girl and two others. Even though these commercials had been cast in New York, two of the three were to be shot in Los Angeles. This made me feel even more confident about the move.

Michael stayed on in Los Angeles to start work as of January 1, 1988, and found us a nice two-bedroom apartment in Toluca Lake, with a small yard for the boys to play in. He enrolled Chris in Saint Charles Borromeo School, an outstanding parochial school he had kept in mind from previous work trips to Los Angeles. I came out with the kids as soon as possible, on a flight, as I'll never forget, on which Mickey kept throwing up. Our baby had roseola and insisted that our plane mates share the misery.

For the first six months in Los Angeles, our life went well. Chris liked Saint Charles Borromeo School. I was able to enroll in Glendale Community College—a screenwriting class, as it happened—to keep my credits going, as I looked toward transferring to UCLA. I also started having a surprising amount of success in landing new commercials—I was the new girl in town and everyone seemed to want me.

I also went out on calls for television shows and movies and was pretty horrible, I have to admit, at giving cold readings. I was too nervous and had acquired some bad acting habits from my days on *All My Children.*

Michael and I avoided the old fights of the past, but we took on new, lavish habits. We loved going out to dinner, often with other people, and it was common for us to spend seven hundred dollars on a meal. Much of the expense came from the liquor bill, because we were still downing ten Jack Daniel's and Cokes in an evening.

Not long after Michael was hired on *General Hospital,* the show was given to a new producer. Actors know that when new people take over, there are bound to be changes. Michael had a two-year contract, but, as in all actors' contracts, the two years were divided into a series of short-term options. He could be dropped the next time his contract came up for renewal at the beginning of the summer.

We had completely changed our lives to make the move to Los Angeles, and we were naturally concerned about whether Michael would be affected by the rumored shake-up at *General Hospital.* We asked the head of casting at ABC out to lunch. She must have known why, and when we asked, she was ready to tell us that Michael's job was secure. No problems, no worries, we were going to be okay.

For a good five months, Michael and I had been doing the New York thing by taking taxis everywhere in Los Angeles—we still didn't own a car. I had been looking at a cool Buick Reatta for some time. Once the ABC casting director gave us the thumbs-up, I went out the next morning and bought the car.

That very afternoon Michael received his pink slip—he was being dropped from the show.

Now we had an apartment in New York, one in L.A., a new car, and no job once again. Nothing came along quickly. We spent another summer with neither of us working.

Then Michael auditioned for the lead villain in *The Further Adventures of Zorro,* a Family Channel production that would be shooting in Spain. He landed the role. Before we knew it, I had a part on *Days of Our Lives,* playing Marina Toscano opposite Stephen Nichols' Patch.

We should have been happy and grateful, but our professional success placed another tremendous strain on our marriage, especially the prospect of Michael being gone all fall. I was worried about what he might get up to in Spain and he was worried about the Los Angeles scene swirling around me. We couldn't have named what we were going through at the time, but it has one: separation anxiety. Alternately, we clung to one another, trying to ward off the impending separation, and then pushed each other away, to protect ourselves from being damaged emotionally. We started voicing our fears through barbs: "You might find yourself already replaced when you get back," I remember saying.

One night, we went out with our friend Chris Holder to the Magic Castle. That night has inspired a running joke between us: Go to the Magic Castle and poof! You're an idiot!

We stayed for a long time at the bar, drinking tin jigger kamikazes—that lime-flavored firewater. Michael and Chris were playing stump the Magic Piano. "Irma" is a "ghost playing piano" that can jingle out just about any song. If you can call out a song that stumps the piano, you win a free round of drinks. Chris and Michael are both musical theater buffs with elephantine memories, and they kept stumping the piano and downing kamikazes.

When Michael went to the men's room, a man started up a conversation with me. I let the conversation go on, my memory of what this inevitably led to with Michael having crashed and burned with the kamikazes.

On the way home in the car (how we didn't kill ourselves and others on those evenings, I'll never know), we began fighting. "When you act like that with a guy, Hunter," Michael said, "I don't know what you're thinking. That you don't care about our marriage any more? That it's dead?"

"I'm the one who *does* care. You don't. You're constantly mean to me. Ever since we got married, I feel like I'm just not good enough for you. You want me to work, but you don't respect my work. You do the same kind of parts, but you're the *real* actor. So you did a few plays on Broadway. So what? I'm tired of hearing it. You're leaving the family to play in a damn kiddie series."

"I'm talking about the way you act with other men, Hunter."

"I'm talking about the way you act with *me*."

"And I'm *not* leaving the family. You're the one who's threatening to replace me."

"For a smart man, you are so unbelievably stupid. I was teasing, asshole."

"You *are* a tease, Miss Wet Britches. Don't you know that hurts?"

"*God! Michael!* I cannot believe it. You're hurting me. Every flick of your finger tells me how much you despise me. That I'm just this beautiful mannequin to you. Do you know how much *that* hurts?"

When we pulled up in front of the house, we were still yelling at one another. We found ourselves halfway out into the street in our angry dance. Finally, Michael said, "Okay, Hunter, what is it you want? Do you want to kill me? Would that make you feel better? If I've hurt you, maybe you better hurt me. What do you want to do? You want to kill me? You want to kick me in the balls?" He spread his arms and legs wide. "Come on, then. Go ahead. Kick me in the balls. If that will make you feel better, go ahead. Give it your best shot! Come on!"

I was wearing four-inch spike heels, but I could still move, and I took a running start at him and planted my pointed toe in his crotch with enough force to lift him off the ground. He fell onto his back, writhing in agony.

I went into the house and greeted our baby-sitter. I asked her how the kids had been.

"Mrs. Tylo?"

"Yes."

"Your husband. He's in the street out there."

"Oh, I know. He'll get up and come in when he wants to." I didn't know whether he was being dramatic or what, and I didn't care.

The baby-sitter cleared out as quickly as possible. Michael finally came in. When I confronted him, I could see murder in his eyes. Before he could speak, I said, "Look, let's admit it. It's just over. I'll send you the divorce papers in Spain. Don't come back here, the place will be cleaned out. I know how to do this. You know I do. So get the hell out tonight and don't come back. There's nothing here for either of us anymore. Nothing. Everything's empty. What we had's gone. Totally gone."

"Really?" he said, gathering himself. His eyes fell on my treasured dining-room table. He went over to the table and placed his hands on the back of one of the black lacquer chairs. "Then you won't be needing this anymore." He picked up the chair and smashed it down on the table.

My hands went up as if to catch the chair. "*Michael, don't!*"

When he saw that he had chosen to smash something I still valued, that he was getting to me, he picked up another chair and smashed it down. For the moment, he seemed possessed of superhuman strength and the chairs virtually exploded as they rained down on the marble top. The marble itself started to crack in the middle.

"Michael. Michael, don't! Don't. Please! Michael!"

My hurt and terror spurred his fury, and he picked up chair after chair until the table itself broke in half, the splintered marble tangled up in its wire mesh underpinning.

"That is it," I said. "That is it!"

I went and got the kids out of bed. I wasn't going to have them stay in that house a moment longer. Chris was in his pajamas, and Mickey in his little drawstring sleeper. They had no idea what was happening. (Both Michael and I are now ashamed of involving them for one moment in our past conflicts.)

I brought them out along with various overnight bags to the living room on our way to the car. "Where are you going?" Michael asked.

"Daddy," Chris said.

"Don't talk to Daddy now, Chris. We have to leave now. I'll explain later. We just have to leave now."

"You're not leaving," Michael shouted. "I am." With a movement too swift for me to resist, he took Mickey out of my overburdened hands and roared off with him in the car.

He was only just out the door when the apartment complex superintendent came around. The police arrived practically on his heels. "My husband's drunk!" I screamed to the police officers. "And he's kidnaped our baby."

The officers promised to put out an APB.

For several long hours, I thought of Michael driving drunk through the streets with Mickey in tow. It was sheer terror.

About 4:00 A.M., our friend Jeff Byron called. "I don't want to get in the middle of anything, but I thought you'd want to know that Michael and Mickey are here. They're fine. They're asleep. They're safe. You don't have to worry any more now. Your baby is safe."

Once our heads cleared from the alcohol and the anger, we confronted yet again how stupid and destructive we could become. We made pledges to one another: to stop smoking, stop drinking, and to begin programs toward greater physical and mental health. We began working out. We went to marriage counseling. We began to see that we were two of a kind: When in doubt, when we felt something we treasured was threatened, when we feared losing one another, we resorted to fighting to test the other's commitment. Fear of loss tempts anyone to craziness; alcohol and fear equals raging insanity.

Before Michael left for Spain in September, we were, once again, more sure in each other's love. We rented a small house in Studio City. As much as we fought each other, we also fought hard to save the relationship, and managed to pull back from completely destroying what we had.

As crazy as Michael might have become during some of our alcohol-abetted fights, his fears about other men were based on real-life pressures. When I began playing Marina Toscano—the once-presumed-dead wife of Stephen Nichols' character, Patch—Michael came to the set to "spray his territory." My costar promised my husband that he would "take care of me" while Michael was in Spain.

There's always a bit of flirtiness between costars on any set. Showing a certain interest helps the other actor feel more comfortable in the emotional and sometimes passionate scenes the two people play together. At the beginning of my time on *Days,* Stephen inquired about my moods, brought me glasses of water, and spent time running lines with me. I always went down to his dressing room to rehearse, because that's an unwritten rule of the theater: the newer actor goes to the longer-running player's space. Stephen had that way about him that suggested he believed himself irresistible to women, so I would also take a pack of cigarettes and sit on the floor and smoke while we rehearsed. All the lighting up and flicking of ashes gave me a way of gesturing outward, increasing my own personal space. I also insisted that the door be kept open—otherwise the room would become too smoky.

One day, I went to work more stylishly made up than usual. My friend Carla was in town. After Michael left for Spain, I was quickly overwhelmed by the demands of taking care of the kids and carrying on a full-time job. (I was still taking a class here and there as well.) Carla came into town to help me reestablish the household's equilibrium and work out a regular routine with Edith Salazar, the wonderful young woman who would be our child-care provider for the next year or so. That day, I was going out to lunch with Carla, so instead of my usual early-morning mufti of T-shirt and sweats, I wore a lacy see-through skirt with black leggings underneath and a silk blouse.

As Stephen Nichols and I began to run lines, he shut the door.

"You better keep it open," I said. "The smoke," and I gestured with my cigarette.

He sat down next to me and began to run lines—except when the scene came to the part where the characters kiss—he actually did it! He had never done that before.

I have no idea where my cigarette landed. I hope it burned a hole straight through his sofa.

I scrambled to my feet.

He looked over at me, disappointed. Was I the biggest prude or what?

"I don't do that. I'm married. I thought you understood that." I was so unnerved I could hardly turn the handle on the door or catch my breath and it felt as if I were in a dream in which the more I tried to escape, the slower and more awkward my movements became. Finally, I was out of there.

An hour later, Carla and I went to lunch at a Mexican restaurant.

She said, "Never tell Michael. He'll think every crazy idea he gets is justified. Never tell him."

After that day, Stephen Nichols' little attentions completely stopped. No more polite inquiries about my well-being, no bringing me a drink, no running lines. In fact, he played our scenes together as if my character were a big nuisance. Patch wanted to go on with his current marriage and the ghost from the past needed to get lost. The writers took the star's cue, and I was quickly written out of the show.

In late November, I went to visit Michael in Spain. We enjoyed each other's company once more, traveling north to France and into Paris. Michael kept asking me what had happened at *Days.* I told him that Marina Toscano made Patch look like he was being unfaithful to his current wife. Marina cast his heroic character into too much doubt. The writers thought better of what they had thought would be a good idea.

Michael knew that the writing on a show is never so cut-and-dried. "What happened?" he kept asking.

One night, after a bottle of wine, I told him. I was feeling romantic, wanting him to desire me, and not above letting him know others did.

"That shit," he said. "That unbelievable shit."

Later, when Michael came back from Spain, he asked for permission to call Stephen Nichols.

He called Stephen, and I have to give the man credit, he didn't deny it. Michael then told him where he could get off.

Michael came home from the *Zorro* location in December and had six months before he needed to be back. We both auditioned for other roles during this time. It looked like he was going to be cast in the remake of *Dark Shadows,* but then the part was given to the hot actor Ben Cross, from *Chariots of Fire.*

My agent at the time, Bud Moss, called to say that I was up for the female lead in a new Steven Seagal movie. The casting people liked my look and I went to read for Steven, his writers Michael Grais and Mark Victor, and the casting director. We met in the offices of the producers who created the *Naked Gun* films. The reading took place in a corner office with huge windows; they wanted to see what the actresses truly looked like in the glaring light of day. I thought the reading went well; everyone seemed pleased.

I knew that appearing in such a high-budget production would be good for my career, and so I did a little research. I rented the videos of two of Seagal's earlier films. I noticed that "the girl" usually became a pawn in the plot, her life put in danger by the bad guys Seagal was determined to vanquish. Her body was also exploited by the filmmakers. There was always at least one nude scene, the girl totally naked, Seagal almost fully dressed. The camera work always allowed the viewer a lingering view of the woman's breasts. At the time, I didn't mind doing naked love scenes, if lighting or other artifices were used to preserve the actors' dignity. If I landed the part, I was hoping to talk to Seagal about the in-your-face breast shots. But that was down the line, I told myself.

Bud Moss called to say that everyone involved in the production really liked me. Seagal himself was so impressed that he wanted to spend his personal time working with me. There would be one more meeting in the next couple of days before the role was cast—the meeting with the people putting up the money. Seagal wanted me to come by his office on the Warner Brothers lot any time between 6:30 and 7:30 to run lines. He wanted to cinch the part for me.

"In the morning?" That seemed awfully early, and I'm not a morning person.

"No, no, Hunter," my agent said. "In the evening."

"In the evening?"

"It's his *personal* time."

"It's mine, too, and I'll want to be home for dinner."

"Seagal is a powerful man," my agent said.

"But that's not professional. Nobody schedules meetings after regular office hours. Not to run lines, at least."

"I'll call them. Maybe we can find another time."

Within the hour, my agent called me back. "You're putting us in a spot, Hunter. His people tell me that Steven is insulted you would think this unprofessional. He's trying to do you a favor. He's extremely busy and that's the only time he has. You'd better go."

"Bud?"

"*Go.* You're a big girl, you can take care of yourself."

So I went the next day to meet with Steven Seagal in his bungalow—which turned out to be more like a condo. I arrived as his secretary was leaving.

Steven invited me into his office and began showing off mementos from his previous pictures and photos of himself from his life in the Orient, where he learned to be an aikido master. He explained that he wasn't just an actor, or an actor-producer, but actually president of a subsidiary company within Warner Brothers. All this had come about because he was truly a martial arts *sensei*. He had also been a soldier of fortune and lived the life depicted in his films. Warner Brothers wanted to put a person who had lived that life into their actions films, and that's why the opportunity had opened up for him.

From the wandering tour around his office, I finally made it to the chair in front of his desk. I pulled my script out from my briefcase and placed it over my knees. I began thumbing through it. "What scenes do you want to go over? I have that long speech in scene fifteen. That's a good moment for the character. That would be a good scene to do for the money people, don't you think?"

He picked up a picture of a beautiful raven-haired woman holding a newborn. "You recognize Kelly LeBrock, my wife, don't you? You know what made her famous? She's got a great body and she was willing to show her tits in *The Woman in Red.* Half the audience—the male half—fell over when they saw her tits."

How to reply to that?

He told me he had worked with an actress who refused to show her breasts in one of his movies.

"That wasn't the best experience. People say she's going to be a big star, but I doubt it. She wouldn't show her tits."

I was nodding. Why was I nodding?

"Now, you, you've got beautiful tits. I mean, I haven't seen them, but I can tell. You show your tits in my movie, your life will never be the same."

I tried to talk about the script again.

He stood up and came around behind my chair. He began rubbing my shoulders. "I don't want to work on the script until you're more relaxed. I can see how tight you are. Do you want a drink? Or we could listen to some music."

He momentarily disappeared and suddenly there was soft music and the lights went down. Like that, his office became a *pad*.

"Steven . . ."

"I know shiatsu and every other kind of massage technique. It's part of the life of a warrior. Here, I'll show you."

He disappeared again and came back with a massage table above his head. He set it up in the middle of the office and patted the table. "Get right up. Come on. You'll feel so much better."

All I could think was, I have to let this guy show what a ninja master he is. He's telling me who he is and wants to know that I approve. He can be whoever the hell he wants, I suppose.

I scurried onto the table, lying on my stomach. He began to massage my body, from my scalp down to my calves. I had to admit that as a masseur, he did know his stuff. I started relaxing despite myself.

However, when he flipped me over on my back, every muscle about went into spasm. My heart was whamming in my chest. I tried to control my breathing, not wanting him to see how flustered I was. It was an extremely uncomfortable situation and I was off that massage table with a flying gymnast's dismount. "I think I'm relaxed enough," I said. "I don't think I'm going to get more relaxed. Not tonight. Not ever, if you know what I mean. But I'll see you at the audition tomorrow. I'll see you."

I beat it out of there.

The next afternoon, I brought Michael with me to the seedy hotel on Fairfax where the money people decided to meet with the four actresses up for the part. Steven came out into the courtyard, where we were all walking around, taking a last look at our lines.

He was still friendly until I introduced him to Michael. He wasn't pleased to see my husband.

When my time to read before the money people came, I asked to do that long speech I had wanted to rehearse with Steven the night before. Every time I started into the long speech, he broke things off by raising a question, coughing, or suddenly seemed to be lost in his spot on the page as he read with me. I took three or four starts at it, until I closed my script. "I think we're done," I said. "I'm done."

As I was walking out, I glanced at the casting director, who was looking at me like, "What happened? You were so great in the first reading." Until that day, she and I had one of those professional friendships in Hollywood, in which it's clear through callbacks and repeated auditions that someone's rooting for you to land a part. But after that day, she never contacted me again. I've always wondered if she told the financial backers, "This is the one you are really going to like," and I had embarrassed her.

I couldn't have done otherwise.

During the first six months of 1989, while Michael was home from the *Zorro* set, we both failed to attract any additional work. We thought we'd move back to New York, since we still had the apartment there, and Michael's return trip from Spain—on the one two-week break that broke up the shooting schedule—would be shortened by six and one-half hours of flying time. In the end, we thought, Los Angeles hadn't been particularly good to us. We started packing up the house.

Bud Moss scheduled one last audition for me. It was for a short-term part on *The Bold and the Beautiful*. I explained to Bud that Michael and I were moving away from Los Angeles, and asked him to thank the producers of *The Bold and the Beautiful* and tell them maybe later.

Bud wouldn't hear of me missing the audition, though. "Even if you are moving back to New York, Hunter," he said, "you don't want to get the reputation of an actress who blows off auditions. That's death everywhere in the industry, whether you're in New York or Hoboken. Make an appearance. Go. Treat these people with respect."

I went. The owners of the show, Mr. and Mrs. Bell, were there, as well as Brad Bell, Jr., the directors, and most of the writers. A big group. They sat in a semicircle and watched me do my audition piece.

I could feel the onset of a migraine and I went through the audition with no expectations—as I had at my first successful Dallas audition for *All My Children*. For once, I was relaxed, because I didn't think I could take the role even if it was offered, and for that reason, perhaps, I must have nailed the part.

As I was coming out of the studio, the senior Mr. Bell stopped me, placed a kindly hand on my forearm, and said, "Has anyone ever told you that you are incredibly beautiful?" His attention was fatherly and made me feel great. I thanked him and I meant it.

The day the movers came to clear out our stuff in Studio City, I received a phone call from Bud. "They want you," he said.

"Who?"

"The Bells. *The Bold and the Beautiful*."

"Bud, this is exactly what I didn't want to happen. I'm moving. I told you. In fact, the movers are *here*."

After I said more words to the same effect, he hung up.

He called back. "Hunter, they are going to make it a contract role. A two-year deal. They are offering a lot of money per show."

The money was significant enough that I had to think about it. I called out to Michael. He came over and we talked briefly about what had happened. "We have *Zorro*," he said. "The *B&B* money's nice and we could have used it plenty a while ago, but it's not enough to cancel everything now."

I was looking forward to New York and Fordham again. "Bud, tell them they are angels. But we can't. We can't stay."

After a couple of hours, Bud called back again. "They've upped the offer, Hunter. And they understand your situation. They're willing to do whatever it takes to keep you here. They'll pay for the deposit on another apartment. They'll get you into a furnished apartment until you can move your own stuff into a new place. This is unbelievable. They are dying to hire you."

I talked with Michael again. As we spoke, the moving van pulled away from the curb. We were standing by a phone sitting on a naked floor in a completely empty house. Our furniture was headed for New York. But all those expensive dinners had done a number on our credit cards. Even though we had *Zorro*, we also had a lot of financial catching up to do. The kind of money we were talking about now demanded another look. In fact, the offer was so good, we couldn't afford to say no.

"What about the furniture?" I asked.

"Let it go," Michael said. "We'll store it in the New York place. We'll move into a furnished apartment and ship our stuff back later. With your salary, we can do it. It's kind of crazy, but we can do it."

So I became Dr. Taylor Hamilton Hayes Forrester.

12

*R*ight after Michael returned to Spain, in June of 1990, I checked my voice mail and found a message from my sister, Elizabeth. My father had suffered a stroke the night before, on Sunday.

I called my family in Fort Worth to find out how serious the situation was. My parents had recently visited with us during the Easter season, and my mother kept warning me that my father wasn't doing well. By this time, he had a collection of health problems, including diabetes and heart disease. I could see that he lacked his old energy, but otherwise he looked well. He had suffered small strokes before. Perhaps this was simply another one.

My mother told me that my dad was in the hospital, in a coma. The EEGs indicated to the doctors that his brain hadn't suffered catastrophic damage; he should be able to recover. My mom said that he could squeeze her hand twice for "yes" and once for "no" in response to questions. They knew he was aware of what was going on around him, in some sense. He just wouldn't wake up.

"Should I come there?" I asked.

"No, not yet," my mother said. "I don't think it's that serious. We'll let you know if there are any changes."

I was scheduled to work all that week and to shoot a Clarion lip-stick commercial that Saturday. I let the producers at *The Bold and the Beautiful* know they might have to revise my shooting sched-ule, and I was ready to dump the commercial at a moment's notice. I thought a thousand times of doing so, in fact, but decided to heed my family's advice.

On Wednesday evening of that week, I was out in the car with Chris and Mickey, coming home with a take-out dinner. At a stop-light on Ventura Boulevard, I suddenly had an overwhelming sense that something was wrong; I felt that everything—the world it-self—had been diminished. "Daddy's died," I thought. I knew I had to get home and call as fast as possible, although I had no doubt of what had happened.

When the boys and I walked into the living room, the phone was ringing. My sister was calling with the sad news: My father had passed away. The doctors believed he had suffered another stroke, a massive one this time. Elizabeth could hardly speak. She's the most emotional one in our family, the one who keeps album after album of pressed flowers and other mementos—the one who still has her Brownie uniform. She cannot stand loss. She was wailing and sobbing.

Hearing the news, I dropped to my knees. I was overwhelmed with grief, too, but I knew that I had to try to comfort Elizabeth. "Where's Mom?" I asked. "Where's Leland?" I knew she would need her husband's help to get through this.

I felt the need of my own husband. During the phone call, my boys sat stock-still on the couch. My dad had been Chris's most en-during father figure, and hearing me talk in hushed whispers about his "Poppy" froze him. Little Mickey picked up on his mood as well. The whole family needed Michael.

I called the *Zorro* set in Spain and told an assistant director what had happened and that Michael should call home immediately.

Michael returned my call within the hour. "I'll come right home," he said. "I know how much he meant to you. I loved him, too." Michael meant it; my dad and he had grown close.

By the next morning, though, Michael had to renege on his promise. "They're not going to let me get away," he said. "They won't hear of it. They have my scenes scheduled at locations that are only available as scheduled. They say my leaving now would be prohibitively expensive. I'm sorry, Hunter. I'd give anything to come home and be with you now. You know that?"

"Do I?" I was instantly ticked off.

"What can I *do?*"

"You could talk to them again."

"Okay, I'll try."

After a little while, he called back with the same story. "But Hunter, look, if you can't get through the funeral without me, I'll walk off the set. I'll walk off and come home. I'm serious. That's the only option they're leaving me with, and I'll do it if you want."

Walking off a set for any reason is virtually a career-ending decision in Hollywood. Whatever Michael decided, I would have to go through the grieving essentially alone. His willingness to put the fate of his working life in my hands satisfied me for a time. Later, although I tried to remind myself of his genuine pleadings to be excused from the set, I couldn't adopt the same view. I became deeply resentful about Michael's letting work keep him from the funeral.

Chris, Mickey, and I flew to Fort Worth as soon as possible. Now nine years of age, Chris began acting up on the trip immediately. He kicked the back of the seat in front of him, called out "Hey, waitress" to the flight attendant, and screamed at her about the in-flight meal.

When the boys and I went to the viewing together, I brought Chris up to the coffin with me. My father looked bloated and stuffed as the result of the mortician's art. I saw, as my mother had told me, that she had slipped an envelope filled with his children's baby pictures into my dad's pocket. I began petting his hair and saying, "Good-bye, Daddy, good-bye."

Chris, who was standing next to me, said, "He looks so stupid." He reached out his hand and touched Poppy's cheek. "Oooh!" he screamed. "He's hard as a rock!"

"Chris!"

"*Ooooh,* his hands are cold. What did they *do* to Poppy?"

I grabbed him by the scruff of his neck and took him into the hallway. "What do you think you are doing? This is a sad time. Mimi and Mommy are sad. You've been acting like this ever since we started out on this trip and I'm sick of your behavior. What is wrong with you?"

He looked up at me, his face still hard, expressionless.

"It's because you are sad, isn't it? We're all sad. We're going to miss Poppy very much. It's hard to start missing Poppy, but we have to. Let yourself be sad, Chris. I know that's what you are really feeling."

My little boy collapsed on the floor and began to cry and cry. The tears sprang out of my eyes again once more, too. What were we going to do without Poppy?

Everyone in the family thought my mother might fall apart, but she rebounded from my father's death almost too well. She carried on with plans my father and she had made to build a new, smaller, more easily managed house. She went back to school for a nursing degree and would remarry within a year and a half.

Chris, Mickey, and I flew home from the funeral and I shot the Clarion commercial the next day. In it, I was supposed to be bright and perky and say, "Here come Julie's lips!" I'd get the line out and then collapse into tears. My makeup would be retouched and then I'd pretend to be cheery for a few more seconds on film before dissolving once more—the next day was Sunday, Father's Day, and it was almost too much to get through the shoot.

Later in the summer, three-year-old Mickey was enrolled at a Montessori preschool. One day when he came home, he had blisters at his hairline. When I took off his clothes, I saw that the blisters covered his stomach and legs as well. Chicken pox. Chris came down with it the next day.

I called my mother to ask whether I had ever contracted the disease. Not that she remembered.

I was at work two days after Mickey's outbreak when I scratched my scalp and felt the itchy pox. I went home from work immediately, of course, not wanting to infect others. I had already seen Mickey rebound from his flu-like symptoms of the first day and I didn't anticipate being gone from work long.

Late in the afternoon, I remember telling Chris to make Mickey some soup in the microwave. I was too nauseated to eat and couldn't lift my head from the couch.

The next thing I knew, my mother was putting cold compresses on my forehead. I had been out for twenty-four hours. My resourceful nine-year-old Chris managed to fish my organizer out of my bag and called Michael in Spain. My husband sent the alert back across the Atlantic to my mother in Texas, and she was on a plane and in my home before I came to consciousness once more.

When Michael returned from Spain at the end of the summer, I let him know how unhappy I was that he hadn't been there for me when I needed him most: at my father's funeral and during the chicken-pox episode. This was hard to say, because Michael had a great time playing Louis Ramone, the evil Alcalde in *Zorro,* and his stage training showed itself to great effect. Although I slammed him about starring in a "kiddie series," Michael brought his character to life in a memorable way, making an invaluable contribution to the kind of production I most value now. The show was a hit and would have gone on if people, especially Michael, hadn't opted out because of the long stints away from home.

To his credit, Michael put family ahead of career and told the *Zorro* producers that he wouldn't be coming back. I should have been more aware at the time of how much this cost him; I'm afraid I dwelt mostly on my resentments from my father's death and the chicken-pox blackout.

In 1991, I started working with the acting coach Ivana Chubbuck. During my years in Los Angeles, I had auditioned enough to understand that my acting skills needed improvement, especially if I wanted to do guest spots on prime-time shows or movies in addition to my work on *The Bold and the Beautiful.* New York soaps have their own technique, which is broader and more stagy than either prime time or films. In my years on *Days of Our Lives,* I had come to rely too heavily on stock expressions and responses.

Ivana began teaching me film technique, especially how to bring my personal experience to a role, informing the character's experience with my own.

The additional work began paying off. The writers on *The Bold and the Beautiful* and the show's viewers took a new interest in my character. I began working many more days out of each week and my fan mail increased exponentially. My acting "spoke" much more deeply of life's reality, and provided a means for the viewer to confront buried aspects of her own experience. Providing that type of entertainment had more substance to it. I began letting go of my veterinarian dreams. I was an actress, for as long as the profession would have me.

Michael was also enjoying a period of success. In 1992, he was cast as Blade on *The Young and the Restless,* the other show the Bells owned and produced for CBS. We began working in the same building again, on adjacent sets.

In the spring of 1992, Kimberlin Brown Pelzer crossed over to *The Bold and the Beautiful* from *The Young and the Restless.* With straight, silky brown hair, wide, inviting eyes, and a toned and shapely figure, she played the knockout villainess Sheila Carter. She brought a tremendous new vitality to *The Bold and the Beautiful*'s story lines.

Soon after she came onto our show, she started knocking on my dressing-room door, asking whether I'd like to go out for lunch and in other ways indicating that she would like to be friends. I thought that was great. I have lived most of my life without women friends close by and I longed to do the whole girlfriend bit. I felt starved, in fact, for that type of friendship. Kimberlin had a wicked sense of humor, and I liked the way she cracked everyone up with her bawdy jokes.

When Michael and I went out to dinner the first time with Kimberlin and her husband, Gary, at the Coyote Cafe in Laurel Canyon, I found Gary to be the sweetest man, and all man—a former football player and now a BMW-driving businessman. I felt grateful that here at last Michael and I had found a couple with whom we could be close friends—a couple whose position in life was much like ours. Within a month of meeting Kimberlin, we became fast friends and the two couples became an every-weekend dinner group.

Soon after our first dinners together, I was working our new German shepherd puppy, Max, in the backyard of our Studio City home, when Kimberlin peeped over the fence. "Hunter," she said, "I have to talk to you."

I could tell she was upset. I went to the front and let her in. "Honey," I said, "come in, what's wrong?" Michael came around as well and asked what was troubling her.

"Oh, it's nothing," she said. "I don't want to talk about it."

I thought she'd probably be more comfortable telling me first, so I suggested we go into the backyard. I was working the puppy, we could talk there.

I gave her a glass of iced tea and time to compose herself, as I taught Max to sit, to heel, to stay. Kimberlin had her face buried in her hands, and every time I inquired once more, she put her hand up: she needed another moment. Finally, she told me she was worried about Gary.

Michael, seeing us talking, came into the backyard. The tears were flowing down Kimberlin's cheeks.

Kimberlin told us that Gary had a business all set up, a boat business down in San Diego. Gary had gained the leasing rights to the docks at a major resort on Mission Bay. He had run this type of business before, with great success. Now, after months of development, his financial backing had fallen apart and he needed help to buy the boats.

"Maybe we could invest," Michael said.

"Yeah," I said, "we could be in the boat business together. That sounds fun!"

Kimberlin started to brighten up. "Do you think so?" She gave us more and more details about this business, and it sounded better and better. Gary and her brother would be running it. We could be mostly silent partners, although Michael might take a hand in the company's management. We could help out a friend and earn extra money for ourselves as well, it seemed; the boat business appeared to be a win-win situation.

We had a series of more formal meetings on the boat business after this, and came "on board" as investors and partners. We helped buy a slew of power boats, pontoon boats, kayaks, etc.

Soon after this, Kimberlin and I were both up for the same Pantene commercial. The advertising company narrowed the field initially through photographs. They needed a woman with long, dark hair and also someone recognizable—a woman with whom the viewer would already identify. Kimberlin and I were among the final four candidates.

At that stage, the advertising company made hypothetical offers to each actress's agent. They wanted to know whether the actress would be available for two different shoots in Thailand: a test in September and the real thing in mid-December. (They had an Asian director who had perfected the art of shooting hair to look like glass.) They offered each actress a buyout deal: a set amount of money to show the commercials they developed as many times as they liked, with no residuals. The buyout terms were generous, though; the actress who was eventually picked would be receiving a big chunk of change.

I'll never know quite what happened in all the negotiations that went on. It's my impression that *The Bold and the Beautiful* producers may have told Pantene's advertising company that Kimberlin could not take that much time away from the show. She was new and working almost every day. They were still setting up the story line for her. This may or may not have been a factor. At any rate, Pantene picked me.

Kimberlin came to me and she was suspicious about my role in the final outcome. "Hunter, I just want to know, did you tell Brad

Bell to tell the Pantene people that I wasn't available? Or did you get to influence who would be available? Because I heard you put your two cents in somehow."

"No, no, no, Kimberlin. My commercial agent asked Brad if I could have the time off. He said yes. That's all I know about it."

I thought Kimberlin was insecure and let the matter go. I'm not sure she ever did, though.

Over time, Kimberlin and I began to make graphic sexual jokes for "whoever" might be our audience, according to their own sexual preferences (including encouraging people to "come out of the closet"). This coarse jesting led to sexual topics and material I had never seen before.

We got most involved in reading a series of erotic fairy tales by Anne Rice that were filled with graphic, and often sadistic, sex scenes.

Under this influence, Michael's and my sex life came to be about nothing more than simple gratification. At first, I thought I was learning how to give my husband more pleasure. Then I found myself not caring about his pleasure; I was much more interested in my own. Even within marriage, our sexual lives became selfish in a way that would have damaging effects. At the time, I had no idea this would be the case; I thought we were being introduced to a wonderful new world of pleasure.

When the Pelzers and the Tylos went out to dinner, we started doing "body shots," licking salt off another person's inside wrist or neck and then slamming back a shot of tequila. We'd start doing body shots off our husbands. Then Kimberlin and I would do them off each other. Then we'd trade husbands for the purpose. We did this at fashionable restaurants like Spago and Bistro Garden. Our evenings usually became wilder and wilder, with us whipping our bras out from underneath our blouses and tossing them to onlookers. Desperate waiters often appeared, asking, "Okay, can I bring coffee now?"

I thought our newfound high life liberating. We didn't have to be so jealous anymore. Sexuality could really be a harmless diversion and didn't always have to be about love.

Certain events in our new life would sometimes bring me up short, though. I threw a lavish forty-fourth birthday party for Michael at the Moonlight Tango Cafe. By the end of the night, everyone was dancing in a huge conga line. Michael got so smashed that he couldn't walk, and had to be dragged through the door into the car. Before that, though, I saw a woman I hardly knew, someone who was volunteering to run a fan club for us, lick salt off Michael's cheek and pass on the tequila for the sake of sucking Michael's lips. She was kissing him right there in front of me! That took the bloom off. Partly in revenge, I took a post-party picture of Michael passed out on our bed in his underwear.

On my way into work one day, I called in to a radio station that was offering a pair of Guns n' Roses tickets to the fourth caller. I had them on my speed dial and punched. I actually won front-row seats. When I walked into work, the first thing I did was ask Kimberlin if she wanted to go with me.

We rented a limousine and went first to an Italian restaurant for pasta and many, many drinks. I think we flirted with every man in the place as a preliminary to the evening's entertainment. We were totally smashed by the time we started out for the concert.

"Welcome to the jungle," I roared out later that evening with all the Guns n' Roses fans. Welcome to the out-of-control jungle. My life was changing in many destructive ways, but all appeared calm—or "plastered over"—on the surface.

At Christmas, Kimberlin and I exchanged lavish gifts, jewelry from Tiffany and Waterford crystal. We were the best of friends.

Late that next winter, in February of 1993, Gary and Kimberlin came back from a trip to Las Vegas with tales of the great housing values there. We could have a house that would cost three to four million in Los Angeles for three to four hundred thousand in Vegas. A new community of homes was being built around Lake Las Vegas.

I had a long-held dream of owning a great, big, beautiful mansion of a home, and we had actually waited to buy until we could have much more of what we wanted. The pricing in Vegas tempted us.

The Pelzers and the Tylos went for a weekend to Las Vegas and stayed at the Rio Hotel, where the Pelzers had friends who let us have the rooms at a discount. We had a super time together and saw that Gary and Kimberlin were right; we could have ten times the house in Vegas that we could have in Los Angeles.

The Pelzers and the Tylos began looking at lots together. At first, our idea was to build back-to-back, with our homes fronting parallel streets. I thought this idea indicated how close Kimberlin wanted to be. She wanted to do the Lucy and Ethel thing! I thought that was so sweet.

Eventually, Michael and I found an oversized lot that had been left undeveloped because of the difficulty of finding an appropriate floor plan. The Pelzers bought another lot one door down—we would be separated by a policeman and his family.

I became competitive with Kimberlin over what our houses would look like. She was going to have a huge, marble foyer. Well, then, I would have a double staircase straight out of *Gone with the Wind*'s Tara. She was going to have a library with every wall covered in cherry wood bookcases. I would have built-in terrariums in the living room, in which I could put exotic reptiles and chameleons from Indonesia. The base price of our homes was about $250,000 and soon soared to more than half a million dollars from our add-ons and upgrades.

As quickly and securely as I thought Kimberlin and I had bonded, we stopped being friends for such slight reasons that I'm still mystified about them to this day. The nub of it seemed to be that Kimberlin couldn't take confrontation. On a couple of social outings, I felt she slighted me by going off with other friends— "ditching me," as a junior high schooler might do to someone whom she wanted to "get lost." When these incidents cropped up, I told her that I thought she was being discourteous. This truth-telling, which all real friendships require, canceled ours.

When Michael and I finally moved into our Vegas house in December of 1993, we felt a natural pride. The experience was shadowed, though, by how estranged we felt from our one-door-down neighbors.

Part Four

13

In 1994, three months after we moved into the Vegas house, I was offered a lead role in the miniseries *The Maharaja's Daughter.* Titanus Pictures, an Italian company that produced Sophia Loren's early films and many biblical movies, wanted me for a sixteen-week shoot, eight weeks in Canada and eight in India. I would be costarring with Bruce Boxleitner and the well-known Indian actor Kabir Bedi, who played the bad guy Gobinda in the James Bond film *Octopussy*.

The opportunity might open up more film work, I thought. It seemed worth taking the time off from *The Bold and the Beautiful,* especially as I could commute back and forth from Canada during the last part of the shoot. I prepared to go away to India at the end of February, to a little town called Udaipur in Rajasthan. Udaipur is known for its Lake Palace, a white jewel in the midst of serene Pichola Lake. The Lake Palace, which is now a luxury hotel, has often been used as a movie setting.

Seeing India for the first time is difficult to put into words. The moment I got off the plane in Udaipur, I was overwhelmed by the sensation of being in a highly spiritual land. The air carried a host of flowery scents I could not recognize. Even the old European car that took me to the hotel along roads whose pavements sank into white, powdery soil reinforced my sense of being transported into a dreamlike world.

The production company put us up at the Shivniwas Palace, originally a guest house for invitees of the maharajas. It sits close by the City Palace, the main residence of the area's maharaja. In fact, I met him at parties several times. In his palace, he showed us a lavish room full of solid heart-cut lead crystal chairs with little silk cushions, sofas, china cabinets, and chandeliers, a display of brilliant dazzling decadence.

The old car pulled up before an immense stone building surmounted with towers and cupolas, with giant wooden doors. The palace is built around an impressive, semicircular courtyard that contains a long, tiled pool. In the evening, tables are set up around the pool and the hotel's guests are entertained by traditional Indian musicians. Everyone from Jackie Onassis to Queen Elizabeth II has stayed there. I walked across a mosaic floor that must have taken decades to lay. At every turn, I saw beautiful fountains, cusped arches, inlaid stones, and stained glass. I felt as though I had arrived in fairyland.

I was startled to see langur monkeys everywhere I looked— monkeys hanging upside down, monkeys sitting on a porch, monkeys swinging by one leg. They were cute black monkeys with white faces, or white with black faces, or silver with red faces, and they were everywhere.

As I was led to my room, a sweet, bread-like scent overtook me, a kind of cinnamon spice aroma so potent I can still remember it now. I was told by my Italian and Indian hosts that the maharaja kept his harem here at one time and carried on orgies by the pool. One or more of his consorts had been kept in the room where I'd be staying.

My room featured a gorgeous canopy bed set in an alcove. Alcoves and niches of every size were carved in the walls throughout the hotel, some with little banisters and intricate detail. Every doorway—even the one leading to my bathroom—was framed with a carved arch at the top, the door fitting like a puzzle piece.

A sliding patio door in my room led out to a beautiful balcony overlooking some gardens. Pichola Lake spread out beyond, with its Lake Palace, which was lit up at night as if anticipating the sunrises that enveloped its shoulders. The first moment I looked out, a flock of demoiselle cranes—dove gray with white hoods—crossed the sky.

As I unpacked, I came across a gift from my friend and the children's nanny, Leanne, a beautiful Easter-egg-shaped candle holder with a cross carved into the front for the candlelight to glow through. She had given it to me before I left, along with a small Bible. "You're going to be there during Easter and you might get lonely." She also gave me a crucifix to put on the wall over my bed. I set these gifts and pictures of the kids, Michael, and the then-new Las Vegas house in the room's surrounding niches.

My sense of being almost magically transported into another world came as a particular relief at this time, as the years between my marriage to Michael and this passage to India—from 1987 to 1994—had brought with them a sense that I was losing my way.

In particular, I couldn't help looking at my life through the dark lens of a family tragedy. Five months before, I had received a phone call at two o'clock in the morning. My brother-in-law Leland had just killed himself in front of my sister, Elizabeth. On the sofa in their dimly lit living room, Leland laid back and put his gun in his mouth. Just before he did it, he had said something like, "No, I'm not going to do that." He may have been planning to kill my sister first and then himself. Fortunately, he changed his mind, but my sister had to live with the terrible aftermath—the unanswered and perhaps forever unanswerable questions.

There had been marital problems in the past, fighting on and off; at one time, my brother-in-law told Elizabeth he wanted a divorce. It seems Leland may have been having an affair with a counselor he started seeing because of his suicidal thoughts. That surely didn't help. He also felt depressed over the limitations of his job prospects. But my sister said things were calm at the time of his suicide.

Leland's family felt my sister and our family were to blame, that she drove him to it, our family drove him to it. She hadn't had children with him, had she? They had been married for fifteen years.

I spent many late nights on the phone with my sister, sometimes all night, because she was close to a nervous breakdown and was having nightmares.

My boys were having nightmares, too, especially Chris, who adored Leland. Both Chris and Mickey used to visit Leland and Elizabeth in Tennessee. He took them hunting and taught them how to shoot and how to clean a gun. He taught them everything about guns. (A month earlier, Leland had given *me* a PPKS handgun as a gift.) At first, we told Chris that Leland's death was an accident, but, bewildered, he would say, "But Mom, he showed me so many times not to point the gun at my face, ever."

I was completely devastated by Leland's death. I began to distrust life more and more. Even my own marriage felt at risk. Nothing, as people around me kept tirelessly repeating, is forever. Everything seemed so unsure, so unstable. You never knew when someone would freak out and betray you. The very things that could never happen in a million years happened all the time.

My sister kept asking why God would allow such a thing to happen. I wanted to know that, too, but I didn't have any answers.

Then Christmastime rolled around, with what had become the usual—no, habitual—partying. After Michael and I moved to Los Angeles and my career began to gain momentum as the result of being hired on *The Bold and the Beautiful,* we began to live a life devoted, at least in part, to going out and being noticed. We showed up at the latest fashionable restaurant or dance club with a group of our show-business friends. Then we'd drink way too much. The drinking led to flirting. Sometimes the drinking and the flirting were one and the same thing. Our friends liked to do body shots. After a while, the body shots would become extramarital. This type of flirting led to serious jealousies and suspicions. In one particular instance, a friend of Michael's hit on me—all the while claiming to be his good pal. I could only wonder what other women might be suggesting to Michael in the conga lines that usually closed down our revels.

Most disturbing, I suppose, was the fact that Michael came to accept the freewheeling flirtations, whereas once he tore my head off for wearing black-seamed hose to an audition. He was spending more and more time with his buddies playing golf. As we built our custom dream house in Las Vegas, most of the time we spent together was spent hungover, walking around the construction site, deciding on new, unplanned-for materials—tile, countertops, flooring—that would send the house's costs soaring ever higher. Otherwise, we were commuting back and forth on different shooting schedules. The partying didn't slow down after we moved, either. Almost every night, someone dropped by with a bottle of Jack Daniel's, which invariably became a dead soldier by evening's end.

That Christmas, I was reluctant to join in the frivolity. I kept feeling more and more disturbed about the life we were living. Then Michael got pretty smashed at one of our Christmas parties. It was embarrassing. I was trying not to drink like that anymore.

I began trying to get the family to go to church again. We had stopped going two years before after someone broke into our garage and stole all our bicycles while we were at church one Sunday. Michael wasn't inclined to begin again. Sunday was one of the few days he could count on being home to play golf.

Michael's increasing tendency to live his life—at least the part of it he enjoyed—apart from me kept prompting the question I had first asked after Leland's death. *Who's to say Michael won't flip out one day? Won't leave me. Won't . . .*

I found myself in this mansion-like house with all of its marble, crystal chandeliers and expensive carpeting, its wooden doors, bay windows, and a giant double circular staircase that met at a landing and then descended with a railing like something out of *Gone with the Wind*—and I wondered why we had bothered. We were living anything but a dream in that dream home.

My misgivings partly stemmed from a fortune-teller Michael and I were calling regularly. One of our neighbors encouraged

Michael and me to call Shirley, who lived somewhere in Pennsylvania. We only had to send a twenty-five-dollar check at the end of the month and we could find out what was going on in our lives. The neighbor claimed this fortune-teller had been dead-on accurate about many things in his life.

We began calling as a lark. She immediately started predicting problems with one of my friends, and I did have the friendship that was going sour with Kimberlin Brown. Then the fortune-teller revealed that one of my family members would die soon—well ahead of Leland's suicide. "It's going to be a shock," the fortune-teller said.

"What do you mean? Who? What?" I asked her in alarm.

"I don't think it's a member of your immediate family, but someone close. An older man. He has brown eyes. It's going to be like a plane crash—something out of the blue. I don't really know who it is. That's all I can tell you. There's going to be a death."

This frightened me, and her ability to see into the future frightened me more once Leland died.

I didn't stop calling, though, because she was also telling me good things. She told me Chris had a phenomenal talent for music, something I didn't discover for another two years, not before we put a piano in the house and he taught himself to play. She told me details about the home we were building, and she knew that I desperately wanted to have a baby girl some day. I hadn't mentioned anything about my hopes for another child.

She also told me I would soon be offered a role in a big film. "You're going to go to a foreign country. You're going to be there for a period of time. You're going to become famous. You're going to work with a big-name star."

I was thinking, "Yeah, right." But I was also laughing; I enjoyed the thought.

She went on to say there would be another man, a dark man of a different nationality, who would cause problems for me. She wasn't warning me, just telling me matter-of-factly. As she read my tarot cards over the phone, she foresaw divorce or serious marital problems.

*M*y mom named me Deborah, after a prophetess from the Bible (Personal)

*I*n 1990 with *The Bold and the Beautiful* costar Ronn Moss shortly after the loss of my father (Maureen Donaldson)

"*R*oyal Family" portrait from 1992 (Maureen Donaldson)

*S*eemingly happy couple
in 1992
(Maureen Donaldson)

"*B*est of friends" with
Kimberlin Brown Pelzer
in 1993 (Hutchins Photo
Agency)

*B*eginning of the end with Michael in 1993 (Hutchins Photo Agency)

*A*rt imitating life with my pet boa Kingfish in *B&B* episode in 1994 (Hutchins Photo Agency)

*P*ost-India: sporting my new ear-piercings by Jetu. Kabir Bedi starred on *B&B* and *The Maharaja's Daughter* (Jill Johnson/Hutchins Photo Agency)

*S*ex plus money *doesn't* equal happiness. Photo taken during 1994 Indian summer separation from Michael (Personal)

*H*appy reunion: October 1995 reconciliation dinner with *(left to right)* Vegas friends, Bill and Gigi Smith and John Sousa IV (Personal)

*F*riends and family celebrate our 1995 New Year's Eve Wedding Vow Renewal
(Personal)

*G*loria Allred had tagged me,
"A pioneer in the footsteps of
Susan B. Anthony"
(Kate Turning/Turning Pictures)

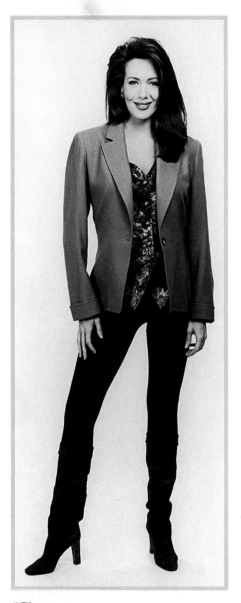

"Trick" trial outfit photo that was taken in the third week of the trial, when I was thirty-four weeks pregnant (Dennis Mukai)

Trial "Miracle Bra" outfit —six weeks to deliver! (Dennis Mukai)

*E*ight-and-a-half-
month-pregnant
"Sexy Vixen"
(Dennis Mukai)

*(Below) C*ouldn't look
sexy pregnant?
(Dennis Mukai)

*F*our days from the birth of Bella, with *B&B* friends John Zak and Ronn Moss
(Hutchins Photo Agency)

*W*ild Emmy hair, 1997,
one month pregnant with Katya
(Kathy Hutchins/Hutchins Photo Agency)

*B*urning the midnight oil with Ronn Moss on *B&B* after a day in court,
November 1997 (Hutchins Photo Agency)

*F*iftieth surprise birthday party I
threw for Michael in October 1998
(Maureen Donaldson)

*M*asking difficult times—two months
after Kat's diagnosis
(Maureen Donaldson)

*H*iding a broken heart: my dear Katya during chemo
(John Russo)

*G*lamour during tragedy: Katya had only recently lost her right eye (John Russo)

"*M*iracles Event" to raise money for retinoblastoma in August 1998
(Kathy Hutchins/Hutchins Photo Agency)

*M*y baby dolls! Bella and Kat (John Russo)

How did she know all these things?

She told me her gift was from God. Even then, I wondered if it could be, because I knew that the Old Testament taught that sooth-saying is an abomination to God.

Before I left for India, I spoke with Michael about having another child. After Mickey was born, we decided our love life would improve if we didn't have to worry about pregnancy all the time. Michael was willing to have a vasectomy and did. I had come to regret this decision. In fact, as I began to see that my childbearing years wouldn't last forever, I became ever more eager to have another child.

Much of my anxiety over the direction our family was headed in resolved itself into this one issue. Our attitude toward having additional children said everything about our basic commitments. Were we building a family or constructing a pleasure dome where we'd bump into each other once in a while?

I told Michael this would be a great time to have his vasectomy reversed. We could start trying to have a little girl when I returned from India.

But Michael told me no. "I'm not reversing it. I told you if we had a child, that would be it. I'm not reversing it. Two boys are enough," he said.

"Wouldn't you like to have a baby daughter?"

"We're having a hard enough time taking care of the two boys. Particularly with all the commuting. No, Hunter, I just don't want to have any more. Not right now, at least."

I didn't let go that easily. I begged him. Then fought him.

He'd only say, "I'm not ready. We'll do it later."

The first couple of weeks in India went well. I was doing my job, getting my work done, and really enjoying myself without feeling too homesick. I put through a call every morning at 6:00 A.M. my time to catch the kids just before they went to bed. We always thought that was fun, me telling them good morning and them saying good night.

As Easter Sunday neared in India, I heard about the Indian spring carnival called Holi. The carnival's spirit is something like Mardi Gras, with all castes mixing together and people playing practical jokes on one another. All over India, the people run through the streets, throwing red powder and colored liquids on one another. Holi includes parades and other events.

I mentioned to some Indian men that I thought this was a strange custom. They replied, "It's like your Easter. You dye Easter eggs different colors. We dye each other." (There are actually deeper similarities. Easter celebrates the death and resurrection of Jesus. Holi celebrates the gods' propitiation—the appeasement of their anger—through animal sacrifice. The red powders and liquids are substitutes for the blood that used to be used.)

I wanted to participate in Holi; it sounded fun.

But my director thought otherwise. "You are not doing that," he told me. "I know what that stuff is. It stains your skin. If you get any on your face, I can't shoot you tomorrow."

I suggested we shoot on Tuesday instead. I tried to convince him that participating in this festival would help me understand my role, since my character was supposed to be half Indian. (That's how the story line explained my Western looks.)

The director was adamant about me staying in my room on Easter.

When I got to the set the next day, I was glad. Everybody's skin was stained, as the director had foreseen.

During one shoot, we had to take a boat across the lake, out to the Lake Palace Hotel. In the middle of April, the Indian summer was in full bloom and some days the temperature climbed to one hundred and ten degrees. I understood why the maharaja had gone to such trouble to build a palace that would catch the lake's cooling breezes.

At the Lake Palace, I met a man who spoke very good English with a British accent. He was an old man, with the contented face of a Buddha. He asked me if I would like to smoke a joint.

"I've never cared for the stuff," I said.

"Have you ever tried opium?" he asked.

"No way. I wouldn't touch any of that."

"Oh, come on," he said, coaxing. "Maybe some night we sit out by the Shivniwas pool and we can smoke it."

"Whatever," I said, not thinking much more about it.

He came to my hotel a few nights later. The crew hung out around this pool every night and drank. There were tables with candlelight, lights strung in the trees, a musician playing the sitar. I really began to enjoy the food, becoming familiar enough to pick from the menu. Before I left Los Angeles, I was told to take a shot of whiskey with my meals; the alcohol would kill any unusual bacteria in my stomach and I would avoid dysentery.

As I was hanging out drinking on this night, this well-educated Indian asked again, "Do you want to try the joint? It's very fun and not addictive."

I said, "Okay."

We walked out to the back of the courtyard, although I'm sure nobody but the director—the only other American there—would have thought anything of our opium dalliance. I took two puffs. I had tried marijuana off and on in the past, but I was never into drugs. I don't like them, and I know their dangers. But I was just having fun, I was away from home . . . who would know?

The opium made me feel truly weird. I wasn't hallucinating, but I felt drawn into an even more exotic world, where everything felt ethereal and profoundly pleasant. Something else in me shifted as well, something that lay far deeper than passing sensations. I knew I had broken a promise to myself never to do anything like that. I began to learn how fragile such promises can be.

A few days later, I had one scene in which my character was kidnapped and thrown into a cave. We had to drive a bit to get to this cave, located near Udargos, not far from the Ganges River. We actually went to an Indian graveyard, although it looked more like a temple site, with a maze of sculpted walls. Nearby, a little river flowed, and a big, steep set of stairs led to other parts of the caves and grounds. We were in a huge burial and shrine complex. I felt wary somehow from the minute I got there—it was too spooky.

When I arrived on the set that day, the crew told me I would be working with my choice of three snakes. In this particular scene, I had been knocked out by the bad guys and thrown into this cave. Then I was to wake up and escape. Part of the escape involved my character seeing a snake, grabbing it, and throwing it at the guard's face.

I was nervous but still ready to do the scene. After all, I love reptiles.

Everyone on the set, especially the Indians, were really fascinated. "You're not afraid?" they kept asking me.

"No way," I told them. "I have snakes. I have tegus. I had alligators once."

They told me they had brought in several different snakes. I didn't necessarily have to handle a cobra. The cobra was revered and feared as the pet of the god Shiva.

"What shop do you get them from?" I asked.

"Shop?" they asked.

"Where do you get them, then?"

One of the men had been sent out to catch snakes in the fields. Even though he was working on a movie set, the snake catcher dressed in toga-like rags, as did most of the crew.

They took me to a trailer outside the burial grounds to look at the snakes they had collected. Of course, I wanted the nastiest-looking snake possible to make my character look tough. They had snakes I had never seen before, and I knew a lot about snakes. One was an extremely long, skinny, bright emerald green snake. It was highly poisonous. The men assured me, though, that they had defanged all the snakes.

I was most impressed by the baskets full of cobras—yes, ten baskets containing cobras, straight out of an old movie.

"Which one do you like?" the snake catcher asked me, taking the top off the basket and rattling it so that the snakes stuck their heads up, their hoods flared, ready to strike.

I knew enough about cobras to realize they can bite and spit up to thirty feet, causing grave harm—from blindness to death—if aggravated. I asked about the fangs again just to be sure, and again the snake catcher reassured me.

"No, no, no, we pull their teeth out."

I settled on this one black cobra. He was gorgeous, all smooth and shiny, quite beautiful. Cobras' scales are very different from those of other snakes; they are smooth as black glass. He had a bright horseshoe marking on his back and frowning eyes with deep, menacing eyebrows. Cobras just look cool. It's as if they're asking, who wants to mess with me?

Yet without his hood flared, while he was crawling on the ground, he was actually very friendly, calm, and not easily aggravated. We had a hard time getting him to flare his hood because he was so nice. He mainly wanted to keep going down the back of my shirt to get warm. That snake took to me and I liked him, too.

"Let's use the cobra," I said, "but they're going to want one that flares his hood. Will this one's hood open?"

The snake catcher nodded, took the snake and rattled a big old, cheap watch on his wrist in its face. Immediately, the snake drew back, flaring his hood. I stared in awe. When he opened his mouth and hissed, I saw a hole in the back of his throat open. The snakes I kept at home never hissed, but cobras do. He reared in position and waved around as if teasing. He was a fascinating creature.

I asked, "How do I grab him? Will he bite?"

"Yes, he'll bite," the snake catcher answered. He gave me a few quick tips about picking him up.

"How do you catch them?" I wondered.

"I just grab them around the back of the hood," he answered.

"Don't you ever get bitten?" I asked.

"Sometimes," he said.

I noticed how unhealthy he looked. But most Indians did. This snake catcher had hardly any teeth, as if he were defanged himself. I couldn't help but wonder how much his profession had to do with his ill health.

After choosing the black cobra, I carried it around the set for a while to gain its trust before doing the scene, wrapped around my waist like a belt or draped around my shoulders and neck.

Everybody was amazed that I wasn't afraid of the snake. They respected that black cobra because of its association with the god Shiva. They seemed to think my familiarity with the creature could only be attributed to my own spirituality.

When the time came to do the scene, I had to lie on the ground as though I had been tossed there. They painted dirt and bruise marks on my skin to make it appear as though I had been beaten up. My character was to wake up slowly and discover the snake. The director told me the snake would be in the corner, but he wouldn't tell me exactly where. He wanted to capture my surprise on camera. The crew wanted to shoot the entire sequence of me figuring out how to pick up this aggravated cobra with its hood flared in one long take.

The snake catcher had shown me how to pick the cobra up from the floor when it was calm. But I still didn't know exactly how I would do this when the snake was agitated, with its hood flared. It was so wide! A boa constrictor won't turn around to bite when grabbed behind the jaws. Perhaps that applied to the cobra as well. I'll just figure that part out when I get to it, I thought. The flared hood would indicate where his jaws were, and since he didn't have any teeth, everything would be fine.

Just before the director shouted "Roll," I heard the snake catcher's watch rattling. I knew they were agitating the snake somewhere off camera. When we were rolling, I jumped up on cue, acting groggy and disoriented. After discovering the snake and conceiving the idea of using it for my escape, I went to grab it. But where would I grab that thing? Its whole hood was flared and there didn't appear to be a good way of reaching around behind the jaws.

The director and crew looked as though everything were going great.

I decided just to grab it. When I did, it turned around with its head within its hood and bit me. Immediately. With teeth.

When I realized I had been bitten, the thought flashed through my mind that certainly they had taken out the poison sac. I didn't get upset, and I went ahead and started to run out of frame as directed.

"Reset," shouted the director.

They wanted to shoot it over; they had missed something.

I looked down and saw blood running out of the wound on my hand.

"Does this thing have teeth?" I called out.

One of the crew ran over saying, "Let me see." They were looking at my hand, looking in the snake's mouth, speaking in Hindu and English. "Yes, something bit her, something scratched her."

I started to get mad. *Oh, my God,* I thought, panic beginning to rise. I'm going to die. I'm going to die. I've been wearing this thing the whole day and it has its teeth!

When the snake bit me, one of those looking after me put his mouth on the wound, sucked out the poison, and spat repeatedly. As he kept inspecting and wiping off my wound, I recognized him as one of the stunt men for the movie.

When he looked up at me, I saw how dark he was. This was my first encounter with Mehendra, the fortune-teller's "dark man of another nationality." I could almost hear her words. Mehendra could be a problem for me because I found him extremely handsome.

I could tell he came from a higher class, as he was much more educated, well-dressed, and healthy than the other crew members. He spoke two or three languages: Hindi, Italian, and very clear English. When he spoke to me, his education and intelligence were obvious. From that moment, Mehendra became my caretaker. He seemed truly concerned for me.

Another man—I think he was something like an animal trainer—finally ripped out the snake's teeth and cleaned out the empty sockets.

We needed to redo the scene. The incident held up our shooting schedule for two to three hours. I didn't become afraid of the snake, though. By the time we actually reshot the scene, that snake and I had bonded once more. I took the snake in its basket back to the hotel with me.

As we finished the scene, I felt reasonably well. When I went back to my room, though, I developed a migraine and started to feel terrible. In fact, I became so traumatized that the Indian Film liaison, Aruna, fetched a doctor to administer an injection of valium to calm me down.

Mehendra stayed to take care of me. He cautioned me against trusting people too easily and getting sucked into dangerous situations. They had hired "those idiots" with the snakes off the streets without really knowing who they were. There were no unions or guilds to certify these people as professionals. While there are several club-like affiliations, Mehendra said there was no reliable mechanism for checking out anyone's professional credibility.

Mehendra took care of me for several days as I struggled to regain my health after I became ill, either from the snake bite or dysentery or malaria—no one could ever tell me for sure. The more I was around Mehendra, the more I noticed how everyone around him looked up to him as a leader.

Through conversations with him, I learned that he had a great respect for spiritual matters. In India, one of the hallmarks of spirituality is the wish to dedicate one's self to serving the gods. But because this is difficult to live out, those who actually do are considered enlightened. They become spiritual leaders to those around them, much like a guru. Mehendra assumed this role with the people around him. It impressed me that he was so highly respected.

As I came to know him better, Mehendra told me that not only did he live his life for his gods but that he would also die for his gods.

"I pray when I'm in the bathroom. I pray when I'm in the shower. I pray when I'm doing anything. I pray all the time. I talk to the gods," he said.

Every morning, he followed a certain ritual. He would use paint or ashes on his forehead, sometimes all over his face. That took some getting used to, but it made a significant impression on me. I thought of Michael, who didn't even want to go to church anymore. Here was a guy who said he lived his whole life for his gods. Wow, that's inspiring, I thought. He is a deeply spiritual person.

As I got to know him, Mehendra began to teach me all about his gods, telling me what each one did, what they had done for him, the great powers they possessed. I felt drawn to his beliefs. I learned that Shiva died when a cobra bit his mouth, which is why he's always painted blue. Mehendra introduced me to Rama (or Vishnu), the head god, and Sita, his wife. Mehendra brought me images and statuettes of the gods—a boxful as a gift one day. These included a *shivalinga* (a phallic representation of Shiva) made of brass, a cobra with its hood flared, and various icons for specific gods, small cards with colorful drawings or paintings and real gold accents. He showed me how to worship his gods, explaining that women are particularly gifted at influencing them. "Take off your shoes," Mehendra told me. "You have to wash your feet first. You count the number of times you say the sacred name AUM—the Hindu trinity—with these beads. Good things happen when you do this."

Mehendra instructed me to pick fresh flowers and sprinkle these around the statues, and to provide them with food, such as bread and fresh cow's milk. The milk was to be poured over the top of the statues so that it flowed down into a dish while the worshiper prayed and chanted the sacred name. Long sticks of sandalwood incense were lit and placed on specially formed niches.

He showed me that I could change aspects of my life by serving these gods. Hanuman would bring good fortune, good luck, because of his devotion. Ganesh, the elephant god, was especially good at bringing success in life. I tried worshiping his gods, performing the sunrise ceremony each morning, and things on the set began to change as I wished. I felt a new sense of power.

The more I watched and learned from Mehendra, the more I thought he must be enlightened. He knows so much more about his faith than I do about mine. He's someone anyone could look up to.

When he went away intermittently to work on other films, I

missed him more than I was missing Michael. Experiencing so many strange changes in such a compressed time frame, and being cut off from the familiar, led me to change my mind and my whole way of thinking about my lifelong beliefs. I'm an adult, I figured. I'm changing because I know the truth now.

Mehendra began to come around to the hotel much more frequently because he was handling the production's horses. He asked me whether I would like to go horseback riding some time, and I agreed because I loved horses.

We began to spend a lot of time together over a two-week period, having dinner most nights. Things moved quickly, to the point that I soon thought I was falling in love with him.

In the midst of—or maybe *because of*—this spiritual awakening I was experiencing, I became convinced of it. Although nothing physical had happened between us at this point, we began to say "I love you." All the recent losses in my life and all my longings for a new kind of stability seemed to get caught up and jumbled with my feelings for him.

I was even beginning to make plans with him. I knew that many Indian families sell their young daughters to brokers who promise good-paying jobs for them in foreign countries. Often, these young girls are sold into prostitution—virtual slavery. This broke my heart. I wanted to have a little girl so much. Perhaps I could save a child from prostitution through adoption.

I asked Mehendra to help me find a little girl to adopt. He told me I could go out to any village and people would sell their little girls without a thought.

"For how much?" I asked.

"Twenty-five dollars," he said. "If you've got American money, I've seen them sold for ten dollars."

I wanted to go right then. I couldn't stand it. This is awful, I thought. I've got to save one; at least one, one or two. Mehendra warned me that there might be problems, however. I must go through the government, he said; Aruna knew people who could pull strings. He wanted me to wait and see.

Mehendra soon had to leave to direct the stunts on another picture (he supervised the stunt work on up to fifty pictures at a time). During his absence, I became friends with another Indian man, Nassir, who was the associate director for our movie. He and I would sit out by the pool discussing spiritual matters. He spoke about Jesus and his confusion about religion. He told me many stories about gurus who had helped him and temples he had visited where he had witnessed many bizarre and inexplicable occurrences, such as people being levitated. I thought Hinduism sounded better and better.

This one particular night, Nassir and I proceeded to get drunk, and I returned to my hotel room alone. Mehendra had devised a little temple for the Hindu gods for me. I decided to incorporate all the Christian things Leanne sent with me, thinking, *Well, they're all gods. They should all be the same.* I placed the crucifix right smack in the middle, propped against the back wall, surrounded by the *shivalinga* and all the little pictures, statues, and brass figurines.

With Mehendra gone, I had some time to sit and think about Michael. My thoughts went from bad to worse. One night, I was sitting in my room drinking. Nothing lasts forever, anyway, I told myself. I might as well end my marriage now. I've already found somebody else I like better. I'll tell Michael . . . I guess I'm going to have to tell him eventually.

I certainly never expected Michael to call so soon, much less at the precise moment I was having these thoughts. It was about 10:00 P.M. when the phone rang.

We began to talk and the conversation turned unpleasant. Michael had to be in Los Angeles and I hadn't arranged for a nanny to care for the kids during the time he was away. Leanne had other commitments now. He didn't know what to do.

He was finding out how much work I really did at home. He was being inconvenienced by my absence and didn't like it. Good, now he knows how much he depends on me, I thought.

To complicate matters, the phone lines in India were not always reliable. I'd pick up the phone some days to find the line dead. Michael and I hadn't talked in four days at that point because I hadn't been able get through. Now that he had finally gotten through, he wanted to know where the hell I'd been. That elicited "none of your damn business" from me, of course.

That telephone conversation dredged up every problem I had ever had with Michael. This guy won't quit drinking. (Boy, that was the pot calling the kettle black!) He won't take the kids to the church he claims to believe in.

I decided to see how breaking up might feel. "What if I don't want to be with you anymore?"

I said it just to see what he'd say. I had never said anything like that.

"Well, if that's the way you feel, then fine," he answered. "Good, go. Stay in India. I don't care."

That's all I needed to hear. "Really? You dare me? You're daring me?"

I taunted and aggravated him; he retaliated. What else could he do? The fight escalated to the point where I was saying things like, "What if I never come back? What if I leave you?"

"Fine, good. Stay there. Stay in India, you like it so much," he said.

Then I started talking about how great a place India really was . . . did he know all about these gods? Ganesh and Hanuman and Kali and Durga Bhagwati were powerful. What if he needed a hex broken or the power to charm someone? Did he know what to do? (Of course, I had just learned all this two days ago and I tried to sound like a lifelong Hindu.)

"Okay, that's it," Michael said. "You are coming home. You are getting on the next plane and coming home. I don't care if you never work again. This stuff is lethal." By then, the conversation had gone on for three hours.

I told him where he could stick it.

"Then I'm coming there. You must be totally screwed up to be saying all this garbage."

"No, you're not," I said. "You know what? I'll have you barred. I can have you arrested here. I know the lady who has all the pull in this town. I can get you arrested. I can truly have you locked away in a third-world country and you will never get out! You don't think I'll do it? Just go ahead and show up!"

He knew I wasn't kidding. When I'm acting like a brat, then I'll do whatever, just to prove I can.

The conversation got even worse. I found myself saying, "I don't love you anymore." I knew I didn't mean it; I just wanted to see if I could make him cry. I was drunk and ready to do as much damage as possible. The more we talked, the more cruel I became.

I finally told him, "I think I'm in love with someone else. I don't love you anymore."

"Fine," he said. But then he cried. I had finally made him cry.

Then I felt bad and I kept saying, "I'm sorry, I'm sorry, I'm sorry." But even I didn't know whether I was sorry to have said those things or because our relationship had degenerated to this point.

At the time Michael called, his parents were visiting. After our conversation, Michael proceeded to get smashed right in front of his mother, Margaret. She knew that I had done exactly what I said I would never do. As of right then, Margaret hated me, and with good reason.

14

My acting teacher, Ivana, called soon after Michael and I had our hateful telephone conversation. She had flown to Vegas to hang out at our new home, and found everyone there in an uproar.

"What's going on there, Hunter?"

"What do you mean? I'm *working.*"

"Honey, I'm really getting worried about you. I'm hearing things and I'm a little concerned and I want to know if you're okay. Do you need me to come there?"

"What things?"

"I'm hearing things about you having an affair. Michael says it's true."

"We're not having an affair. Not really. Not yet. But I have met someone."

"You can't fool around with Michael's affections this way, Hunter. He's a mess. He's drinking every night."

"I've had it with him," I said. "I've already told him this. If nothing else, we at least need a separation. I'm tired of his crap. You know my problems with Michael." I had voiced my complaints about Michael to Ivana on many occasions.

"Hunter, what's going on? What do you want? I mean, you don't want to leave Michael? Do you?"

"I don't really know. I just don't know right now."

"Hunter," she said, "I know you still love Michael. You may have problems with him, but don't be stupid. Please don't be stupid. I'm not trying to scare you or upset you, but Michael has been dating another woman."

"Dating?"

"I'm not sure what that means, either. But I think he has a girl-friend."

"*What?*"

"It's a waitress from the Mirage."

I knew then that she wasn't kidding. I knew she was my friend and I trusted her. "What do you mean, a waitress?" I asked, getting angry. "Who? Who is it?"

"I don't know, just some waitress from the Mirage Hotel," Ivana answered.

"A tacky waitress from the Strip? What does she look like?" I demanded.

"She's really pretty, Hunter," Ivana replied. "She's blond and pretty. I'm serious, Hunter. You've either got to come home or you've got to let Michael come there. You've got to stop this because this woman is after your husband. He started seeing her right after you told him you wanted to split up."

"Well," I said, "if it's that easy, then he doesn't love me."

How could he bail on me so quickly? I wondered. I'm the one who's found someone else. I'm supposed to be in control here. He's not supposed to be interested in anyone else. He's supposed to be over there miserable and crying and sad. He's already going out? He's already replaced me with some bimbo from the Mirage Hotel?

"Look, Ivana, I'm in India for another month and I'm just going to enjoy myself while I'm here," I said, determined now.

When Mehendra returned, he told me he was in love with me, that all he thought about was me. He brought me gifts, including many beautiful saris. I had bought one sari to wear to a welcoming party for the cast and crew at the palace one night. I also wore some of the costume jewelry from the movie. Because Mehendra had seen this and liked it, he bought me four or five expensive saris made with fabric imported from Bangladesh.

Our affair began. Mehendra was sexy and passionate. For a time, I relished being romanced. He always brought me gifts: gifts, gifts, and more gifts. Often, I didn't even know what the gifts were or whether they were of any value, but I enjoyed his thoughtfulness. Mehendra learned that I knew a little something about jewels, because I once bought some loose gemstones—rubies and sapphires and emeralds—very inexpensively at a local shop. (One sapphire was almost half a karat, but I paid only forty dollars for it simply because it needed a little polishing.) Mehendra knew where to find high-quality, polished, beautiful loose stones, which he brought to me frequently.

He became ever more helpful. Because his family owned all the horses used for the movie, he would select the best horse for me, show me how to handle it, and send me off to practice. Mehendra also protected me from being taken advantage of on the set. He made sure that incidents like being bitten by the cobra never happened again.

Mehendra's fifty different projects kept him traveling back and forth from other locations. He worked with his brother Jetu, a very talented dancer who was in charge of all the dance numbers for *The Maharaja's Daughter.* Jetu didn't like me at first and I soon found out why. Mehendra had a wife and children at home. Mehendra's and Jetu's father had cheated on their mother as well and Jetu remembered too clearly how he had felt.

As Mehendra continued to shower me with gifts and we became more and more attached, I didn't feel wrong about any of it despite the fact that I was still married. I simply felt I had moved on. My former life, my former home, all seemed so far away—on the other side of the world. My marriage existed in another realm, one belonging to the past. I was moving on, making plans. Somehow, I would get my boys back eventually, and if I ended up losing my job at *The Bold and the Beautiful,* I'd find work through Titanus in Italy. I was going to make this relationship with Mehendra work.

I kept calling my children and sometimes Michael called me, but I wouldn't talk to him. My other Indian friend, the assistant director, Nassir, watched my whole relationship with Mehendra develop.

Once, when Michael called, I handed the phone to Nassir. "Here, talk to my friend," I said.

Nassir talked at length with Michael and tried to reassure him that this was just a phase, something that happens to people when they come to India. Afterward, Nassir said to me, "That man loves you. You'd be a fool to leave him."

Even though I was deeply involved with Mehendra, I did confront him about being married and not telling me. It was complicated enough that I was married.

"It's no big problem," Mehendra reassured me. "Shiva will protect us. We're going to be fine. I can have two wives."

"I don't think I want you to have two wives," I said. "We don't do that in America."

Mehendra's wife, Shifali, once called my room at the Shivniwas. "May I speak to Hunter?" asked an Indian woman's voice.

When I identified myself, her first words were, "You better stay away from my husband." Somebody must have told her what was going on, perhaps one of the other Indian men on the film crew. Maybe Jetu.

"Who is this?" I demanded.

"I am Shifali. I am his wife."

"Yes, Mehendra's told me about you," I said, trying to be brazen.

"We have two children, Hunter. You're going to break up my family. You're going to destroy my life, Hunter," she said to me. "Do you know what happens to an Indian woman when she becomes divorced? I'll be an outcast, Hunter. I'll be . . . I'll have nothing. I'll have no money."

I knew there were many implications for her. I felt slightly guilty. But I was annoyed at her calling my name repeatedly. "Mehendra doesn't love you," I said. "He doesn't want you. Your marriage is one big problem to him and has been for a long time."

But she kept calling my name and begging and threatening. "Don't threaten me," I said. "Or I really will take him away from you. I can do that. You know I can."

"Then I will kill myself," she said. "I will kill myself and I will kill the children if you do this to my family."

For an Indian woman, I knew, this might not be overstatement. Women in India often went to extremes to manifest their love—or to protect their station in life. What if she wasn't kidding? Can I live with that? I asked myself. What am I doing to her family?

Aruna, the Indian-crew coordinator, and Mehendra were good friends. Toward the end of the shoot, when she heard that Mehendra was instructing me about the Hindu gods, she told me what she described as a "wonderful story" about her aunt throwing herself on her husband's funeral pyre.

Aruna told this to me as a beautiful love story demonstrating how a Hindu woman shows courage and dignity. Her aunt wore a white robe and appeared more beautiful than she ever had in her entire life on this day. She spoke of the bells her aunt wore on every toe, how she walked, how she was completely at ease, serene, even peaceful. The other mourners kept saying, "Ahhh, don't do it. Don't do it." Aruna acted this out very dramatically, whispering "Don't," to emulate the mourners. Her aunt replied simply by throwing herself on the pyre in front of all the family. As she was telling me this, I grew more and more horrified. But all the Indians sitting nearby agreed with Aruna that it was indeed a beautiful story.

Aruna told me, "You haven't seen anything yet. We must take

you and show you a temple. Tomorrow, I will come to pick you up. We will get a nice car."

Aruna's husband was a high-ranking political figure—he was the one I was counting on to throw Michael in jail if he visited. Aruna picked up Mehendra and me in a sleek, late-model Mercedes. I brought my video camera along, excited to be going to a famous place tourists rarely see.

We drove past huts, down dirt roads that looked recently cleared. I saw one hut where a family was bathing in a dark pond full of reeds. They're probably putting more dirt on than they're getting off, I thought.

People lined the sides of the road, sitting and eating rice out of dishes. Children, babies, even infants lay scattered in the grass fields. No one seemed to be watching them. A goat stood chewing grass right beside a little infant lying in a basket like baby Moses. In another place, I saw a baby lying in a hammock. What if it fell?

I saw men wearing nothing but diaper-like cloths, and women with tunics beautifully draped and tied. We passed several women walking down a dirt path with huge baskets full of bananas on their heads. Their baskets must have weighed thirty pounds. They had babies strapped to their backs as well, and one woman was leading a camel.

Their husbands walked leisurely along behind in their turbans, smoking cigarettes. I couldn't believe it.

"Oh, yes, oh, yes," Aruna nodded approvingly. "That's the way it's done here. Isn't that great? Women are so strong."

To get to the temple, we passed through a hilltop clearing with children playing everywhere, running through an open area full of wildflowers. Spread before us lay a vast expanse of land dotted with huts and an occasional white structure.

We got out of the car to walk into the field where the children were playing. Large blocks of marble marked this place as an ancient site of worship. Erotic carvings decorated the blocks, Kama Sutra–type graphic imagery. I had heard of these erotic images but had never actually seen them. Whoa, I thought, I didn't know any-body could do that! Right in the midst of what seemed heavy duty pornography were eight- and nine-year-old children running wild and playing, no parents in sight.

Only one man was around, standing beside a beat-up old Volvo. He appeared to be watching over the children.

The children ran up to me, hands outstretched, begging. "Lady, lady, lady! Hey, lady!" I immediately gave them some coins, of course. They took the money and ran away laughing, straight to this man.

We walked on into an ancient temple that lay at the field's end. Aruna hired a guide to show me around the grounds, although she knew enough to keep up a running commentary as we walked. Both Aruna and the guide explained who the gods were and how each god was worshiped. I ran my videotape, although I felt un-comfortable and disturbed. Why had one man been watching over those impoverished children?

I was drawn to a large slab of concrete under a giant awning. We walked farther, into more intricate, maze-like parts of the temple, but I kept returning to this particular slab for reasons unknown to me. In my video of this occasion, the camera focuses on the slab, then zooms away, then comes back again—over and over.

"What's this for, Aruna?" I asked.

The guide Aruna hired to accompany us around the temple said, "It's for the sacrifice."

"They kill goats here?"

"No," the guide answered, "the little girls that we sacrifice here."

I saw there were stains on the slab, streaks of brown and red. I didn't know if these marks were from long ago or a week ago, but I came to understand—from conversations this day and later on—that these people still sacrificed children, specifically, little girls. The guide went on to explain this very graphically, and I captured it on tape. "This is where we sacrifice the virgins. This is where they are sacrificed to the gods."

"And they're always girls?" I asked. "They're always virgins?"

"Yes," he said, "between the ages of five and twelve, usually seven-year-olds." Then he added, "Do you know how they're killed?"

"No," I answered, although I didn't really want to know any more at this point. I was horrified. "This must have happened a long time ago."

"No. They still do it today," he said, going on to explain in his broken English how all the people gather around with stones and beat at the child's head until it splits open.

I felt sick, and in my mind's eye I saw my brother-in-law Leland put the gun into his mouth. There were too many hellish possibilities in this world. No one controlled what happened here. These people's culture taught them that the gods wanted such sacrifices. And women throwing themselves on their husbands' funeral pyres. I had thought we were talking about the same God—just different manifestations of the same spirit. But if there were gods, they might have interests other than love and peace. They might delight in stonings. Perhaps I really did need to serve them, in order to avoid their retaliating against my indifference. Leland didn't believe in God or the gods, and he took his life—or they made his life one he wanted to take.

I was thrown into tremendous confusion. My guides could see this happening, that I was already affected deeply. As we were leaving, I understood that the children up on the hill belonged to that man, that they were there to do nothing else but beg. Who knew what the fate of the little girls among the children would be? I was overwhelmed with horror that day.

I should have let the matter go, I suppose, but in the car on the way back, I returned to the subject of how some Indians sell their daughters. Although Mehendra and Aruna sensed my confusion and pain, they didn't back away from the subject. They told me a story about children being sold to Arabs who sexually abused them and then literally threw them out of speeding cars or hotel windows to their deaths.

Once more, I was disgusted and traumatized. It was like being spiritually raped. I came back to the hotel shaking and crying.

Back in my room, I remember standing before the shrine Mehendra and I had put together. It felt like I was asking the statues, Will the real God please stand up? There was only one God, I knew. Even the Indians said this. Weren't these other gods just aspects of the God I already worshiped? Or were they something else? Why did the Hindu gods need offerings? How jealous were they?

At the end of the shoot, I called home one day to speak with the boys. Kimberlin—with whom I'd been fighting, remember—answered the phone.

"What are you doing there?" I asked.

"I'm not sure," she answered. "Tell me what you're doing there."

I kept begging off. "I don't want to talk about it," I said. "It's none of your business."

She proceeded to ask me a lot of questions about my affair. "Are you really going to divorce Michael?"

"I don't want to talk about it with you," I kept repeating.

I never did talk to the boys that day. Later, Michael and I pieced together that Kimberlin had freely embellished what I said, what I hadn't said, and what she had heard through other sources.

I learned later that my house became a site of collective mourning. Our friends—good friends, real friends—brought Michael casseroles and flowers, as if a death had occurred in the family. Many people were rallying to his support.

After I finished the shoot in India, I had two weeks of down time. I could have come back to America, but I didn't want to deal with what was going on at home.

Mehendra asked me to travel with him into the area where he grew up. He wanted me to meet his mother and take me to see the Taj Mahal.

On the last leg of this trip, we went down to Bombay (now called Mumbai) and stayed in his family home. Shifali was gone, visiting her parents with the children.

After traveling the countryside, I was taken to a temple in a small town outside of Jaipur, a place called Mehendi Kabaligi. (I am uncertain of the spelling—it could be a town or small community or simply the name of the temple. I only know I'll never forget the place.) "I'm going to show you a temple where there are ghosts in people," Mehendra told me. He described to me how people went to this temple after eating food that allowed a "ghost" to enter their bodies. They believed they had to go into this temple and pay money to get the ghost out.

Before we went, Mehendra and Jetu camouflaged my face with mud to disguise my white skin. They put my hair up in a turban, placed a fake earring in my nose, and gave me a long tunic to wear so that I looked like a boy. They asked me to hide my hands so that I wouldn't give away the fact that I was a woman. Mehendra and Jetu had discovered this temple as children. It was not far from their home.

As we approached, I suddenly had the overwhelming sense that I should ask to be covered with the blood of Jesus. I don't know why. I didn't even really understand what this meant. Nobody taught me this in the Presbyterian church. Nevertheless, just before I stepped into the temple, I found myself repeating over and over under my breath, "Cover me with the blood of Jesus. Cover me with the blood of Jesus."

As I stood in the temple, I saw water covering a tile floor with a bonfire burning in the middle. (Many Hindu temples are built over sacred wells.) We had to cross the tile floor to get to a dry concrete section.

I can only describe the scene as something out of a surreal movie. The faces of the gods on the walls seemed to waver in and out of the flames of bonfires. Many people were screaming. Over their screams, a man was reading from an ancient, sacred tablet. Another was levitating.

While I was still standing on the tile section, more water started to pour out from underneath the tile. I knew with certainty that this water should not touch me, that there was something evil about it. "I plead the blood of Jesus," I found myself mumbling in the midst of people wailing and screaming.

My guides were saying, "Hurry, hurry. Hop." We hopped over the water to get farther into the temple. All the while, without knowing why, I continued to ask to be covered with the blood of Jesus either under my breath or in my head. Strangely, in every room I walked into, people would stop and stare at me. A man floating cross-legged above the floor looked straight at me but with blank eyes. A woman was upside down against one wall, and yet her dress did not fall around her.

My hosts wanted to take me upstairs to see more, to see worse cases of "ghost possession." Everything I had already encountered went beyond my wildest imagination. The screaming, the continual screaming was horrific. This is what hell must sound like, I thought.

We moved into another area, where pews full of people who had been recently delivered sat. They were singing Hindu hymns. Amid this informal choir, one person who appeared as if her exorcism hadn't been successful suddenly looked at me. Then she got up to walk toward me. "You've got to get out of here," my guides said nervously. "We've got to go."

They kept telling me, "Don't let her touch you! Don't let her touch you!" We ran back to the car and got away as fast as we could. They were calling on their gods Hanuman and Rama. Why had I been pleading the blood of Jesus?

We went back to Bombay, where I started preparing to return home. The day before I was to leave, we visited a jewelry store owned by a friend of Mehendra's. I wanted to buy a necklace, something special from India. I looked at many different Hindu gods on chains, but I chose to buy a cross. In the middle of the shop's jewelry collection was a small cross on a delicate serpentine chain. I put it on immediately. Mehendra bought me an AUM symbol with diamonds, in it.

That evening, we went to dinner. Mehendra had taken me shopping and bought me several beautiful *silvokimis,* the type of dress

Indian women wear, usually wide-legged silk pants under a dress or tunic. We dined at a place in Bombay where film people hang out. We went to several places afterward and had a few beers. Mehendra didn't usually drink. The beer made us both sleepy.

On the way home, we stopped at a hotel for a cup of coffee. Mehendra was going to drop me off at my hotel in Bombay so I could get some sleep before my flight.

During that ride, I was nearly overwhelmed by sadness. I wasn't sure what kind of future Mehendra and I might have. We made promises to call. He said he would come to visit very soon—he might even come to Canada for the second part of the shoot.

Mehendra drove an old, boxy European car—something like a Volvo but of a make I didn't recognize. The night had grown late. I was sitting in the front passenger seat—which is on the left-hand side in India—with my head laid back on the seat. I tried not to go to sleep in case Mehendra needed me to keep him awake. We were working our way through the back streets of Bombay.

As I began to drift off, I heard Mehendra screaming. I opened my eyes and saw we were headed straight for a tree. We were going fast, really fast. I wasn't wearing my seat belt. (Nobody wears them in India because seat belts frequently end up stuffed down into the seats from the towels used to sop up one's sweat.)

As we headed for the tree, I was thinking, *Oh, my God, we're dead. We're dead. We're dead.*

At the last second, Mehendra swerved, causing the car to bank off the side of the tree. We flipped over again and again. I thought it was never going to stop. When is the blow coming? I wondered. When is the final blow going to come? What's it going to feel like to die?

I could hear metal tearing out from the side of the car, glass breaking, even the screams of bystanders. Sparks were flying. I expected the gasoline tank to explode.

Am I going to burn to death? Am I going to—what's going to happen? Is my neck going to break? When it stops, when the final blow comes—that's when I'll know it's over.

In those same fleeting moments, I was also aware of all the bad things I had just done in my life. But I was more obsessed with wondering what it would feel like to die. Never in a million years had I thought that I would die in a car accident in India.

And then we stopped rolling. The noise stopped.

I was upside down. My feet were pinned against the hood. I was extremely uncomfortable. I could see the side window, its shards stuck to a sheet of shredded window tinting—the only reason the glass didn't hit me in the face.

Then I saw people's feet, some with *longes*—an Indian wrap skirt worn mostly by men—around their ankles.

Oh, my God, thank God. Somebody will get me out of here.

My shoulder hurt, but I realized I was alive. I still had to get out of that car. It might still explode. I hate to admit this, but I wasn't even thinking of Mehendra.

Men reached in the window, all talking in Hindi. They pulled me out of one window and pulled Mehendra out the other side. I stared at the car. We should have died. Looking at the car, I couldn't believe we hadn't. The entire car had been flattened, except for the front window area. The windshield hadn't broken, but the back end had been collapsed like a soft tin can.

All the townspeople were asking, "Did that ghost do this to you? Did the ghost do it?" Apparently there was a rumor or legend that a demon or ghost owned this street and frequently caused fatal accidents in this very spot, as many as fifty that year alone. Everyone died in that same spot. Over and over again, this happened.

"Did you see him? Did you see the ghost?" they kept asking.

"I thought I saw a man jump in front of the car, so I swerved," Mehendra said. "That's why I headed toward the tree and that's what caused me to topple the car."

I never saw any ghost. Mehendra only thought he saw someone run in front of the car. But this last ghost story was one too many.

I suffered a broken collarbone, my only injury. The Indian medical workers who took me to Hinduja Hospital suggested they could operate on the shoulder there. Before I agreed, I called my mother in Texas, who by this time had become an emergency room nurse. She warned me, "They are not up to date on the newest anesthesia. You do not want to be operated on there. If you have problems, you'll have no legal recourse as an American."

So I flew all the way back home with absolutely no medication. I changed my flights and went straight home to Fort Worth—to my mom.

Part Five

15

My mom picked me up at the Dallas–Fort Worth Airport. I was in agony, with my left shoulder and arm hitched up at an acute angle in a sling. I cried on the airplane nearly all the way home out of sheer pain. I had no pain relievers—other than Jack Daniel's every few hours to make me sleep—for two days. What had I done to myself? The reality of returning home, my life in a mess, hit me when I saw my mother. She knew everything and was beside herself. What was her daughter doing seeing another man and dabbling in Hinduism?

She took me to the hospital right from the airport, and they immediately gave me a major dose of Demerol. Even though what I had been through frightened my mother, I could tell she was just glad to have me home. For once, she wasn't angry and she didn't judge me. She focused on taking care of me and being my mommy.

We decided that I'd wait to have surgery until I flew home to Las Vegas. My mother wanted to come home with me. I needed her support and even entertained listening to her counsel.

Michael met us at the airport, much to my surprise. I was shocked to see him, but I was glad. I was wearing one of my Indian *silvokimis*—I had left most of my Western clothes in India. Michael eyed what I was wearing as if to say, "Oh. Nice outfit." I barely looked at him when I said, "Hi." I knew I looked weird.

We were uncomfortable, but we tried to be nice—initially. There was so much between us; I wanted to know about the girl from the Mirage and he wanted to know what was happening with the Indian guy. Michael was also angry that I had stayed for the extra two weeks in India. I didn't like to think what he had been imagining, much less consider its accuracy.

Once Michael and I got into the car, our amicable pretenses began to wear off, even in front of my mother. He made fun of my new earring holes at the top of my ears. (Jetu pierced my ears at the top as a symbol of being accepted in the family.) I asked him how much weight he'd gained, boozing it up.

I tried to act as though I didn't care when I asked about Miss Mirage.

"Oh, she's just a friend," he said, minimizing it.

Still, he appeared to be finished with me—he was that cold. I was saddened by the distance between us.

Before we arrived home, about noon Vegas time, I decided I'd be sleeping in the downstairs room. I learned that my sister, Elizabeth, was also coming to town later that day. Elizabeth and I could share the downstairs room and have the late-night sisterly talks she would be anticipating. Even though she had not recovered from Leland's death, she, like everyone else, was worried about me.

It was so good to see Chris and Mickey again. I felt the need to reach out once more, to try to be a mother and a wife again. While I was with our Italian producers, they had taught me how to cook some special pastas and sauces. That night, I would make pasta and we could all sit down together. I wanted to get to know my family again.

As I was cooking, Michael came by and said, "Well, bye. See you later."

Startled, I asked, "Where are you going?"

"I'm going out. I've got a party," he answered.

"I just got home. I'm making dinner," I said, stammering. I was jet-lagged to the max but still cooking. Couldn't he see that?

"I don't want dinner," he said flatly. "I'm going out."

That made me plenty angry.

When I asked where he was going, he said, "Well, you can come over if you want. It's at John Sousa's house."

This was John Sousa IV, descendant of *the* John Philip Sousa, who wrote "The Stars and Stripes Forever" and other famous marches. He was also a friend of Kimberlin's, whom I figured might also be there. I didn't want to see her. She had already tried to force a division between Michael and me.

"No," I said, "go on to your party. I was going to make dinner for us. I thought we could sit down as a family and talk about stuff."

"You've got enough stuff for both of us," he said and went out.

By that time, my sister had arrived. Elizabeth suggested that perhaps she and I could walk down the street to the party after dinner. I said I would think about it.

My mother kept kind of quiet, but I could tell she was extremely troubled and sad.

We proceeded to have a very weird, uncomfortable dinner. Afterward, my sister decided to go down to the party. I told her I might come down later and asked her to call and tell me whether Kimberlin was there.

I cleaned up the kitchen and began unpacking. At about ten o'clock, Gigi Smith brought my sister back smashed, dead drunk. She had had too much red wine too fast and thrown up. She was throwing up on herself even as she came in the door. When she wasn't gagging, she was crying and saying, "I miss Leland. I miss Leland."

In the midst of her drunken sobbing, she also said, "I need my sister and I almost lost you. I would have died if anything happened to you."

I tried to get her straightened up with a pot of coffee. My mother chose that moment to let all her anger out. "You two are the biggest disappointments of my life!"

My sister and I instantly ganged up on her in our own defense. "Oh, yeah, Ms. Denial. Your husband's dead a year and you marry someone else. That was plenty disappointing to us. We'll do whatever we want. You can shut up and get out."

We were all mad at the world. My mother was mad that my dad was gone. I was mad that my marriage was falling apart. Elizabeth was mad at both these things and also at her more fundamental loss. To top it off, our young brother Cliff had just split up with his wife and the divorce papers had been filed. The whole family seemed to have descended into total hell.

The telephone rang. John Sousa called to say, "Tell your damn sister never to come over here again. She just ruined my white Chinese rug. You'll be getting the cleaning bill. Keep her the hell away forever!"

Could it get any worse?

Once my sister sobered up, she began to sound more rational, although she continued to weep and lament the loss of her husband. She had loved him. Why had he done such a thing? "Please tell me why?" she asked.

All I could tell her was the truth: I didn't know. I tried to get her to lie down and go to sleep. We lay on the bed and just held each other for a long time, clinging to each other. She talked about why she had gotten so drunk. "I've never done that at someone's house. I don't know what's wrong with me. I just feel like my whole life is gone—our family is gone. Since Daddy's been gone, our whole family has come apart."

I held her tight, each of us patting each other's hair. We cried together and told each other how much we loved each other. "That girl is over there with Michael. He's over there with her right now," she told me.

This was really one of the things that had her downing glasses of red wine. "That girl is all over him. She told me she wants Michael so I yelled at her. I cussed her out and I told her that she was never going to get him."

She looked at me and pleaded, "Don't lose your family. Try to work it out. Don't do this. Don't do it. It's too foolish."

That made me furious. It was midnight or perhaps one o'clock in the morning. There we were: We had just told off our mother, Michael was off with some other girl (the reason he'd ditched my home-cooked dinner on my first night home), and my boys were probably hearing all this crap. I knew that Mickey had tried to run in front of a car not too long before this. His death wish showed the effect on him of his parents' battles. It seemed like a thousand things were piling up. I was so overwhelmed. Nobody could sleep. My sister was crying, my mother was off sobbing somewhere behind a locked door.

Then I heard the front door shut and I knew it was Michael. I got out of bed, ready to go have words with him.

"What the hell is your problem?" I demanded, confronting him angrily. "I was cooking dinner. I wanted to sit down and talk to you. I haven't seen you in four months. I did all this stuff and then you go off knowing that it was my first evening. You don't even want to talk. You don't care. All you want to do is get over there and meet that bimbo. I cannot believe you did that in front of my mother."

Of course, I had just cussed out my mother, but now I was going after him.

"Hey, your stupid sister came over there and caused all these problems," he said. "She started yelling. That girl wasn't there to see me."

"Oh, puh-leez," I said.

"It's none of your damn business," he snapped back. "You don't want to be with me anymore and you've made up your mind, so to hell with you!"

My mother came out and, upset with all the yelling, began her grand finale speech. "I'm so sick and tired of all of you. I just can't take it anymore." She turned to me and said, "Your daddy would roll over in his grave if he saw you now." Then she began to pack and I knew she was doing her Laura Petrie exit.

It was four o'clock in the morning. Mom called a cab to come pick her up. When the boys woke up, they were wondering, "Where's Mimi? Where's Mimi? She's gone?" They were devastated that my mother had left without saying good-bye.

I knew I, too, would be leaving in a couple of days to finish the film in Canada. Even the project had become a nightmare. I had seen enough of the dailies to know that this miniseries would do anything but help my career. It was turning out to be a piece of junk. The Indian style of acting did not match mine or Bruce Boxleitner's. It just looked stupid.

I hadn't changed my mind about Mehendra or my interest in Hinduism, I'll admit. I brought home my statues and icons to set up a shrine in the downstairs bedroom as he had taught me. They were supposed to make things better. Maybe soon?

My shrine disturbed Michael no end. "What is this crap?"

I loved throwing my spiritual journey into his unenlightened face. We had a fight about the shrine because I had set up my household gods in a built-in wall that Michael had made for the giraffes I'd been collecting since I was three.

My shoulder was still very painful. Over the week, I watched Michael vacillate between feeling that I'd gotten just what I deserved and trying to care for me. I could see that there was something left in his heart for me. What? And how much? I didn't know. However, we were still as emotionally damaged as my shoulder was physically.

After one week of recovery for my shoulder, too brief a time to heal the marriage, I had to finish the film in Canada.

I wanted to take six-year-old Mickey with me to Canada because I realized how upset he had become. He needed me, and I needed him, for that matter.

When I asked Mickey if he wanted to go with me, he said yes. He told me he had missed me so much. I started making plans to take him, packing his bag and getting him ready to go. But I couldn't find his passport anywhere. I knew Michael must have hidden the children's passports.

I was forced to ask Michael point-blank where Mickey's was.

"You're not taking him to Canada," Michael said.

"Yes I am," I said. "I'm taking him. He's going." An awful fight ensued just as the car was coming to take me to the airport.

Mickey went out the front door and started getting into the car.

"Go get his passport right now," I ordered.

Michael only folded his arms and shook his head.

The next moment, a sheriff's deputy arrived to serve me with a restraining order barring me from my house when I returned. Michael had taken legal steps to have me booted out and to limit my visitations with the children. He had planned for the sheriff to serve the papers just as I was leaving. I understand now that Michael was trying to protect the boys because he didn't know what I was going to do next. He didn't know if these Indian people would show up and we would take off someplace with them. He was scared to death because he didn't even know me anymore. *I* didn't even know me.

When the sheriff handed me the document, I saw affixed to it several letters from witnesses attesting to my incapacity as a mother. Of course, Kimberlin had written a dossier all by herself. There were even letters from people we hadn't seen in years. All the letters depicted me as the Hindu from hell, with a long history of being neglectful and abusive. One letter claimed that I provoked fights with Michael while strung out on cocaine—something I have *never* done. I stood there flipping through page after page of the restraining order while my car sat waiting to take me to the airport.

All I could say to Michael was, "You are the biggest liar—that Kimberlin is a backstabbing . . ." I was ready to walk over to her house and throw her letter back in her face.

"Don't you take another step," the sheriff's deputy warned me, intervening. "You'd better get in the car and you'd better go to the airport and when you come back, you're going to have to leave your home."

"I'm not leaving," I said. "That's it. I'm getting my own attorney."

Mickey was freaking out. "I want my mommy! I want to go to Canada! I want to go with Mommy!"

I saw that he would not be allowed to go and knew that I had to make the best of the situation for my son. I calmed Mickey down by telling him I'd be home soon, that everything was going to be okay. The pain I caused him remains with me, searing my memory. How had everything gone so wrong—so fast?

In June of 1994, while I was in Canada, I contacted the famous attorney Barry Rothman. He promised I'd be the big winner in the divorce.

"I can get you out of this whole thing and this guy will get nothing," he told me. "Don't worry about it. You're the breadwinner. You're going to win. You're going to get everything."

Quickly, Michael's and my problems became a competition between attorneys. "He can't throw you out of your house," my attorney assured me. "He can't freeze your funds. We're going to do this and this and this. He'll be getting nothing. You just watch how fast he cries uncle."

In almost no time, half our savings flew out the window to the attorneys.

Michael proceeded to buy a house for himself as a result of my attorney's threats—and not exactly a small house. It was priced close to the one we had built. He was counting on alimony from me. We were both going nuts, getting in deep financially and shoveling furiously to go deeper.

He was still working on *The Young and the Restless.* Since we suspected that the divorce would come to trial, we started trashing each other in the tabloids, hoping to persuade a future jury that the other person was a schmuck. I told stories about his girlfriend. He talked about my affair. We were cover-story material for weeks.

Barry Rothman managed to have Michael's restraining order overturned. I came back from Canada and took up residence again in our home.

Michael and I, despite the legal proceedings, were still talking off and on. Michael even tried to get me to go out with him on our anniversary, July 7. I found that really odd—also interesting and flattering, but incredibly odd.

"Well, it's our anniversary," he said. "Do you want to go out? It will probably be our last one. We ought to mark the occasion somehow."

I said, "No thanks." I knew that feelings might come up. I was angry and felt I had to maintain my own sense of pride and dignity.

One day, we were standing around in the kitchen, shortly after I had returned from Canada. I was informing Michael of how things were going to be. He could live in his new, big house, but the boys would only be over there on Saturdays and Sundays. They would be with me unless I was working. Whenever I was working in L.A., they would be with Michael. Whatever I wanted, that's what was going to happen.

Chris was there with us. He wanted to know who would take him to school.

I told him Leanne would. I had forgotten that Leanne was getting married at the end of July.

Before I could correct my mistake, Chris suddenly said, "No."

From the way he said it, I had the feeling he meant more than that Leanne would be unavailable.

"No, no. We've already got our rooms. We've picked out our furniture. We're going to be living over with Dad."

I looked at him as if to say, *You are the biggest traitor.* "No, Chris, no," I said. "Wait a minute. No. You're my son. You're going to live here. Don't talk back to me. And don't you tell me how it's going to be. I'll tell you how it's going to be."

But Chris and Mickey both kept saying no. They were determined to live with their dad.

That's when I started to get just plain belligerent. I was losing my kids, too . . . by their own choice.

16

During the shoot in Canada and afterward, upon my return to Las Vegas, I was in contact with Mehendra by phone. Like other women having affairs with married men, I'd hang up the phone whenever his wife answered, but not before I'd hear something like this: "I know that's you, Hunter," Shifali would say. "You may not have Mehendra. You will never have him. Just go away."

Mehendra called me while I was still in Canada to tell me he was going to visit me. "I'm coming to America in July. I'm coming to see you. I'll be there for your birthday."

I let Michael know that friends were coming in and he wouldn't want to be around. Upon my return from Canada, Michael soon decamped anyway—to our Los Angeles apartment, friends' houses, and sometimes hotels on the Strip. He would come back to the house to see the kids only when I was taping shows in Los Angeles.

Mehendra and his brother Jetu, who accompanied him, didn't actually arrive in the States for my birthday. They were there soon afterward, though. When they arrived, in the middle of July, they stopped first in Los Angeles and then came with me to Las Vegas.

In Los Angeles, I took Mehendra to the studio. People at work recognized his good looks. "Oh, he's really cute," they said. Then they'd add, "But you've got to Americanize that boy." I saw Mehendra through their eyes: he was not foreign to them in a prejudicial sense, but lost and out of place. They didn't know what to make of the white powder on his forehead, and someone even tried to wipe it off, thinking he'd encountered wet paint. Mehendra and Jetu found the Los Angeles freeways ridiculous: They kept wondering why everyone stayed in a single lane. They were shocked by our culture and I was surprised to see how nice they found many things I took for granted.

When we arrived in Vegas, I took Mehendra and Jetu to a McDonald's. Mehendra bit into his Big Mac, popped his eyes at me, and choked out, "Is this sheep? Is this lamb?"

I had forgotten that McDonald's in India only serve lamb, keeping the Hindu tradition of never serving beef.

"Oh, no! That's a cow," I admitted.

He spit his mouthful out and he was very angry with me.

Even though he was in America with me carrying on an extramarital affair, Mehendra found American television disgusting and immoral. His comments revealed to me the unthinking way in which Indian men adhered to a double standard. Sexual license was permitted to men, but they expected women to observe strict standards of modesty and submissive behavior. His comments started provoking fights, because I wasn't going to let him get away with that!

Mehendra and I shared the downstairs bedroom, where I had set up my Hindu shrine—not the upstairs bedroom I had shared with Michael. I told myself that we could more easily worship our gods there, but I retained an unwillingness to damage further the intimacy Michael and I had shared. This small reverencing of our marriage kept me at least subliminally aware of how uncomfortable I was with my behavior.

One day, I picked up the phone to make a call and heard Mehendra on the phone with Shifali. He was telling her he loved her and missed her—all the while refusing to divulge what country he was in.

I confronted him about his divided affections.

"I was just saying that to shut her up. She says she's going to kill herself all the time," he said.

"I don't care," I said. "You tell me you love me, but then you get on the phone and tell her that, too. I think I know how much it means in her case. How much does it mean in mine? You must be lying to me. I don't think this is going to work."

"Oh, come on, Hunter," he said. "I'll come back for another visit soon and then I'll get a visa so I can work here."

Mehendra wanted to get a permanent work visa and he was wise to all the ways he could do this. He had to know someone, an American citizen, to get a work permit, and he kept asking me to write a letter to the immigration service. He told me I could do this through my corporation. He knew I liked cobras. He kept telling me I could import cobras under the corporation and he could be my employee. He wanted me to help him get his immigration papers, basically. I started to understand his true motives. He thought he was going to have two bases of operation: what people in the entertainment industry call Bollywood, the Indian film center in Bombay, and Hollywood itself. Then he'd have a wife in each country to keep the cross-continental fires burning. How convenient. *Way too convenient.*

Mehendra and Jetu stayed only until the first week of August, but those weeks stretched on and on. After a while, I had to admit to myself how uncomfortable I was having them around. I had a feeling many will recognize—the dread of having a lover around you don't want anything to do with anymore. I could not wait for him to leave.

He caused me the worst grief on his last day. I had to work that day. We were back in Los Angeles and his flight was leaving at 8:00 P.M. I wouldn't be able to get off work in time to accompany him to the airport. He was expecting that I would, and I felt guilty about bailing on him. To compensate, I hired a nice car so he wouldn't have to take a taxi.

I called the apartment from the makeup room to say, "Listen, I'm not going to be able to ride with you to the airport. I got you a car. I'll just talk to you when you get back to Bombay."

He was instantly angry. "Damn it, I come all the way over here, Hunter, and I cannot believe you would send me to the airport without even coming to say good-bye or wish me a good voyage."

He made me guilty enough that I decided to run over to the apartment and tell him good-bye. Otherwise, I feared, he might not leave. Sometimes on *The Bold and the Beautiful,* we work late and take an hour-long dinner break. This particular evening, we would only be taking a half-hour break, from 6:00 P.M. to 6:30, in order to get back to work and finish the day quickly.

I left as soon as I could—right at six o'clock—and drove to the apartment to tell him good-bye.

He looked relieved.

"I can't ride in the car," I told him, "but I just wanted to come tell you guys good-bye. I'm glad you could visit and I hope you had fun."

"I'm not happy, Hunter. Not happy," he said. "I want you to ride in the car with us."

"No." I was firm. "I have to get back to work."

"What kind of a job is this?" he demanded. "In India, you can walk off a job and nobody can do anything." (That's precisely why it takes forever to shoot a film over there. There's no such thing as a strict schedule, as there is in America.)

Mehendra made a huge scene in front of the apartment building. "You don't love me? You don't want to be with me anymore, Hunter?"

"Please, just stop it. Just get in the car and go. You'll miss your plane." I was desperate to get them *gone.*

The fit he pitched kept me there until 6:45 P.M.

I finally arrived back at the studio about ten minutes before seven. When I returned to work, everyone was freaking out. They had called my dressing room. They had scoured the commissary. They had people looking everywhere. When somebody said my car was gone, everyone began to panic, thinking something had happened to me. It also costs a small fortune to keep an entire studio idle for even a few minutes.

The show's supervising producer, John Zak, discovering why I had left, let me have it, and with good reason. John was a friend of mine who had always stood up for me in the past. But this was too much to ask, even of him. "Do you know how unprofessional this is, Hunter? Everyone on this show, not only your fellow cast members, but also the crew and support staff, have worked twelve hours already, and they need to get home, not to mention the fact that we were worried sick about you. No one acts this way on this show. I'm embarrassed for you, and you should be, too. We all have a personal and professional responsibility to each other. Please start taking it seriously."

I could only stand there and take it, because I knew I deserved this. The people on the show knew what had happened in India. I had to take more time off than my "out" allowed because of the shoulder surgery I finally had when I returned from Canada. And to top it all off, my attitude since returning to the show had been haughty and arrogant. I knew I deserved everything John was saying and a whole lot more.

I admitted to myself that this was my fault, the result of my selfishness and total lack of regard for other people's feelings. I felt disgusted with myself. I stood there silently, nodding my head, yes, yes, you're right.

Finally, I looked up at him and said, "You're absolutely right. I'm the biggest jerk that ever lived. In fact, you couldn't be more right."

He hugged me and looked straight into my eyes, "I am worried about you."

I went back and shot my scenes, but could barely concentrate.

After that, the first thing I wanted to do was look for Michael. I knew that he had been staying at Kimberlin's apartment in L.A.

I went back to my apartment that night, drank a couple of glasses of wine, and considered going over to see him. I called Kimberlin's number. No one answered, but somehow I knew he was there.

So I drove over the hill from Hollywood to Studio City, stopping at a liquor store on the way to buy a bottle of wine. I bought a bottle of Pommard because that was our favorite wine. I also picked up a couple of stemmed plastic wineglasses. I wanted Michael to know that Mehendra was gone, and I figured he would know that simply by my showing up.

When I rang the buzzer, I heard his familiar voice. "Yes?"

"Listen," I said, "it's me. Can you come down here for a minute and talk?"

Silence.

Finally, he said, "What do you want? Are you after another fight?"

"No," I said. "*No*. I just want to talk to you. I just want to see you for a minute."

He came downstairs and we sat on the steps. "Here," I said, pouring him a little glass of wine. We sat on the stairs and had a cigarette together—one of our rituals.

"This is really weird," Michael kept saying. "Why are you doing this?"

"I don't know," I answered honestly. "I just wanted to visit."

"This is just weird," he repeated. "You know, we're getting a divorce. Why do you want to talk? Why are you being nice now?"

"I don't know," I said. "I just want to talk. I don't know."

I must have hung out there for nearly two hours. We talked about different plans for registering the boys for school. We talked about getting stuff out of the garage, some old pictures and junk, and some abandoned exercise equipment gathering dust. I asked him how much that exercise equipment cost and we were trying to figure out what to do about the money. But we didn't fight. There were no accusations. There were periods of quiet as we drank the wine and smoked and looked up at the sky, where the stars spread out above the tall funereal cypresses on the hills. All I knew was that I wanted to keep sitting there with him.

Toward the end of that evening, he looked at me and said, "You are so beautiful." He looked like he wanted to kiss me. Then he stared down at the ground. "I must be the biggest jerk alive." He stubbed out his cigarette. "I've got to go. I'll see you later."

"Wait, Michael." I leaned forward and gave him a little kiss. I could see this shocked him.

"Why did you come here?"

I couldn't explain why.

"I've got to go," he said. "Thanks for the drink . . . and whatever else this was."

17

Just after this gesture toward reconciliation, Michael confirmed to a reporter that I had been staying with Mehendra in our Las Vegas home. Of course, I had given Mehendra a tour of the studio, so I put Michael in a spot where he was going to be asked about the affair. Still, I felt Michael stabbed me in the back. That didn't have to come out—not from him.

One day, he came over to *The Bold and the Beautiful* makeup room from his adjacent *The Young and the Restless* set. He caught my attention and said, "Hi. You want to go have some lunch?"

"You piece of shit," I said, without warning, without preamble. I wanted everyone to know how angry I was. I wanted to embarrass him. "I know what you said. I know about the story that's coming out. You are such a *jackass!* I was trying to be nice to you. When are you going to stop trashing me in the rags? I thought we were past that, but you have to get your licks in, don't you? Your male pride's been hurt so you've got to tell everyone what a *victim* you are."

He was dumbstruck, his arms at his sides. He couldn't find a breath to reply with.

"That's it!" I screamed at him. "I want you to get all of your crap out of the house in Vegas. You go shack up with your little Mirage Mabel. You've had your tongue hanging out over her for months now. Go the hell ahead already. But get every blasted golf tee and every other little niggling piece of shit of yours out! It's *my* house. *I want you out of it!*"

This fight and others, in which Michael gave as good as he got, eventually led to Michael's being dropped from *The Young and the Restless,* as I've said. Of course, we weren't thinking of the long-term consequences of our behavior at the time. We were so lost in our anger that we craved any audience—including our cowork-ers—as witnesses to our own destruction. We thought we could turn them into a Greek chorus, echoing our points of view.

We made the people in the studio take sides. Who was on Hunter's side? Who on Michael's? We were on scorched-earth campaigns in our divorce war.

When I came back to our home in Las Vegas from L.A., Michael had done as I asked: All the pictures were off the wall. All our wedding stuff was gone. All the pictures of the two of us with our kids. They were all gone. His clothes were also gone from the closet. That didn't affect me as deeply as the visual reminders of our life together. I remember that among these were poster-sized cartoon caricatures somebody had drawn of the two of us. I had never liked them. Now I missed them. I thought briefly of my first husband, Tom, and what he must have felt when he came home to a stripped apartment.

I called a few people, trying to find out where Michael was. I tried not to act worried or shaken. Somebody told me that sometimes Michael would go to Boom Town, or to the Rio, or to the Mirage.

"Why are you asking?" my informant wanted to know.

I didn't know why.

In August, in the midst of trying to work out the details of splitting up, Nan came into our home as our new nanny. Leanne was now happily married. (Sadly, I missed her wedding because the Bombay brothers were in town.) After the divorce was finalized, Nan would become Michael's employee over at his new house, which was still being built. Until then, she was working for us both. Michael and I were now trying to get along for the sake of the children and to facilitate the transition we'd all be making. Our once-more-reasonable talks about taking care of the kids in these new circumstances left me thinking that Michael wasn't such a bad guy. He'd only been a jerk in a difficult situation, in which I had driven him to extremes.

Nan the nanny had worked at fifty different jobs: airlines ticket agent, home-care nurse, flight attendant, cab driver, security guard. She was short and obese. She favored print blouses with flouncy bow-tied collars and wore the same pare of black pants every day. She had coal-black hair and pasty skin, and penciled in her nonexistent eyebrows with single sharp thin lines. She had a gruff voice and smoked one cigarette after another, each pasted to her lips in its turn. She dropped ashes everywhere. When she swept up, she cornered the dust ahead of her while leaving a cindery trail behind. She made an effort at cooking for Michael, preparing big roasts and pan gravy, but when I was in the house she served fish sticks. Nan's great talent was reading tarot cards.

Nan didn't want Michael and me to get back together—the breakup meant permanent employment at his new place. She began reading our tarot cards to us separately. Her readings for me said that Michael was seeing another woman and that I was really in love with someone else. A man was coming into my life.

Her readings of Michael's cards promised new romances and an upturn in his career.

She was given to leaving phone messages for Michael from other women where I could see them.

When I found these, I'd ask Michael, "Who the hell is this?"

He didn't know. I didn't know whether I could trust his answers. I suspected that Nan might have been planting half (or more) of the messages, but I didn't know that, either.

Gradually, we began to realize that this woman was plenty weird. When Gigi Smith came over, I would tell her my suspicions about

Nan's machinations. Gigi thought Nan was probably in love with Michael.

We started teasing Michael about expecting Nan to come around the corner in his new house one day wearing nothing but a teddy. Plus the cigarette on her lip.

My friend Carla from Dallas called. I met Carla back in the days of Don Shook's acting classes and we had been planning to share an apartment when *All My Children* called. Later, she married a wealthy man named Adam Rourk, and they had a little daughter, Abby. When we first became friends, Carla and I used to go to parties together, flirt with guys, and then shut them down, the stuff girls do when they are young and stupid. We had stayed in touch ever since and visited often. I considered Carla one of my very best friends.

Carla said she had been praying for me for a long time. "You've got to get your life together," she said. "I gave my life to the Lord this last year. I do nothing but think about ways that I can do what God wants me to do. I read my Bible every day and I read it every night. You need to turn to God, Hunter."

What kind of a brain wipe would that be? was my immediate reaction. What is wrong with the world? Even my best friend is weird and boring now. What is her problem?

Yet her words didn't really leave me. I knew my friend well enough to know that she would never do anything seriously weird. There must be something that she's going through in her life that makes her need this way of coping, I thought.

She wanted to come see me at the end of September. She was making plans. "I just feel—I hope you're not going to think I'm weird—but I just feel that I need to pray over your house."

"Okay," I said, thinking, *Whatever.* "Come on out."

Even though I extended the invitation, I wondered how I would cope with her religious dramatics.

When she came into town, I picked her up and right away I told her what a jerk Michael was being. "He's still blaming me," I said. "He's never going to forgive me. He's never, ever going to forgive me. So you can forget about any reconciliation. It's just a matter of time before the divorce is final. We're trying to act friendly toward one another and believe me, we're not succeeding."

I knew that Carla was a fanatic about cleanliness. Her daughter and she would be staying in the downstairs bedroom, which had black lacquer furniture. Before she arrived, I told Nan to prepare the place in the way she'd like. I asked Nan to dust—and not to smoke as she did so—and to change the sheets. I emphasized that my friend liked things spotlessly clean. Also, because Mehendra and I had burned tons of sandalwood incense as we worshiped our gods (who were still installed), the room stunk. I wanted Nan to deodorize and air it. She also needed to clean the bathroom and put out fresh towels—white ones, Carla's preferred color—and towels decorated with Sesame Street characters for her daughter. I wanted to show Carla how much I cared down to the last detail.

Carla and her daughter arrived and we had a nice evening together. She told me that when she got up in the morning she'd spend some time reading the Bible. When I saw her at breakfast, she talked about her Bible reading and showed me, in the manner of being a friend and sharing an interest, some passages that had impressed her. She made me feel more comfortable about her new-found enthusiasm.

That morning, after Carla arrived, I went to the gym with Gigi about ten o'clock. Carla stayed home with Abby.

While I was gone, Nan offered to lay out her tarot cards for Carla.

"Oh, I don't believe in that," Carla said.

Nan said, "It's just for fun. It's a game and sometimes it's true."

"Actually, Nan," Carla said, "I'd like you to put the cards away. In fact, I'm worried that you do such a thing in my friend's house. It's nothing to be played with."

Nan started laying her cards out. "You'd better look at this," she said. "You need to look at this because there's some bad news here."

"No, I told you, I don't want to. Stop it. Put them away. The Bible says that divination is an abomination before the Lord. It's in Deuteronomy. Put them away, *please!*"

Nan's pasty faced turned the color of a red helium balloon, but she put the cards away. Her anger didn't abate but could be felt in the house as a presence. When Carla rounded a corner, Nan was suddenly there to confront her. "I didn't want to say this, but I don't think this is a good time for you to visit."

"Oh?" Carla said.

"No. Anyway, Hunter doesn't really want you here. She told me you were a clean freak and your daughter was a brat and you're just causing trouble by being here. You can talk to her about the Bible all day long, but that's not the kind of help Hunter needs. And it's not what she wants. She can't wait until you leave. So why don't you just go now?"

"I think you're the one who should leave," Carla said. "You're Hunter's employee. It's not your place to talk to a guest like this, now, is it?"

When I came home, I could tell there was ice in the air. Carla seemed to be in her room praying.

Nan was in the hallway, washing a wall, smoking and flicking ashes.

Carla came out of her room and told me Nan had tried to run her off. She told me what Nan had reported me saying about her. The way she had taken my words and twisted and embellished them confirmed my suspicions about her planting made-up phone messages to Michael and lying in other ways about his activities.

I went into the hallway and confronted her about what she had said. Carla was at my side, as was Gigi. When Nan protested her innocence, Gigi started citing chapter and verse about the lies Nan had told her as well. Evidently, Nan was depicting me to *all* my friends as self-serving and mean-spirited.

Nan turned back to the wall and acted as if she were going to ignore us.

I said, "Nan, get your stuff and get the hell out of my house right now! Get out!"

She looked at me. "I can't go," she said.

"Yes you can, and you damn well better!" I chased her out of the hallway.

Nan made a call and boxed up the stuff she had in the guest room, where she'd been staying.

A big black car with tinted windows pulled up. We couldn't see the driver. Nan got in the car and drove away, and we never saw her again.

Carla told me later that she prayed before doing anything, and she felt God told her to let me know about Nan's lies. She said, "That woman was evil."

"I know that," I said, and I did, although my notions about evil were completely vague. Still, I had no doubt that she was right about Nan.

Then Carla said, "And Hunter, you get rid of those icons and statues in the downstairs guest room."

Was that important? I began to think it might be.

18

During Carla's stay and immediately afterward, I began to reflect once more on my relationship with Michael. I saw that I had been wrong—terribly wrong—about Mehendra. It kept coming back to me that once Mehendra left, the first person I wanted—needed—to see was Michael. When we drank the bottle of Pommard together, I knew he still loved me. I knew it whenever we discussed arrangements for the boys; I could see it in his willingness to go deeper than the immense pain my infidelity had caused him and find the strength to act out of love. The way I had been justifying my own anger—by imagining his own catting around—disappeared with Nan and her sham phone messages.

Also, I saw what our breakup was doing to Chris and Mickey. Not only had Mickey expressed a death wish by running out in front of cars, both boys had signaled their unhappiness by throwing eggs at neighbors' vehicles, pocketing small items in stores, and opting out of their schoolwork. Michael and I were screwing up our kids big time, and I began to regret my part in this more and more.

I had heard through Gigi Smith and others that Michael had been attending Mass at Saint Thomas More Catholic church. This man, who wouldn't go back to church with our family, was now showing up every Sunday—no matter how much he might have had to drink the night before. I wondered whether he was praying that we would reconcile—or that God would take me out of this world in a hurry. I had no "official" suggestion of his having positive intentions; we had reached a divorce settlement and expected the decree back from the court about the first of the year. Legalities have never stopped Michael from much in his life, though.

Even if he was praying about our marriage and the reconciliation of our relationship, did I want to be reconciled? I knew I didn't want the relationship we had settled for. But if I had explored finding a way out of the relationship, I had been motivated by wanting the relationship to be better—not dead. I still cared for Michael. Every jealous thought, every screaming indictment, every register of extreme emotion, even the hateful ones, told me I still cared.

Saturday night, I cried from 3:30 until 6:30 A.M. over my loss of Michael. I missed my husband more than ever and I knew that he was truly my soulmate. But how could I find him? Then I remembered Gigi telling me about seeing him at Mass. I thought I would take a chance. Our marriage was worth at least that much. I decided to find Michael one Sunday morning in Las Vegas. If he was really attending Saint Thomas More every Sunday, I could show up for the first Mass and wait until he appeared.

I headed off for the eight o'clock Mass and waited in the parking lot. I saw him pull in at 9:25 for the next Mass. I was out of my car before he exited his.

I saw him grimace when he caught sight of me. He must have thought I was going to make another scene.

"Michael, hi, I'd like to talk."

"What's there to talk about? Don't you think we're through talking? Really, I hope to God we are. It hasn't been that pleasant an experience the last year. You know what I mean?"

"Michael, please, I don't mean like that. I want to talk about everything. Everything. Let's go get coffee," I said. "Or we could wait until after the service. Whatever you want to do."

"Let's go now," Michael said.

We went to a coffee shop. We sat outside in uncomfortable white wrought-iron chairs. An awkward silence followed. Michael still was suspicious of my intentions, I could tell.

I couldn't take it. "Michael, I miss us. I want everything back," I said. "I was wrong about a lot of things." I sniffed back a flood of tears. "I want everything back like it was."

He put his hand across the table and grasped mine. "You sure you want to say that?"

"I have to say it. You're going to have to forgive me. Can you?" Before, he might have cited, chapter and verse, the many reasons he couldn't. Now, such a gentleness had come over him that I half expected what he said in turn.

"I need your forgiveness as well. There were two sides to this."

"Is this possible?" I asked.

"Why not? We'll fool them all. We'll beat the whole damn system, lawyers included."

He smiled at me. We were close to home.

That night, I had to leave for L.A. This time, Michael and I made the trip together. It felt so good to be in his arms again. When we arrived in L.A. and settled into the apartment, Michael didn't waste any time reminding me of his soft kisses and his passionate lovemaking.

He moved back into our home permanently the following week. We began to attend Saint Thomas More weekly as a family. I was surprised that the priest's homilies kept showing me concrete actions I could take to help rebuild our family. Like Carla, I also began reading the Bible off and on. I needed to know what kept a family together, what made it safe and secure. I saw that changing some of our basic behaviors—not drinking excessively, not putting ourselves in situations where flirting might cause jealousies, not making decisions apart from each other—would go a long way to effect the healing we so much needed.

I began to see that the Christian faith provided, among other things, good advice about the way life is and how to make life work. I kept in touch with Carla. She was overjoyed at Michael's and my reconciliation and made useful suggestions as to how we could find out more about *why* practicing the Christian faith would help us. She recommended that I visit the Church on the Way when I was in Los Angeles. Its pastor, Jack Hayford, had a reputation as a tremendous teacher.

I wasn't sure about attending any church that called itself the Church on the Way. It sounded almost cultlike. When I called the church's line, I got a recording that explained that the church had two campuses and a blizzard of different programs. I wasn't sure what to make of it. I attended this church for the first time on a Wednesday night. I went without Michael, because he was at home in Las Vegas with the kids.

Jack Hayford's sermon happened to be about broken families and how the world's mind-set conspires to tear families apart. I sat there nodding: *yes, yes, hello, been there, know what you're saying.* He said there is no way to repair a family on your own, that only God can do this. God created the family, created man and woman, and He created the family to be run in a specific way. He said we could see how evil wanted to divide families through the narrative of Adam and Eve in the Garden of Eden. Satan came along and caused dissension between Adam and Eve, so they were blaming each other. The only way to fix the family, he went on, is by walking every day with the Lord and letting the husband be the spiritual leader of the family. The father should lead in the family's spiritual life, although the mother has unique gifts for the family's nurturing. She has a role to play that only she *can* play. His remarks spoke directly to my own situation.

That particular month, the church was focusing on healing families, even offering a special Saturday night service for the whole family, a special time when the church's leadership would pray over each family member.

I told Michael about this church. "I really like this, although it's a little different," I said cautiously. "Some people may seem a little fanatical, but the pastor's messages are really good. I really feel the Holy Spirit and the power of God in that place."

I particularly liked the way the congregation sang. It struck me that the congregation's full-throated singing resonated with what Heaven must be like. Their singing, praising, and thanking God was so . . . real, so wonderful.

I was sure Michael would think I was nuts. He had only gone to Catholic churches. "I wouldn't mind going there with you. I'll be glad to."

From then on, we tried to arrange our schedules so that we were only away from the kids on Wednesday nights, when we would go to these midweek church services together. We started attending regularly, and I began to notice dramatic changes in Michael. Instead of using his anger to control the children, he started to become more spiritual, praying with the children, something I had never seen him do. In fact, at first he would only do this privately and not in front of me.

Then, one Wednesday, the pastor's sermon touched on the need for husbands and wives to pray together. My first reaction was, that's too weird. I could never pray in front of him and he wouldn't pray in front of me because that's a private thing.

We still had difficult days, when we would fight and bring up hurtful memories to each other. That sermon came to mind as we reached the end of such a day. Our bickering went on until I finally said, "You know, we are never going to get past some of these things until we confess them before God." I was convinced that we needed to get down on our knees as a couple, read the Bible together, and ask forgiveness, even confess out loud those things we had done to hurt each other.

We both felt *extremely* strange, but we tried it anyway. We didn't have anything else to lose. Michael knelt on one side of the bed and I knelt on the other. We put a Bible in the middle and I said, "Just open it and read something."

Although he wasn't looking for anything in particular, he just happened to open to the famous passage in Corinthians about husbands and wives. Husbands were to love their wives as Christ loves the Church. Then I read another passage from I John 2:7–11, in which we are counseled that loving God AND our brothers encompasses all of God's other commandments. That we are to forgive each other, as God forgives us.

Then we started to confess aloud everything we had done to hurt each other. We had said, "I'm so sorry" and "I love you" many times in the past month. Confessing our faults to each other in the context of prayer proved a far more profound and healing experience. I cried a lot, having to face what I had done. Michael was similarly moved. It seemed as if God was joining us together in a new unity that was only possible because we had submitted our relationship to God's authority. Neither of us was in control; God was. Major healing in our relationship came about that night.

In November, I once again brought up the idea of having another child, perhaps a girl.

This time, Michael said, "Yes, I'll do that." He suggested having his vasectomy reversed later the next year.

"No," I told him. "I want you to prove to me you are serious. You've been 'considering this' the past three years. Please do this for me. Let's have another baby—please," I cried.

He made an appointment, and by the end of November his vasectomy had been successfully reversed. The doctor reported that the operation went well and that there should be no problem in having another child. Of course, this turned out not to be the case, but Michael's willingness to go through that stinging, uncomfortable operation showed me that he truly believed and cared about my commitment to be his wife again and my desire as a woman to further nurture our family.

If we had signed the papers, our divorce would have been final on New Year's Day, 1995. Instead, we invited Father Ken Morris, C.S.V., to come lead us through a renewal of our wedding vows on New Year's Eve. We sent out beautiful formal invitations, each adorned with a little ribbon bow tie inviting guests to a celebration at John Sousa's home after the ceremony.

Before the priest led us through the ceremony, he performed a house blessing, going through every room and sprinkling it with holy water.

Because of Michael's upbringing, a Catholic ceremony meant so much to him. The ceremony was even more real to him than the first one. It was to me as well, even though I had been raised as a Presbyterian. The ceremony expressed that we would not have been together at all if it had not been for God's blessing in our lives.

Throughout that next year, Michael and I became ever more serious in seeking to know God. I had once thought of Carla's daily Bible reading and prayer as a brain wipe, but now I increasingly depended on these practices for seeing me through the day.

I didn't become an instant saint—hardly. In fact, through much of 1995, Michael and I were both preoccupied with injuries from the past and their ongoing effects, especially our entanglements with Kimberlin and Gary Pelzer. As Michael and I began to talk over all the circumstances that contributed to our near breakup, I learned that my once good friend Kimberlin had helped worsen the rift. Once Michael started dating the Mirage girl, Kimberlin put together dinner parties for the new couple and the Pelzers. When Michael was distraught one day, she took aside our children, Chris and Mickey, and told them they should be loyal to their father. She told Michael stories that increased his jealousy and distrust. Hence the rumors flew, going even to my employer, Brad Bell, Jr., that I had gone crazy in India.

Since Kimberlin and my friendship wasn't healing, we decided that withdrawing from the boat business was the wisest course.

Michael told Gary we wanted our investment back. I followed up with a heated phone call from my L.A. apartment. In my sarcastic sense of humor I demanded our money or we'd sink his boat business.

Soon afterward, when I arrived at work on a Monday, everyone was looking at me as if I were in deep trouble. I was told I needed to call Brad Bell, Jr.

"What did you say to Gary?" he asked.

"What do you mean?"

"Kimberlin came to work today with a bodyguard. She said you made a threatening call and she feared for her safety."

"What?"

"If any of the cast members feel threatened, they have a right to bring a bodyguard. You're going to have to put up with it."

I protested long and loud to this, but there was nothing Brad could do. Kimberlin's bodyguard, a huge Charles Atlas figure, positioned himself between us in the makeup room, his arms crossed, his expression relentlessly menacing. His presence totally rattled me.

When I went home that night, I told Michael what had happened. We considered what course to take. Michael suggested I should hire my own bodyguard—a bigger one, a giant. No, what would really be funny would be to hire a short bodyguard, a tiny one, a midget. After we quit laughing, we looked at each other and asked, "Could that be done?"

A friend happened to know of a short person who worked as a private eye, bodyguard, and sometime actor—he was an Ewok in *Star Wars*.

He wore black pants, a big cowboy hat, and silver-tipped boots, and he stood about as high as my waist. He was also one of the nicest men I've ever met. He understood the situation and for a week, he followed me around the studio, interposing himself between Kimberlin's bodyguard and me. He'd ask me, "How are you feeling, Hunter? Do you need anything, Hunter? Are you feeling safe, Hunter?"

The laughter this brought about in the studio hallways ended Kimberlin's bodyguard gambit. The incident even made it into *TV Guide*.

The Sunday after the week of dueling bodyguards, I went to church with Michael and heard Father Ken preach on the Scripture. "Why do you look at the speck of sawdust in your brother's eye and pay no attention to the plank in your own eye?" (Matthew 7:3). He spoke eloquently about the fact that a truly spiritual life begins with sorrow for one's own misdeeds, rather than with the act of blaming others for their perceived faults.

The next week, Father Ken preached about loving one's enemies. "If you love those who love you, what reward will you get? Are not even the tax collectors doing that?" Jesus asked. "And if you greet only your brothers, what are you doing more than others? Do not even pagans do that?" (Matthew 5:46–47). If I wanted to lead a godly life, I couldn't pursue vengeance. I had to show love even in a situation where I felt none. Before the sermon ended, I was crying and shaking and I knew what I had to do.

I went home and wrote Kimberlin a five-page letter. I was trying to change my life—to live a more spiritual one—and I had become convinced that I had to let go of all the hate and anger in my heart.

Michael carried the letter down to the Pelzers. "Don't slam the door, Gary," he said, when Gary answered the doorbell. "Hunter's written Kimberlin a letter. Just read it. You'll like what's in it."

In the early evening, I was outside training another dog; Max had run away and we acquired a keeshond puppy, Bear. I saw Kimberlin walk out of her house and I thought she must be walking over. I had followed God's direction and now we would be able to become friends once more.

Kimberlin went to the mailbox and then she turned around and went inside her house again. The world—and faith—wasn't that simple, as I was to learn many times.

Gary did show up that evening with a bottle of champagne. He thanked us and told us that he'd return our investment as soon as possible, which he did. He also said that the letter "meant more to Kimberlin than perhaps Hunter will ever know," which remains true, since Kimberlin and I have never discussed the matter.

By August of 1995, even though Michael and I began taking steps to live Christian lives, our old jealousies and resentments started cropping up again. Michael and I were having trouble keeping our emphasis on God and not on material possessions. I bought a Cadillac I didn't need, one wheel of which promptly fell off. (If I had driven the car another mile, it might have killed me.)

We had made new friends, as well, who kept up the pattern of trying to wreck our commitment to one another—Michael's best bud at the time, who'll remain nameless, kept shamelessly hitting on me.

One day, I went into our home office in Las Vegas and absent-mindedly stared at the computer screen. Michael's philandering pal had installed a screen saver on our computer. The screen saver scrolled a message that read, "Sex plus money equals happiness."

I watched that message flash by a few times, remembering how we used to laugh about that, and it occurred to me that we had really bought into that. I must have watched the message cycle by about twenty times, scrolling slowly over the screen, when it started to hit me. *That is such a lie. That is the biggest lie I have ever seen in my life and it's on my screen saver, and we've been living it!*

I was determined to change that screen saver. I didn't know how to do this, and sought help in the computer program's help menu. When I figured out what to do, I changed the screen saver to read, "Jesus is in control of our lives." Until that moment, this hadn't been a sentiment I would ever have thought of, much less embraced, but I realized then that over the last year I had been slowly coming to this conclusion. In this moment, my Christian commitments crystallized for me. I had once worshiped at the shrine of sex and money. Now I wanted God, as God is understood in the Christian faith, to direct my actions.

As I watched the new words scroll by several times, I could feel something akin to hands reaching up and lifting blinders from my eyes. In that moment, I felt completely different about the whole world. Everything seemed to be revealed for what it really was, and everything I once valued no longer seemed worthwhile. All of a sudden, our house, for example, wasn't a big status symbol of success. It was just a house. It was just walls with paint. All of a sudden, I could see the truth—that our home centered in the love our family shared.

I got down on my knees. "You are the true living God and I know who You are," I prayed. "Will you help me? Will you help me walk with You? I can't keep living my life like this. I know You want to help me and I know You've been there but I am asking You now."

Ever so clearly, I heard God say, "Just pick up My word and let Me talk to you."

I took the Bible from a shelf. The first thing I opened to was Deuteronomy 6:4–9. I was certain this passage was for me as I read, "Teach my commands to your children and write them on the lintels and the door frames at home where you will see them when you are going in and going out." I hadn't been doing that, I realized. I hadn't been teaching my kids what's right and wrong. No wonder they were getting in trouble. No wonder they were cussing us out when they got in trouble. No wonder they were pocketing things from the store. These were my children, my boys, whom I love with all my heart, but I wasn't being their mother. I wasn't teaching them. That was the key to the beginning, to turning the whole household around, and I knew it.

Then I read on. "You will have no gods before me. I am a jealous God."

That's when I knew where part of the confusion was coming from. I understood that I needed to go into that downstairs room and get rid of all that stuff from India. They had been worshiped. I understood this was not good. "I am a jealous God" kept ringing in my ears.

So I went in the downstairs bedroom and got every one of them. Some were valuable, made of glass or painted with twenty-four-karat gold, but I took every one of them out to the garage. I knew God was leading me to do it. I either broke or stomped on them, saying, "You are not God. You are not the God of Israel. You are not Jesus. You are not the God of the Bible. You are not God."

I was stomping on a brass *shivalinga* when I had the strangest feeling. It was as if something were being released or banished from the house. I went inside and could feel what seemed an unnaturally cold wind rushing out of the open windows. I couldn't be sure of what was happening, but whatever it was, it went far beyond my experience of the world. I reflected on the priest's house blessing of the past New Year's Eve and thought such a ceremony might have been more necessary than I had supposed.

I told Michael about this creepy experience somewhat hesitantly.

He responded, "Hey, what do you think the Catholic Church has been doing all the time? They have to exorcise people. They wouldn't do it if they didn't think demons were real."

After the "computer screen exorcism," my life turned completely around, and I mean *completely*.

I started thinking about my entire life in the context of what God might want, especially because the fall of 1995, from the day of the computer screen revelation, saw a second flowering in my marriage, for which I was profoundly thankful. Not only were Michael and I getting along, we had never been in love so deeply. Most marriages don't survive what we had been through, and many that do limp along ever after. We had never been so happy.

Because of this, I began to take spiritual risks. Another way of saying it might be that I began to show my appreciation to God in ways that made me feel somewhat foolish, even though I felt compelled to do them. One extremely hot day in November of 1995, I was out watering the yard in Las Vegas in my tennis shoes and old clothes. I looked around that day and began to appreciate, truly appreciate, all the great things God had given me. I had not been a good person, and yet God had given me a career in a business in which most people have to claw and scratch their way to the top. I repaid God by trying to glorify and promote myself. Now I was willing to do something different and I wanted to tell God this in a noteworthy manner. I was already investigating other opportunities apart from *The Bold and the Beautiful* and I needed to tell God that I wanted Him in control of whatever transition I might be making.

I went upstairs to my bedroom, into my walk-in closet, and closed the door. There was just enough room for one person between the rows of clothes crammed along both sides. All my husband's jackets and suits hung on the bottom half of one side, with my skirts and jackets—labeled Donna Karan, Giorgio Armani, and Liz Claiborne—up above. On the opposite wall hung dozens of long, elegant gowns and other expensive things I saved for parties and photo opportunities. My *extensive* shoe collection—a source of pride—was strewn all over the floor of the closet and filled a wall of built-in shelving interspersed with stacks of folded sweaters. I love shoes. Shoes are my fashion hallmark, and they nearly obliterated the closet floor, along with wadded-up clothing, exercise equipment, and stacks of old scripts and acting journals. I knelt down to sweep all this stuff out of my way, bulldozing the shoes into a mountain below the hanging clothes, shoving papers into the corner, moving everything out of the way. I got down on my knees. I had learned that King David prayed before the Lord with his face to the ground. I thought I'd try this.

I lay on the floor, flat on my stomach, with my face in the carpet and my hands out to see how it would feel. What happens when you do this? I wondered. Am I becoming a fanatic or something? Yes, probably, I decided.

But as I lay there on my face in my bursting-at-the-seams closet, I started talking to God. *God, this is kind of scary. But You've done so much for me and my family. Let me do something that will help You help other people. I want You to take my career. I'm going to hand it to You because I've done it my way and You have already been so gracious and You didn't let that career fall apart. Everything else was falling apart, but not that. But now I'm handing it to You and I want You to take it and let it do something that will achieve great things. I want to be a bright light in the darkness. I want You to use my voice in a way that will make it a big voice—but always for You. I want to do something that will help other people and I would like to be able to be an inspiration to other people. So You take my career. If You want to take it away from me, that's fine, too. If You want to take me to another show, even if it's a family show—which I used to think was boring and stupid—that's okay. I don't care if I'm famous. I just want to make a living for my family and I'd also like to do something differ-ent so my interest can be piqued again. I just want You to help me and do what You want me to do.*

In my heart of hearts, I knew that God heard me. There was something compelling about the manner in which David had prayed before God. I kept hearing sermons about how God thought David had a great heart for the Lord, therefore the Lord blessed David and helped him. God says that David was a man af-ter His own heart. I wanted to have a great heart for the Lord, too.

Even as I lay on the floor, I sensed that God respected this ges-ture, that God would honor it. He loved what I was doing, as fool-ish as it might appear to others. I was filled with a deep sense that if I dared lift my face from the carpet, I might see God standing there and I knew that that would frighten me to death. I kept my face down and continued to pour out my heart. My life had been heading straight down the toilet, and then had been changed through no power of my own. My children had been saved and turned around. Chris's rebelliousness and Mickey's death wish, all their anger at what had been happening between their father and me, all of these wounds had been healed. So I thanked God for that and I gave myself to God in a new way.

On December 19, 1995, I was sitting on my bed in the Los Ange-les apartment and praying. I had been reading Psalm 127, which talks about how, if the father is the head of the family, his wife will be like an olive tree and all of the children its fruits around the family's table. I had my hands up in the most ancient Christian at-titude of prayer—I didn't do that very often, but once again I was trying out something that at first felt strange to me. I continued thanking God for the new life He had given me. I also told God that if there was anything I hadn't confessed to Him, I wanted Him to forgive those things and take their effects away from me, to cleanse me so that I would be useful to Him.

I felt a tingling power come into my hands that shook me. I felt as though I had been gently electrocuted—that's a contradiction, I know, but the sensation was at once powerful and also healing. The power went all through my body, and I specifically felt it in my hands and feet, around my head, and in my sides, the places of Jesus's wounds. Then I felt as if something strange happened to my ovaries—a sensation akin to the one women have when they are ovulating, except far more immediate. The power felt as if it were burning me at the places of Jesus's wounds. It left an aching feeling in those areas after the burning sensation subsided. This nearly freaked me out. It lasted perhaps only thirty seconds, but was more intense than anything I had ever experienced.

I knew I had been shaken by the living power of God Almighty, and I was so afraid that I fell off the bed and put my face on the floor. I said, "Don't scare me, God, don't scare me." I thanked God for having given me this experience of His power, but I also asked Him to take it away. It was too much for me.

After I calmed down, I called Michael in Las Vegas and I told him what had happened. He explained the Catholic Church's understanding of the stigmata. Fortunately, I felt, I hadn't received any visible wounds, but my experience bore some relation to what he was telling me.

I also asked my pastor at the Church on the Way about this, and he confirmed for me that I had been touched by God's power. My pastor said that experiences like this usually happen when someone's heart is completely open to God and the person is praising God. I explained more about the experience, and he suggested that the Lord might have used the experience to effect some type of healing in my body.

I would think about this many times—ponder it—after finding out in the next three months that I was pregnant. Michael and I had been trying to have a child ever since his vasectomy had been reversed a full year before. It wasn't until I had this experience in prayer that I was able to conceive.

Part Six

19

So, in the spring of 1996, when I thought about solving Spelling Entertainment's problem by aborting my child, I felt an intense shame. I remembered all that God had done for Michael and me in restoring our marriage. Michael had become willing once more to see our love embodied in a new baby, and had his vasectomy reversed. I even had reason to believe that my experience of God's power in prayer played a role in conceiving the child I was now carrying. How could I think this way? I knew how wrong I was and that any situation in which a mother could be tempted toward choosing against bearing her children must be abhorrent.

Do you think you are the only one? God asked. *The first woman to find herself having a difficult time sacrificing career advancement and financial security in favor of having a baby? This is what I want you to do for me,* God seemed to be saying. *This is your battle.*

I would fight that battle, then, with God's help. Before I stood up from the bed where I was sitting, I knew that my life had irrevocably taken a new direction. I began searching for the new job that led to *Melrose Place* thinking my faith might be shown through new acting opportunities. Something much harder and more real was being asked of me. This task required that I put myself in God's hands in a way that could only be described as all too real. I was willing. But man, I was scared.

I knew that I had to stick up for a woman's right not to be discriminated against because of pregnancy, but of course I couldn't know what measures this would entail. I had to tell the Spelling people they had been wrong. I felt no compulsion to expose them as wrong, though. I hoped to make my position clear and prompt them to think better of the position they had taken. That's all I felt was necessary. The whole matter could have been concluded at this point, and at every point in between until it actually was finished, if Spelling Entertainment had only thought better of its action.

When I told my manager, Marv Dauer, that I wanted to stand up for myself and my child, Marv backed me from the very first. He was indignant for me, as well as very protective and completely supportive. He couldn't believe this had happened and he pledged to stand behind me one hundred percent, wherever the situation led.

From the outset, he advised me to get legal counsel. I didn't want to do something that drastic right away. I kept thinking, if they'll just talk to me on the phone, I know we can work this out. Marv placed the call, but no one ever returned it. They slammed the door in my face.

"Maybe you're right," I finally said to Marv. "They are the ones who have breached the contract—not me. So I probably do need legal advice."

Marv recommended Paul Gleason. I called him from my home in Las Vegas, and told him what had happened.

He responded unequivocally. "Hunter, what they are doing *is* against the law. You can't be fired for becoming pregnant; there can't be language in a contract that forbids you to get pregnant. This is outrageous."

It just so happened that I had recently read a section on the Pregnancy Discrimination Act that I found in a book on motherhood. I asked, "This is covered under the Pregnancy Discrimination law, right?"

He said, "Yes, but this goes beyond that." He began explaining the legal grounds for contesting my firing.

The question then became: What do we do? How do we get Spelling Entertainment's attention? They seemed to assume that their letter was the last word and that they wouldn't be hearing from us again. Their reasoning seemed to be that if they ignored me, I would just go away. The pregnancy had branded me as a completely worthless "thing" in their eyes.

In a three-way phone call with Marv and Mr. Gleason, we concluded that we'd have to threaten a lawsuit and name a figure. Money was the only thing that would make them listen. As a giant corporation, they were used to blowing people off. They had such a huge war chest, after all—who would fight them? This meant that we needed to make the dollar amount attention-getting. We would put together a letter outlining the illegality of their action, showing how I was professionally and financially inconvenienced by losing an entire pilot season as well as several other projects. The letter included the statement that we wanted to work something out, to talk about other options. We also included a letter I had received that released me from a major product endorsement, on the grounds that the sponsors had been falsely informed about my being on *Melrose Place.* The contract was for $250,000 and depended upon my *Melrose Place* starring role. Our letter assured them that a financial settlement would be requested if Spelling chose not to respond.

By adding up the potential income from all of my missed opportunities as well as from the first season of the contract, we arrived at a settlement figure: $1 million. When Paul Gleason faxed a draft of the letter to me, I was stunned by the figure. "Oh, my gosh. Don't you think that's a little bit heavy-handed?" I gasped. But Mr. Gleason and Marv made the point, and I had to agree, that Spelling Entertainment wouldn't take us seriously unless our actions could cost them big money.

Before sending the letter, I felt obliged to contact my talent agency, Innovative Artists. Scott Harris had let me know that he couldn't take my side because he had other clients to protect. I understood that. I wanted to extend him the courtesy of previewing the letter in case he got a phone call from Spelling.

In my mind, I saw someone, even Aaron Spelling, perhaps, reading the letter and saying, "Wait, wait, wait. Now just wait. There's a misunderstanding. I didn't know this was going on. I never would have let this happen. Let's not make threats at each other. Let's work it out." I thought perhaps this would be the next phone call, but, in any case, I wanted the talent agency to understand what was happening.

I faxed a copy of the letter over to them, and a cover sheet with an informal note explaining the contents. I wrote that we had to do this, or "else we will have no leverage to negotiate anything." I was trying to make clear to Scott Harris that, as Marv, Paul, and I had decided, the threat of a financial penalty seemed to be the only way to make these people listen and respond to me. This statement would be taken out of context and come back to haunt me.

My contract with *The Bold and the Beautiful* didn't end until June 13. When I received my script for the first part of May, I saw that my character was being written out a whole month early. I was terrified. I would now be a month behind in income.

I hadn't told anyone that I had been fired from *Melrose*, because I still hoped we could work something out, but rumors were circulating anyway. When I walked through the hallway at CBS, I wondered if this person or that person knew anything. I wanted to ask Brad Bell why my character was being written out early, but I didn't want to look desperate, either.

Then I heard from Frank Tobin, who handled the show's public relations. "Hunter, your last day is this Thursday. They're going to have a big party for you after work that day. It's supposed to be a surprise, but I just wanted you to know so you can dress the way you want to—the photographers are all going to be there."

In what I will admit was a moment of pride, I had previously made the big announcement of my move to *Melrose* and prime time. People would be asking questions at the party. What was I to say? I didn't want to go to the party, I was so embarrassed. Several people came up and said, "I'm sorry about what happened." I told them, "Well, you know, nobody knows what's happening."

However the story eventually came out, everyone would have a private opinion. She was fired for being pregnant? they'd say. Yeah, right. What did she really do? I had participated in enough gossip sessions myself to anticipate the whispers.

In my character's penultimate scene on the show, the writers worked in an allusion to her supposed move. Another character comments to Taylor (my character), "Well, you're going to try to move on and forget about Ridge" (Taylor's ex-husband).

"Yeah," Taylor answers.

"Where are you going to move?"

"Oh, I don't know. I'm thinking of looking for an apartment down on Melrose."

I felt like *such* an idiot.

My last scene on *The Bold and the Beautiful* featured my character, Taylor Hayes, all by herself in an office. It was hard for me not to cry in that scene because everybody had been coming up to me throughout the day, giving me big good-bye hugs and gifts. "Oh, God bless you," they said. "You're going to be a big star. You're going to do so well. Will you still come by and see us? You won't think your soap opera friends are stupid and ignore us like the other people?"

"Of course not," I kept saying, trying to appear happy. "I'll come back and visit." I took the gifts they so kindly offered feeling stupid and guilty.

Somehow, I got through that last scene, then I went to my dressing room to change. I was crying and couldn't keep my mascara from running. I had been crying in the scene, so I was already there emotionally. (Even on a normal day, it's difficult to come out of character. You just can't jump from one mood to the next. You'd be schizophrenic if you did.) Being pregnant made me even more emotional anyway. Everything seemed twice as big. I was a basket case.

I had been on *The Bold and the Beautiful* long enough for the other cast members and crew to become like an extended family. My emotions told me that I had grown even closer to them than I had realized. Sure, we had had our fights, our ups and downs, but then we'd make up, just like a family.

I was anxious about getting through the party and made sure Michael would be there with me. We arrived at the restaurant, Le Colonial, a French-Vietnamese place on Beverly Boulevard near San Vicente. Lo and behold, almost everybody from the show was there: my enemies as well as my friends. (Even though I had made up with most people from my former days of acting like a jerk, like anybody else I had disagreements and unresolved conflicts with people.) I had gone to other going-away parties and usually lots of people had to miss them. But this time everybody came. They applauded as Michael and I came in.

Either they really like me or they're really glad I'm leaving, I thought. Or else they know what's going on and they want to see how I handle this.

The food at the party was wonderful, and even my bosses the senior Mr. and Mrs. Bell were there. Friends asked me to pose for pictures. Magazine photographers had knowing looks: they didn't say anything, but I could see they knew. Please don't talk about it! I implored them silently. For some reason, nobody did.

Then the time came for different people to get up in the middle of the room—many of them tipsy—and tell stories about the guest of honor.

I dreaded the stories at first, but as they went on I couldn't help thinking, I really have had a great time here. These people loved me, and now this is gone too. My friend Teddy Morales, a cameraman, was the first one to recognize that I had truly changed. Scott Reeves from *The Young and the Restless* helped me in this, too. Sometimes Teddy and Scott would pray with me at lunch when I felt the old arrogance coming on or when the desire to get whacked on Jack Daniel's seemed too powerful to resist.

I knew the guests would soon want to hear from me. I had less than nothing to say. I was living a lie. These people were wasting their evening. They should have been home with their families. I wasn't going anywhere, except off the show. And here they all were celebrating my success.

The show's true creative force, Brad Bell, Jr., got up and gave a wonderful and sad speech about how my absence would affect the cast and crew, and wished me much success. In closing, he added, "Hunter's been so wonderful and faithful. We just love her. We want to give her this little gift of appreciation."

He was holding a little bag from Tiffany. My eyes were tearing and I was getting choked up. It's probably a key ring, I thought— or hoped. The show had an account at Tiffany and often gave *The Bold and the Beautiful* key rings as gifts. I really didn't want to open it right then, but Brad indicated with a nod of his head that he wanted me to do so.

I gave in and pulled out a velvet box. Obviously, Brad had wanted to do something very special, which touched me even more. I opened the box, and there lay a silver cross pendant with diamonds. It was gorgeous. I shattered into tears. To me, the gift said: Even though I should be mad at you for leaving, I'm proud of you. You did a lot of good work for me and in spite of everything, I care about you and I honor and respect your new religious commitments. That meant everything to me. It was the most beautiful moment that I've ever had with anybody I've worked with. I gave him the biggest possible hug, and then hugged his parents—his father was the one who originally hired me. I got a big hug from the senior Brad Bell in return, and I could see how much the family cared for me.

At the same time, I couldn't get over the feeling of living a lie. I didn't want to limit the Spelling people's choices by discussing the situation, but I didn't want to mislead my friends either. I didn't mean to mock the loving gestures of all these people. I didn't want to make them feel like fools for applauding my "success."

The caterers brought out a cake made by Hanson's, my favorite bakery. The cake had a picture of Melrose Street on it and a message wishing me "Good Luck on Melrose Place." Needless to say, I couldn't eat it.

Everybody was standing around wolfing down cake and enjoying it while I was feeling lower than I'd ever felt in my life. "This is so great! Thank you all!" I said, playing out my role in this charade.

Luckily, I had an airplane to catch.

As we walked away from the party, Michael said, "Thank God we're out of there."

Paul Gleason's letter on my behalf finally elicited a response from Spelling Entertainment, but one I found so unworkable as to be insulting.

Since I couldn't work for them that year, in their opinion, they were offering to hire me the following year on similar terms. They promised to come up with another character. The letter promised a lot, but it also required a lot. One clause specified that I couldn't bring any action against Spelling to recover damages . . . ever. "For all of eternity" was the way Mr. Gleason defined it to me. In addition, if I accepted this settlement offer, I wouldn't be able to work on another show or even do commercials for a whole year without getting Spelling's prior approval. In that context, studios turned down people's requests all the time—they never wanted to dilute the talent's value through overexposure or association with a competitor's venture. Plus, really, I had already stepped on their toes. Couldn't they have been setting me up to punish me by turning down every opportunity that might come my way?

What do they think I'm going to do for a whole year? I wondered. If I signed this, I'd be sitting, doing nothing. How was I going to put food on the table? Should I just call all my creditors and tell them I'll get their checks to them next year? Should I tell the same thing to my doctor and the hospital?

"I cannot sign this," I told Paul Gleason flatly.

"It's not so bad," he suggested. "You get a raise on each show."

"But what am I going to do for a year? If I don't work for a year, I'll lose all my health insurance."

I think Paul—as I began to call him—like many people assumed that the famous Tylos could well afford to lay low for a year. He didn't understand that we didn't have any money saved. The divorce that never was cost us what we had accumulated. We were still living well, but right on the edge of what we had coming in.

Once I explained, Paul understood.

We sent a reply telling them that they would need to make a provision for my income that next year effective immediately until the start of that contract. The letter also asked, once again, what character I would be playing the following year. I wanted to make sure that they would commit themselves to a character I felt I could play. There had been too much miscommunication about this already, and I didn't want to submit myself to a situation in which the producers could exact their revenge by way of a degrading character or scripts.

A series of conversations ensued between Paul Gleason and Spelling's attorney for these negotiations, Paul Grossman. (A man named Bill Waldo also represented Spelling and seemed to control the proceedings, although he remained in the background.) I wasn't privy to all that went on, only to the last draft of the settlement offer. Marv, Paul Gleason, Michael, and I had to sign a nondisclosure agreement saying that we would never discuss what we read.

As I've said, I wanted a holding fee—income for that next year—since they wanted me to sit idle. Studios actually do this all the time. My original contract with Spelling included a guarantee of thirteen weeks, with salary totaling $108,000. The *Melrose* season ran thirty-four episodes, so if I was kept on for at least a season—a far shorter time than everyone at first envisioned—I would have made a good deal more than twice this amount. Still, we thought it reasonable to base our holding fee on the guarantee that they wanted to tell me they didn't have to pay. Contractually, I was guaranteed a "pay or play" deal. Since we believed Spelling was the one breaching the contract, we felt they owed us the $108,000. They came back with a counteroffer of $54,000.

So what they were saying was: Start a year later. We'll give you half of what we already owe you, and you still may lose your health benefits, but you can get them back later. Deal with it.

I felt they were merely throwing me a bone and I said so. It was just enough to tempt me to compromise. It also sent the message, "Don't mess with us. We don't need you. You have to dance to our tune and take what we offer."

I might have felt differently if someone had taken the time to talk with me personally. In fact, I'm sure I would have if executive producer Frank South or Aaron Spelling—or even Jonathan Levin—had sat down with me and said, "Look, we care about how you have been affected by this. You made a commitment to us. Even though we can't find a way to work with you while you're pregnant, we want to help you make ends meet until the baby's delivered. Then we'll be off and running!"

Instead, I was being treated as a commodity—not a woman with a husband and children. They didn't care that I was pregnant, that all of this was putting added stress on my pregnancy.

And I was under enormous stress. I was having cramps and pain that would double me over. I worried constantly that something might happen to the baby. This isn't worth it, I thought more than a few times. I need to get away from this. I'm going to lose the baby. I became enraged that my child's life wasn't valuable enough for them to take into account.

It wasn't that they weren't taking this seriously. They were dead serious about playing hardball.

When we turned the offer down, their next letter cited their interpretation of the law and, in so many words, dared us to sue. They took their offer off the table.

After Spelling Entertainment's lawyers walked away from negotiations, Paul Gleason realized he couldn't be of any further help. Anybody who knows anything about the legal process would understand that my hiring Mr. Gleason meant that I never wanted to bring suit. Paul Gleason is principally a defense attorney for employers. He wasn't prepared to fight for me, even if I wanted him to.

When the legal threat looked as if it had played itself out, Marv suggested another game plan. He wanted me to hold a press conference at which I could tell the world I was wrongly fired. He thought this might put a new type of pressure on Spelling Entertainment to work something out.

Marv and I met with Paul Gleason one final time at a restaurant on Little Santa Monica, a dark hole-in-the-wall with big old leathery circular booths in dark corners, a place for business lunches and trysts.

Marv brought a public relations person. "Look," Marv said, "holding a press conference is the only way to save your reputation and keep people from starting ugly rumors that you were fired for other reasons. You've got to know who you're dealing with. They may already be painting a picture of you that you won't like about why you were fired. It is probably already in the works because they're going to cover their butts. They've got their own staff who are paid to do that every day."

Perhaps he was right. Perhaps the time had come to make an announcement that I'd been fired for becoming pregnant and put an end to all the speculation. Besides, it was time to let people know that I was available for other work.

I gave the public relations woman some background.

"Oh, oh, these press people are going to eat this up," she said. "I can't believe they're even doing this. This is so bad. I can't believe they would do this to a pregnant woman." She was getting all geared up. She started coaching me on how to make the Spelling people look bad.

Right then I did a one-eighty. I didn't like this new direction, after all. Tattling to the world on Spelling was not going to change anything. I didn't say anything for a while, but I was thinking, No, no. I don't want to do a press conference. I don't want this "He did this to me and he won't do that" stuff. This is not the right direction. This is starting to get into scandal and finger-pointing. That's not what this is about. This is a serious legal issue.

Paul Gleason agreed. "I think you have no choice other than forget it or get a heavy-duty, powerhouse, major-league employment attorney. You do not mess with Paul Grossman. I tried playing hardball with them and they're not budging. You're not going to move them now with anything short of filing a lawsuit."

He laughed the press conference idea off the table. "That isn't going to do a thing," he said. "It won't do anything but aggravate them even more. And they'll kill you in the press. Even with our friend's expertise here, they'll outgun you all down the line. They're *big*. They can even get the other actors to bad-mouth you."

The conversation turned to a discussion of powerhouse attorneys. Who would want to defend me?

Marv kept bringing up someone named Gloria Allred. I thought I remembered the name from the O.J. trial—something involving his murdered wife, Nicole Brown?

I didn't know who she was, but I noticed that every time Marv said her name, Paul nodded his head in agreement. "That's a possibility," he said. "She is a very strong possibility."

Marv said, "I'm going to take care of this. I'll call her and get Hunter an appointment."

He made an appointment for the next day at three o'clock. We were to take all the papers we had, all the information we could possibly collect, and meet with someone named Dolores Leal.

I had been in attorneys' offices before, but when I got off the elevator on the fifteenth floor of this Wilshire Boulevard building, I realized Allred, Maroko & Goldberg was going to be different. Their offices took up half of a whole floor. I noticed beautiful, cream-colored marble everywhere, almost like the Spelling place, but without the cameras or the James Bond palm identifiers. This was much more homey. Ms. Allred had added many feminine touches—elegant Victorian furniture, creamy white carpet. I wanted to take off my shoes before I walked on it. The entire office had a pristine sparkle. The lobby was adorned with beautiful Oriental flower arrangements.

We sat in the lobby area, and as I was taking all this in, I thought, I can't afford this. At the same time, I knew I had to trust God to lead me. I had to trust that God would open doors. I found myself silently saying, Okay. Whatever You want to do. Whichever way You want this to go.

Then Dolores Leal opened the door. She was the cutest thing I'd ever seen, small, with a pretty pale Hispanic face and soft pink lips. She wore a beautiful, tasteful business suit and shiny patent-leather pumps. She looked like an actress from *L.A. Law.* Could she be real?

"Hello, I'm Dolores Leal," she said with a warm, friendly smile, extending her hand.

I liked her immediately.

Dolores led us into a huge, beautiful conference room. One entire wall was a window overlooking all of L.A. I walked over to it and found that I could see CBS, my old studio, from her building, and I could see the Hollywood sign on the side of the hill.

The gorgeous, swirled-marble conference table could have easily fit thirty chairs around it. She asked Marv and me to have a seat. So far, Dolores was the only one we'd seen. I couldn't help wondering, who's the Gloria person? Where's Gloria?

"Now tell me what happened," Dolores said, interrupting my thoughts. She took out a notepad and began to write, shuffling through the various papers we handed her as we talked. She wanted to see every last piece of correspondence. As Marv and I outlined the course of events for her, she began to say, "Hmmm. Now, I wonder if that would—yeah, that would fall under the EEOC."

I never heard that phrase before.

"Hmmm, just a minute," she said, and she went out and came back with one of Gloria's partners, Mike Maroko.

They began to carry on a running debate in front of us, tossing ideas around. "Well, what do you think?" Dolores asked Mike. "Isn't this an interesting case?"

As it turned out, Dolores had heard about me two days before from a friend of Paul Gleason's. She thought this was a case that somebody needed to fight. By the time I came to her, she was already dying to get her hands on it.

Dolores and Mike stood arguing and reasoning back and forth in front of us, and I began to see her reasoning strengthen my argument. Dolores looked impassioned. I watched her face. She looked mad and indignant for me. I knew she would fight for me. Very quickly I came to understand that these were the people I needed to be with. After feeling certain that no one would ever believe me, to see this woman shake her head in disgust at every added detail felt so validating.

Marv was getting into the discussion, getting more emotional, and all of a sudden he jumped up and exclaimed, "Yeah, and that's when they suggested an abortion!"

I looked at Marv and said, "What? What? What?" That was the first time I had heard that. "Wait a minute. Now wait. What happened?"

Marv looked like a little kid who had just unintentionally spilled the beans. "Hunter, it's no big deal," he started backtracking in a breathy but still gruff Marv Dauer voice. "I didn't want to upset you. I'm sorry."

I could see that he was angry himself, though, and that he had held this inside for a long time. He was relieved to have it out now. "I didn't want to upset you," he repeated, "and it wasn't really important, but I'm mad that they said it."

"Did they say if she does, she can have her job?" Dolores cut in.

"No," Marv said. "They said it more as an off-the-cuff remark, something like, 'Why doesn't she just go off and have an abortion and then show up for work in July?' Whether or not they meant it, they made the suggestion and then dropped it."

That infuriated Dolores. I saw her face turn red.

Watching Dolores helped me work through many of my own doubts. I had wondered if I was overreacting because I was indignant for myself. I had to weigh things out. What did this mean to me? Was it only that I was mad? Was I making something out of nothing? Or did I really believe I had been wronged and I could help prevent other women from feeling cornered?

The more I heard Dolores talk, the more I knew my case was truly important. She confirmed what I was feeling. I knew I wasn't being unreasonable or acting from selfish motives.

She left and brought back Gloria Allred. In walked a stunning woman with closely cropped, jet-black hair with soft brown highlights, impeccably made up, very elegant, and very Beverly Hills. She was wearing a beautiful Chanel suit. She had a powerful presence that said, I'm in control. Whatever the problem is, I'm going to fix it. She wasn't going to take jack.

After greeting me with a very firm handshake, she stood in the conference room, arms folded, listening and nodding as the others briefed her.

Finally, she looked at me and said, "How did you not go kill these people?"

"It's nice to have someone on my side for once," I said.

The firm's attorneys held a conference among themselves while Marv and I sat at the conference table drinking coffee out of bone china cups. I was hoping and praying we would be able to work something out.

Gloria came back and we all sat at the table. I could sense we were going to cut a deal—or try to. Previously, the attorneys had all been standing. Dolores hadn't been able to contain herself. She had to stand up from the minute we started telling our story. But now we all sat and got down to business.

I don't remember much, but Marv pitched for me. "Listen," he said, "we can't afford to fight these people. What can you do to help us?" he said.

They asked me for a $10,000 retaining fee, which I couldn't afford. Not with what we were facing. But I knew—and now it had been confirmed—that I had a solid case. Somehow, I thought, we'll find a way to get some money.

"The rest of your fees can be on contingency, can't they?" I asked in a quavering voice.

"Yes," Gloria said. "But this is the deal. We get sixty, you get forty, if we persuade them to settle or win a judgment. And you pay all our filing fees and postage and everything else that has to be done." (Later on, I found out that was very expensive. The average cost of the suit's incidentals per month turned out to be around $1,500, but a few months it went as high as $3,000.)

I had to agree to that, because there was no other way I could have done it. What I didn't know at the time was that if I were to lose the case, opposing counsel could ask the plaintiff to pay the defendant's attorney's fees. I could have been responsible for paying for Spelling Entertainment's defense.

Dolores said, "We get to fight Bill Waldo again." They all laughed. They had stock jokes about Spelling's litigator. As in, where's Waldo? This would be their fifth case against him that year.

"You're going to love him," Gloria said.

I wondered what I was getting into.

Later, I learned that there was an ongoing rivalry between these two attorneys' offices. They tried to be as professional as possible, because they saw each other in court frequently and took opposing sides on different issues. Then they would turn around and shake hands and go home. I never could have been an attorney. But Gloria used this to her advantage. Recognizing her opponents only helped her size up the coming battle without flinching.

After we came to an agreement, Gloria suggested we needed to move fast, right away, in fact.

"We're going to start tomorrow," she said. "Hunter, you need to sit down and write out how you feel on paper. Write down everything. Write down why you feel sad, why you feel angry, and the whole series of events. Write it from the standpoint of trying to explain the facts to somebody so that the person wouldn't be inclined to start any rumors."

"That's one of my concerns," I said.

"We have to do a press release," she said, "and we'll use your statement for the release."

A press release? That was exactly what I didn't want to get into, but she felt it was necessary.

"They're going to start a campaign to smear you and kill you because you did this with Paul Gleason," she told me. "That's a no-no. From their perspective, you don't do that. We've got to stop the smear before it gets started. A preemptive strike is the only way to do it."

I had to trust her.

. . .

I went home to write my statement, thinking it would take a while. But I went with the very first draft, writing it in a white heat of inspiration.

Gloria Allred set up the whole press conference down to the last detail. "You come over here," she instructed me on the phone when the time arrived, a few days later. "I'm going to have your makeup checked."

I was a nervous wreck, and paranoid about what I should wear. Already two months pregnant, I had become obsessed with what I looked like. Did my outfit make me look fat? Was my face heavier? On the way down to the law offices, I spent the entire time checking and rechecking myself from side to side, top to bottom.

"Stop it," Michael kept saying. "Stop it, stop it."

In the past couple of days I had been doing things I had never done before, such as putting ice on my eyes every morning. I didn't need to do that. But I was paranoid. I had always been busty during pregnancy, and now I felt ashamed of that. Before, I was proud when that happened.

I probably went through twenty outfits trying to pick out what to wear that day. Nothing seemed right. I knew people would be looking at me closely.

Did you see her at the press conference? Didn't she look huge? Didn't she look awful? We told you she was fat. She's had a material change. Look at her ugly face. That's *material* for you.

We held the press conference in that same meeting room. I ended up wearing a pretty little dress from Friends, with a professional-looking jacket from an inexpensive, trendy Beverly Center shop. The attorneys let me into the conference room through the secure door. They had set up their own security to restrict outside access to the conference area. The door had a foggy glass window, and from the hallway I could make out what looked like *thousands* of people, a sea of people in the conference room holding cameras and lights.

Oh, my goodness.

Among my remarks, I said:

Most women do not publicly announce their pregnancy until they are three or four months along. However, I wanted to give *Melrose Place* the courtesy to let them know immediately.

Now, having been honest and professional, I am portrayed as being irresponsible and incapable of acting and, I suppose, unappealing to look at—in short, ugly.

I didn't do anything wrong, and now I'm being punished for it.

I was very nervous and thought I did a horrible job. I'm sure I stuttered and stammered all the way through the speech. I could barely read my own writing because I was so nervous and upset. I felt like an idiot, a big loser. Yet I was telling the truth. Still, this seemed like the most humiliating reason possible for an actress to appear before twenty or more cameras. CNN was there, as was my old network, CBS, and Court TV. My press conference came shortly after the O.J. Simpson criminal trial. Did I look like Kato Kaelin? was all I could think. Was I going to turn into Kato?

We finished and people began to ask questions. After that, most of the people immediately went their own way, but many of the women present came up to me, despite Gloria's statement that we would not do any one-on-one interviews. Gloria knew I wasn't prepared to deal with too much pressuring. Also, there were areas she didn't want me going into until we had gone through depositions. She didn't want me to be tricked into saying something stupid. Still, some of the women from the press made offhand remarks to me, knowing I couldn't comment.

"I think it's disgusting what they did to you," one said.

"I was fired from an anchor job," another said. "They thought I wouldn't look good on camera."

"Thank God somebody's going to stand up for this."

"We need somebody to do this. Thank you."

Okay, I thought, I'm on the right track.

20

fter the firing, the going-away party, and the press conference, Michael and I had to find a place to live. Since we had sold our house in Las Vegas and were moving out as of June 1, we needed to find another place to go—immediately.

Michael had launched a yearly summer Shakespeare festival at the college in Allentown, Pennsylvania, where he helped start a TV and film department. He would be playing Iago in the festival's *Othello* that summer, which he agreed to do for five hundred dollars a week, originally as a courtesy. As things were shaping up, we would need that five hundred dollars. An offer was in the works that would make him the head of the television and film department he had helped the school create. As far as we could tell, our future might lie in Allentown.

Michael and I had flown to Allentown without the kids in May on a brief scouting trip. In our panic, we bought a house. We were that freaked out. Michael felt as though L.A. had ruined our lives, that we were never going to work there again. "We're dead in L.A.," he said. "I'm going to have to be a college professor for a while. But then we might be able to find work in New York. That town has always been much friendlier to us."

The house in Allentown had plenty of room inside, a nice lot, and even a swimming pool. There was nothing fancy about it, though. All the rooms needed new carpeting and wallpaper, as well as a few minor structural repairs, but we bought it in two days. I can only say that we did it so we could feel comfortable again. We found comfort in knowing that we had a place to go to, and we flew back to Vegas.

We told the boys we had found a house and would be moving to Pennsylvania. We tried to get them excited by telling them Pennsylvania wasn't as blazing hot as Las Vegas. But I could see the boys were severely depressed. They were thinking we were going to be poor. Mom had no job; Dad wouldn't be an actor anymore. They grew quiet. I know they had told their school friends, "My mom's going to be on *Melrose Place.*" Chris, who was now in high school, had found the news particularly useful; he became the hot thing and now he was embarrassed.

We wanted to give the boys hope. Hey, we've got someplace to go, we told them. It's going to be okay. We're going to get out of here so people won't be teasing you. Maybe you'll get free college tuition if your dad becomes a professor. (It sounds lame now to me, too.)

In the meantime, I had made a commitment to go to South Africa for a few days, a deal Marv had made back in December. I was to do some ads for Lux soap. I had nearly forgotten about this. Although Lux soap is no longer marketed in this country, it remains a big seller in South Africa. Apparently, *The Bold and the Beautiful* was a hot show there, so the manufacturers asked me to be the Lux girl. The money I would be paid would help, but most of it would be gone before I ever saw it—to the South African government, agents, Marv, and union dues. The soap campaign would only sustain us for a couple of months. We still didn't know how we'd get through the year. The moving and storage of our furniture was already estimated at about $50,000. We also wanted to get Chris into a school where he could concentrate on his piano, and that wouldn't be cheap. Yet going to South Africa proved a tremendous gift. That window of time gave Michael and me the chance to be together and reflect. We went straight from Allentown to South Africa for twelve days (two weeks in mid-May). Just in time to pack and move.

The Lux people and I shot the commercials on the Seychelles islands. There were some long, hard days when I was on a boat, four months pregnant, wearing a flowing white dress, trying to convey for the cameras that Lux makes you feel fresh as a sea breeze and a dream of desire. Not easy when you're feeling seasick, but I did it and the clients were very happy. They kept telling me that I didn't look pregnant. They said I was glowing and the best Lux girl since Cheryl Tiegs.

As we flew over Madagascar, all I could think of as I looked out our airplane window were the exotic chameleons in the bushes. If we still had our Las Vegas home, I would have been able to fill my living room terrariums at last! I had planned out the backgrounds with black and white squares, polka dots, and a variety of challenges to the chameleons' capacity for camouflage that I knew they could meet spectacularly.

When we arrived in South Africa to do media appearances for Lux, we didn't encounter any apartheid-related political problems. Everything seemed calm. (I know this was more apparent than real, of course.) I was fascinated by Africa, especially since I love animals so much.

Michael took me to Sun City for a day and we went on a short Land Rover safari. We saw lions and elephants but missed out on my favorite, the giraffes. The people at Sun City took great care of us.

During that week and a half, Michael and I tried to forget about everything. We went into our own fantasyland and pretended it wasn't happening. This was our vacation, we told ourselves and others. We were expecting a baby.

The bubble broke when I did an interview and the journalist

asked me about being fired from *Melrose Place.* All the way down here they knew . . . already! I was shocked!

I said, "As you know, I'm pregnant, and when I told the show's producers that I was pregnant, they released me from my contract."

This caused a huge uproar on a talk show one morning. Many people called in. They were disgusted. They said they had never heard of such a thing.

A woman visiting from Sweden said, "Do you know people go to jail in my country for doing that? Do you know how sacred pregnancy is there? Not only does a woman get to keep her job, but she gets six months of paid vacation after it. They honor you for having a child."

When we returned from South Africa, it was time to pack up the Las Vegas house. I watched the movers carry my bed out, broken down into pieces. I watched my dresser go. I realized I didn't know which box contained my jewelry or the pocket watch I had given Michael. When would I ever see these precious things again? We were sending the lot into storage because we wouldn't be moving in to the Pennsylvania home until the end of June.

I also returned to find that Gloria had booked me for the Sally Jessy Raphaël show. I didn't want to do this. The guests usually have their own agendas, movies or books to plug, a political campaign to win, and I didn't want to give any appearance of promoting or campaigning for anything.

Gloria talked me into doing it. "You've got to talk about this to know the other women who need your support. They're going to have other people on the show who have encountered pregnancy discrimination—that's why I booked it.

"Besides," she added, "you'll get two free tickets to the East Coast." That sold me. I needed the transportation because I had just given Gloria $10,000.

Sally put Chris, Mickey, our new dog, Bear, and me up in the St. Moritz hotel. This was the place I'd stayed when I first came to

New York for the *All My Children* audition. I clung to the good memories of that time in this unsettled one.

The show itself turned out to be an eye-opener. There were ten guests, including two couples. One husband and his wife had *both* been fired from the company they worked for when the woman became pregnant. Their boss didn't want to deal with the father being tired the next day from staying up with a crying baby. They both lost their jobs right when they needed them most. I couldn't believe it . . . the father too?

Another woman had been a waitress at a cocktail bar. She was fired the minute her bosses found out she was pregnant, because they said she wouldn't fit into her cocktail outfit or look sexy. She tried to show them ways to fix the costume so that she could still show her legs, but they wouldn't listen. "They told me I was going to get as fat as a house. They told me I would be ugly. They told me my face was going to get fat and they just fired me without ever waiting to see what happened to my body."

That sounds familiar, I thought. I was almost four months pregnant and still wearing a sundress I had worn six months ago.

I will say, however, that throughout this stressful period, I wasn't able to eat the way I would have liked. I was not able to make food choices that a woman in a stable situation can. Normally, I would have eaten something like a raw bell pepper for a snack. But I didn't have time to go to the grocery store and go wash one off and cut it up. I had to stop and get fast food many times. So I was eating poorly and I was aware of gaining more weight than I should have that early in my pregnancy. Also, my workout schedule had gone south. I was used to working out three days a week with light weights. But at this point, I had not exercised in two and a half or three months because of my ever-changing situation. I couldn't have exercised if I had wanted to. I was too tired all the time.

Throughout my pregnancy, every successive month became more and more stressful for me. When I did start to see my stomach showing, I became utterly depressed. There were days when I thought, Maybe they were right. Look at me.

Once I dressed in the morning, depending on the kind of clothing I picked, I could still look sexy and pretty, but I was growing more paranoid with each passing month. I could hide it, but I still always had my doubts. Look at yourself, I could hear them saying. You're fat. You're ugly. Look at your right ankle today, it's all swollen. It's practically bubbling out of your sandal. You're the elephant woman.

I continued to have frequent migraine headaches. I don't think I had one solid night's sleep. There were many nights I would wake up and have to pray to keep myself calm, to keep my fears from running rampant, to keep from chickening out. Many times I thought, I can't go through with this. I can't do this. I can't do this.

Then I'd realize I had chosen this path. There was no turning around. I had to face things. I had to go on. I had to ride this beast.

After doing *Sally,* Chris, Mickey, Bear, and I took a taxi out to Pennsylvania and joined Michael. It was an unstable, truly horrible time. We couldn't move into the new house yet and we had to check in at the Bethlehem, Pennsylvania, Days Inn. Two parents, two kids, and a spastic keeshond puppy in one ten-by-twelve-foot room. Michael could look forward to his Shakespeare festival, but the kids and I hardly knew what to do with ourselves. We had two queen-size beds and all our stuff crammed all over the place. I had four outfits to choose from because all of us were living out of two suitcases. Colored plastic cups, Coke bottles, and cellophane cracker wrappers littered the floor because the kids were constantly eating and drinking to stave off boredom. I started feeling like a real loser. What kind of a life am I going to be able to give the poor kid who's coming?

There were days I was so depressed I thought I was going to die. I kept remembering sending my furniture away into storage, locking the door for the final time on the Las Vegas house.

We tried to cheer up by looking forward to small things. Michael had mailed more clothes that hadn't arrived. The UPS box will be here any day! we told ourselves. We heard that we might be permitted to stay in the Allentown dorms for a couple of days if they could get one of the rooms cleaned up. These incentives helped keep us going, but I would still have moments of depression because here I was, a thirty-three-year-old woman getting excited about the prospect of getting a dorm room.

More than anything, though, I was able to get through this time and others like it because of promises I received through reading my Bible. The Lord promised to protect us, to fight for us when we couldn't fight for ourselves, to be our rock and our shield. This was the fundamental truth, I believed, and I had to learn to depend on that.

There were also moments when I was lying in bed, peaceful and quiet with no traumatizing phone calls or other interruptions, in which I would just put my hands on my tummy and tell myself, *At least I have her.*

Marv called me at the Days Inn in early June to get the motel's fax number. "I've got to send you something," he said excitedly. "I've been talking to Brad Bell."

I said, "Oh. Really?"

He wanted to fax me an offer Brad Bell had made. I was tremendously relieved and flattered. Ashamed. Grateful. They were asking me to come back to *The Bold and the Beautiful.* Ron Weaver was giving me my old position back. They were even allowing me time to make the transition back to Los Angeles through a light schedule at first, in anticipation of signing a long-term contract later. I would be allowed to fly back and forth from Pennsylvania for spot appearances. (Marv had told Brad I didn't live in Los Angeles anymore, since I had also cleaned out my apartment in L.A.) I was amazed.

I called Marv back and said, "He really is willing to do that? Don't they think I'm the loser of the century? Aren't they embarrassed to deal with me? How do they feel about this lawsuit? Doesn't this rub off and affect them in some way?"

"Obviously, they're not affected," Marv said. "They don't care. It's going to be okay."

Now I was in another bind. We had just bought a house. Michael had been gearing up for life as a college professor. How could we just turn around on a dime again? But we definitely needed the money.

When I talked to Michael about it, he was gun-shy and suspicious of anything having to do with L.A. His first reaction was, "You tell them to forget it. We're never going back."

"Michael, we're broke," I said. "We're broke. We're about to have a baby. I can't go through this pregnancy with this kind of instability. I'm telling you, I cannot do it." For two weeks, Michael and I debated how to handle this situation. We came to the conclusion that we needed to get through the pregnancy and make long-term decisions afterward. I would make my spot appearances, but we would also see what happened in Allentown.

I felt nervous about the state of my reputation in L.A. I didn't know if people in the business hated my guts. I knew a lot of people loved Aaron Spelling and I knew they loved *Melrose Place*. I figured I might be considered a pain in the butt by now, the actress who thought she was tough enough to defy the powers that be. Many people thought Aaron Spelling had been one of my biggest supporters, giving me plum guest spots in prime time and then a regular role on a hit series, and I had turned around and bitten the hand that fed me. I would never be able to explain that I knew Aaron had been kind to me in the past, but that he had given this matter over to lawyers who were anything but kind.

Even so, I went back to L.A. I had moved all my furniture out of the apartment on Beverly Boulevard and turned in my keys, but the lease ran through August. I went back to the manager and arranged for the lease to be extended. I ended up sleeping on the floor in a sleeping bag. I looked like a pregnant street lady, moving into an apartment with shopping bags and blankets.

I did a lot of reading and didn't watch TV, because I didn't have a TV. I tried to catch up on my sleep. I enjoyed the solitude, and the time alone in the bare apartment brought me some genuine healing.

My first day back on *The Bold and the Beautiful* came shortly after my birthday in July. I was as nervous as I have ever been in my career. It was humbling to have to go back. Everybody could see my anxiety, it was all over everyone's face, but nobody said anything out loud. They were almost embarrassed for me, that I had to come back. Everybody treated me as if they felt sorry for me, telling me they loved me and giving me big hugs.

In my first scene back on the show, my character was coming back from France after attending a symposium on psychiatry. Ridge, who was my character's ex-husband and a designer, had flown over to France to do a fashion show. The scene had both of us flying home coincidentally on the same plane, and we happened to be assigned seats next to one another. I was to move to my seat, see his coat lying on my chair, and say, "Excuse me, could you move . . ."

Then he would look up and then . . . they're back together once more.

When we did our first rehearsal, he reached over and held my hand, giving it a squeeze. Then we broke character and hugged each other. When I turned away, Brad Bell was walking toward me with a huge bouquet of roses. I thought I was going to die.

The whole crew applauded and welcomed me back. I was overwhelmed by how caring everybody was. We had always joked on the show about other actors who proudly left the show to become stars, and then nothing ever happened. They went to catch the big-time bus and missed it. I felt as though I had caught the big-time bus and gotten dropped off again. Or the door hit me in the face as it opened. All the same, I was welcomed back and it felt great to be home.

Once I had done a few shows, Brad talked to Marv about keeping me there to work more, but Marv was concerned about me flying back and forth.

Then came the first day of my deposition by Spelling Entertainment's counsel. I met Bill Waldo—lead attorney for the defense—for the first time. For hour after hour he badgered me and tried to go on fishing expeditions into my past at every occasion. He proudly displayed the two-feet-tall stack of magazines he had accumulated while researching me. Surely the India garbage was in there, too. He looked at me, wearing a smirky smile. When Dolores Leal objected, he kept telling her she didn't know her case.

When I got home to the little apartment, I was bleeding. I was on the floor, crying, having contractions and bleeding bright, bright red blood. I was in utter agony. I went as quickly as possible to the hospital. I had to have an ultrasound, which showed that my placenta had ruptured. It was diagnosed as a partial placenta previa. I rested, and fortunately the hemorrhage subsided, but not without consequences.

My doctor, Dr. Kessler, told me I couldn't fly anymore. "You may not go back to Pennsylvania," he said firmly. "You may not fly again in your entire pregnancy. Every time you fly, you increase the chances for miscarriage."

That ended my plans to fly back and forth. I never got to see Michael in one of his performances as Iago, which ended with a big finale in July that he was so proud of. Even though we had an empty house in Pennsylvania, we were all going to have to live in an apartment in L.A. We had to fly the kids, who by this time were totally confused, back to L.A. and enroll them in schools quickly. In between legal appointments, depositions, doctor visits, and *The Bold and the Beautiful* tapings, I spent the whole month of August trying to find a school where Chris could develop his musical talent.

During August, we were all together again in a one-bedroom place, this time with no furniture. We were sleeping on blankets and sleeping bags. We had been vagabonds all summer long, and we still were, even though our income situation was improving. We had the dog again, too, shipped all the way back from Pennsylvania, full of ticks from the kennel where he'd been boarded. It turned out that no pets were allowed in our apartment building. We tried to hide the dog on the balcony, but he proceeded to yelp long and loud. It was a nightmare trying to sneak him down the back stairway to take him for a walk.

I started feeling sorry for myself. I was tempted to say, "Woe is me. Look what they've done to me." Instead, all these experiences only served to fuel my fighting fire. It's not woe is me, I thought. It's woe is any woman, woe is any family this happens to.

Everything we went through that summer gave me a settled conviction: This cannot happen to anybody else. If it's the last thing I do, I'll see that it doesn't.

21

My suit against Spelling Entertainment, et al., began on October 30, 1997, in Los Angeles County Superior Court before Judge Fumiko Wasserman. Jury selection and preliminary motions took up the next ten days. On November 10, my lead counsel, Nathan Goldberg, presented our opening argument. My suit alleged that Spelling Entertainment was guilty of pregnancy discrimination, sex discrimination, and breach of contract. On my behalf, the law firm of Allred, Moroko & Goldberg was asking for compensatory and punitive damages.

Eighteen months had passed since my termination in April of 1996. My little girl Izabella—to the defendants' minds, the cause of our conflict—was born one year before the day I started to give my testimony, November 12. I had been back working on *The Bold and the Beautiful* for more than a year and was now under another long-term contract there. Michael and I had moved back permanently to Los Angeles and Chris and Mickey were enrolled in Los Angeles schools.

A stable life reestablished, I still found the trial blindingly stressful, with the next migraine only a pulse away. As I watched the jury being selected during voir dire, I wondered what these ten women and two men must be thinking. They claimed to be neutral, of course—as I would have. But a tremendous amount of negative publicity had already been generated about me in the press. Did they think I was just a big nobody trying to make a buck out of Spelling? For us to win, we would have to present our case in a way the jury could identify with, as if they were living through the experience of pregnancy discrimination themselves.

During the past year, especially during the summer of 1996, I had sat by my attorney, Dolores Leal, as the various potential witnesses were deposed, their preliminary testimony recorded during the legal process called discovery. I came to admire Dolores's tremendous understanding of the law and the way she comported herself. She bore opposing counsel Bill Waldo's often maddening behavior without ever becoming flustered. She didn't let him get away with anything, either. Often, during depositions, I was beside myself, hearing how facts about my past were being twisted to their advantage. But Dolores could calm me with a touch at my elbow.

For the trial itself, Dolores would serve as "second chair." My lead attorney would be Nathan Goldberg, a fit and trim man of about fifty, with a kind face and a natural, impish sense of humor. Nathan's manner is like that of a favorite family doctor: a wise man whose advice, however unsettling, can always be trusted. Being in his company always made me feel secure.

In private conversation, Nathan Goldberg is usually reserved and soft-spoken, although he always has a twinkle in his eye as he detects hidden ironies in what he's hearing. When he rose to speak to the jury for the first time, he became animated in a way that I hadn't anticipated. Suddenly, this Marcus Welby, M.D., type became more like Jerry Seinfeld crossed with Perry Mason.

In his opening statement, Nathan clearly articulated why we had brought suit. "This case," he said, "is about a working mother, my client, Hunter Tylo, who was unfairly deprived of an opportunity to advance her career and unlawfully fired from *Melrose Place*. Why? Simply because she was pregnant."

As Nathan continued, he anticipated the line of reasoning Spelling Entertainment's attorneys, Bill Waldo and Linda Edwards, would pursue. He acknowledged my celebrity, which he knew opposing counsel would use to depict me as a spoiled brat, but Nathan insisted that my real life was much the same as the jury members. Like them, I had to balance work and family and pay my bills. I should be seen, fundamentally, as a working mother.

He went on to summarize the events that had led to the suit. He recalled that, in late 1995 and early 1996, after working on *The Bold and the Beautiful* for six years, I hired a new manager, Marv Dauer, and began looking for other acting jobs. He recounted how Spelling Entertainment expressed their interest in my playing a role on *Melrose Place* and detailed my two phone conversations with executive producer Frank South in which I learned, in a preliminary way, what my role would be.

Then he told the jury how, after finding out I was pregnant in March of 1996, I had informed Spelling Entertainment of the news, in order for them to have as much time as possible to make whatever adjustments might be necessary as we prepared to begin filming in July.

Nathan told the jury how I had then been quickly fired—by fax. "And this was Ms. Tylo's chance," Nathan said. "Her chance to go from the minor leagues of daytime television to the major leagues of prime time. She had worked long and hard for this chance, paid her dues, put in years of work. And they took away that chance, unlawfully, just like that, without any consideration at all."

Nathan cited clause 10(A) in my contract, which opposing counsel would be using as the grounds of my termination. He showed that the "material change in appearance" language in the contract, which we would be hearing so much about, was closely connected to an actor's inability or "incapacity" to fulfill the terms of the contract. I couldn't have been "incapacitated" by my pregnancy with Izabella, he argued, because by July of 1996, when my contract with Spelling called for me to begin work on *Melrose Place,* I had returned to *The Bold and the Beautiful* and worked on my old show throughout my pregnancy. In fact, I returned to work five days after giving birth to Izabella.

Nathan finished his opening statement stressing our major

theme. "A woman today," Nathan said, his voice rising, "doesn't have to make a choice between having a family and having a career. Spelling Television decided, apropos of nothing, without reference to any legal standards, that they weren't going to work with a pregnant actress. But what they forgot—or chose not to pay any attention to—is that the law simply doesn't allow men to make such selfish, foolhardy decisions anymore."

At the end of Nathan's opening statement, I was so grateful. Someone had finally presented my case and hit the nail right on the head. He spoke exactly as I would have if I had had his gifts as an orator and litigator. If the trial accomplished nothing else, at least the truth had now been spoken in public. I was particularly moved when Nathan said that my chance at exercising my gifts as an actress on prime time had been taken away from me. My shoulders started to shake, and I felt so embarrassed, but I just couldn't keep myself from breaking down a little then.

I heard rumors circulating that the *Melrose* people were saying, "See what a soapy, melodramatic actress we picked!"

But I would never break down in public deliberately. I felt humiliated, crying in that dignified courtroom setting.

I saw on the faces of the jury that Nathan's opening argument brought the case to life for them. They were with him all the way, step by step, reason by reason.

The next day, the lead attorney for Spelling Entertainment fired his own opening salvos. Bill Waldo started off with a few jokes, trying to ingratiate himself with the jury. I thought he had a too-ready smile and that his jokes mostly failed; but I had to wonder whether he was being persuasive despite his annoying manner.

He soon came upon his main line of reasoning. "I was struck by at least one thing Mr. Goldberg said on Monday," he said. "In fact, I wrote it down. I'm quoting. He said, 'The law protects all of us.'

"I went home and I thought about it, and thought about it a lot. The law does protect all of us, big-time entertainment companies and producers as well as actresses. Under the law, everyone is equal.

"What the law doesn't do is grant special privileges. The law does not require special privileges for someone who's a celebrity actress. A celebrity has no right to sign a contract and then come in to this court and say I want to pick and choose parts of the contract I like because there's parts of the contract I don't like. The law grants no one any special right to pick and choose."

He went on to point out that Spelling Entertainment and Spelling Television employ many women and these women sometimes become pregnant. Ordinarily, this makes no difference to their work status, because their appearance doesn't pertain to their ability to perform their duties.

Appearance does make a difference, he argued, when it comes to actors and actresses, because actors are hired for their appearance; it's part and parcel of what makes them believable in the roles they play. He pointed to the example of Roseanne Barr. The *Roseanne* show was often number one in the ratings, which it wouldn't have been if Roseanne wasn't a fine actress. But Roseanne couldn't credibly play Miss America.

Spelling Entertainment hired me for my appearance, Bill Waldo argued, and their contract stipulated that if my appearance "materially changed," they had the right to fire me. Beginning and end of story. He admitted that Hollywood producers sometimes, at their own discretion, use body doubles and other means to hide the pregnancies of their actresses, but no producer was under any legal obligation to do so.

Mr. Waldo went through his own version of my hiring and supplied background to the creation of what would have been my new character on *Melrose Place*. He claimed that from November of 1995, the Fox network people, the Spelling Entertainment people, and the executive producer of *Melrose*, Frank South, had been intent on hiring a "sexy vixen" to seduce Heather Locklear's husband away from her. To his mind, it was obvious that a pregnant woman could not play a "sexy vixen."

"So where are we at?" Bill Waldo asked. "This is not a pregnancy discrimination case at all. This is a change-of-appearance case, pure and simple. If a male actor starts to change his appearance by, for example, gaining weight, the male actor is told to take it off. And if the actor doesn't take it off, we take him off. It doesn't matter, male, female, pregnant, not pregnant. Appearance matters.

"The law requires that if somebody enters into an agreement that says they won't change their appearance, and then changes their appearance, our view is that the law ought to enforce the contract.

"The law doesn't require . . ."

At that point, Nathan Goldberg had had enough and stood up. "I'm going to object, Your Honor, to this characterization of what the law requires and doesn't require."

Judge Wasserman responded, "The objection is sustained."

Mr. Waldo finished his statement. "Our view is that *common sense* doesn't require that there be special privileges for someone simply because she is a celebrity actress."

The two opening statements set the stage for most of what would follow. We believed that the jury could identify with me as a working mother. We thought the jury would come to understand what it's like to have your family's future and your own on the line and then be fired by an employer without a thought to the havoc being created.

Our opponents hoped my celebrity status could be used to alienate the jury; to depict me as a spoiled celebrity and themselves as commonsense businesspeople. They tried to stand on strict, if questionable, legalities, while we pursued the broader avenue of society's interests in women's rights and specifically in the rights of pregnant women.

Would a narrow interpretation of the law trump motherhood or would the law be seen as extending its protection to my particular situation? My lawyers told me we were in uncharted territory, even if we had the truth on our side.

22

I began testifying on the third day of the trial, November 12. I wore a cream-colored suit, with two little bows on each side of the pockets at the waistline. It had silk lapels and a short skirt that was tailored, sophisticated, and sexy. As I prepared that morning, I was so nervous that I had trouble making decisions about my makeup and accessories. I wanted to look just right because I knew that if any day of the trial held surprises, this day would.

Nathan decided that Dolores should begin my direct examination. After I took the stand and swore to tell the truth, she began the questioning in what appeared to be an innocuous manner, asking my name and my general place of residence and questions about my family.

"How many children do you have?" Dolores asked.

"Well, that depends on how you look at it."

"Okay."

"Three and a half."

Dolores blinked at me twice and smiled; she didn't know I was going to say that, but she did know where we were headed. "Three and a half. What do you mean, three and a half?"

Every eyeball in the courtroom was glued to me. What is she, nuts? people must have been asking themselves. "I have a sixteen-year-old. I have a nine-year-old. I have a one-year-old as of today. And I am almost eight months pregnant."

The jury gasped. Opposing counsel Bill Waldo's face turned four shades of red. He tried waggling a pen with his fingers to appear nonchalant and then began scribbling furiously on a legal pad. Sally Suchil, in-house counsel for Spelling Entertainment, looked stricken. How could her litigators not know this? Bill Waldo's second chair, Linda Edwards, a prim and proper woman with tightly curled hair and thin lips that went white when she became angry, tilted her head and pulled in her chin as if a huge truck had whipped by her on the highway.

During the months leading up to the trial, my counsel and I kept wondering when Bill Waldo and company were going to figure out that I was pregnant again. I thought they must have known until I heard Waldo's opening statement, in which he made no mention of the fact. Ordinarily, an opposing attorney wants to detonate such an explosive piece of information himself, in order to control the blast.

During this pregnancy, I was able to keep up my exercise regimen and eat properly. My stable home life translated into a weight gain of only twenty-two pounds during the entire pregnancy—only fifteen pounds as of the trial.

In his opening statement, Bill Waldo had mentioned that I had gained forty-six pounds during my pregnancy with Izabella. Later, Mr. Waldo produced charts—huge charts—documenting my weight gain. This surprise announcement of my current pregnancy blew the "pregnant blimp" strategy to smithereens before it could ever be effectively launched. The jury was staring at me, wondering how I could be almost eight months pregnant.

Dolores went on with her questioning and soon we came to what was for me the most important moment of the trial. "Ms. Tylo," Dolores asked, "why did you file this lawsuit?"

"I filed it for two reasons."

"What are those reasons?"

"The first reason is that a law protects pregnant women from being discriminated against. In my situation, I began to understand why that law was put in place and why it's so important. I wanted to see the law upheld.

"The second reason is that I was placed in a position of feeling very threatened, and feeling that my family had been treated as if it were a piece of dirt on the bottom of someone's shoe. There was a brief moment that I'm ashamed of in which I considered having an abortion because I felt that I had done something wrong. I thought, if I'm being told I had breached my contract, what did I do wrong? What can I do to fix it? And I considered having an abortion. And I'm ashamed because I don't believe in it."

I became more and more emotional then. I felt awkward and even foolish. My voice climbed higher, my nose started running, and I broke out in a sweat, so that my hair started sticking to my forehead. I was struggling to control my shaking as I finished explaining. "I look at my little one-year-old daughter sometimes now. She's walking. And I'm so thankful that I didn't have an abortion. And I don't ever want to see a woman put in that position again. Pregnancy is temporary. It is not something that's crippling or debilitating, and it does not make a woman ugly. That's why I filed the lawsuit."

Dolores said, "You've heard Mr. Waldo speak of what an influential man Aaron Spelling is in the entertainment industry. Did that concern you at all in making your decision to file this lawsuit?"

"Of course it did."

"Why?"

"He is very influential. Because of this, my career may be overlooked from this point on. Who knows? But I did feel that the right of a woman to bear her children without being pressured to choose abortion certainly outweighed the value of my career."

I finished giving my direct testimony to Dolores late in the afternoon. We broke for the day. I would be cross-examined by Bill Waldo the following morning.

Unfortunately, I woke up that next morning with the flu. I was nauseated, running a fever, with body aches and a headache to boot. I knew that not appearing might cause the jury to wonder if I were afraid to be cross-examined. At the same time, I didn't want to submit to the expected barrage of hostile questions feeling as though I were going to puke. I called Dolores. She told me to get up, dress, and see how I felt then. She wanted me to come in at least for the afternoon session. I didn't have to look my best, she assured me. It would be more important for the jury to see that I was committed to pursuing this case, even in the midst of illness.

I drank some tea that morning and tried to pull myself together. I had to dress much more simply because I didn't have the energy to contour my eyes and style my hair. So I put on a sweater dress, with a casual jacket, and wore my hair brushed out straight. In the car on the way down, I felt woozy. I had no idea how I would make it through a whole afternoon on the stand, but I was going to try.

As I walked past the jury and the judge to be sworn in, I felt a little uncoordinated, a little dorky—I was that much under the weather—and I nearly knocked over the pitcher of water on the witness stand. I brushed the microphone in a way that made it honk. Of all the days to feel spastic—the day I would be cross-examined by Bill Waldo!

He started off with the usual preliminaries and then hit me with a surprise. "Ms. Tylo, do your recognize this document? It's a fax transmission sheet that you sent to your agent, Scott Harris, right?"

"Yes," I said. I took a deep breath because I could foresee Mr. Waldo's strategy. My courtesy note to Scott about my first attorney's letter to Spelling Entertainment would be interpreted as an attempt at extortion by legal means, not a shot over the bow meant to open up the phone lines.

"You wrote, 'Scott, please look over the following letter.' And there was a letter attached to it, correct?"

"Yes."

"Your note says, 'Please look over the following letter. I feel we have no leverage for negotiating anything, let alone another series, if "the powers that be" do not see the legal ramifications and unlawful actions they have taken in black and white from an attorney. I will call you at 5:00 P.M. today.'"

"Yes."

"Now, were you attempting to threaten legal action against Aaron Spelling for the purpose of negotiation?"

"Nobody was threatening litigation. We were talking about them speaking to us, giving us the courtesy of a phone call, anything, something to discuss. We just wanted to discuss what might be worked out—maybe even a rollover deal."

Bill Waldo objected that I was not answering his question.

Judge Fumiko Wasserman said, "Ms. Tylo, in order for us to avoid my having to strike your answers and then having you repeat answers again, would you listen carefully to the questions? Some of them may require just a yes or no response."

Mr. Waldo resumed his attack. "The language in the letter says, quote, 'I feel that we will have no leverage for negotiating anything, let alone another series.' Simple yes or no. Were you trying to use some threat against Aaron Spelling as leverage for negotiating another series?"

"That question is unclear."

He moved away from me and back again. "You wrote this to Scott Harris, the head of your agency, attaching a letter written by one of your representatives. And you weren't attempting to use anything to negotiate another deal or a series with Aaron Spelling? That wasn't your motivation?"

"That's not the way this letter is meant to be read."

"I see."

"That's not what it *means,*" I said, distraught.

"I see. I see . . . thank you very much Ms. Tylo."

Fortunately, for all the suspicion Bill Waldo was able to create with his "I sees," Dolores enabled me to supply some context as soon as she rose to question me. "Let's look at the phrase, 'I feel that we will have no leverage in negotiating anything.' Would you please explain why you wrote that?"

"The word 'negotiation' means getting the Spelling people to talk with us. We were trying to get them to talk with us about the idea of rolling over the deal, which meant that if they were unhappy with the way I might look, then why didn't we just start the deal in January."

I felt relieved at having said my piece on this score at last, but my insistence that no one would talk to us later opened a trapdoor into a discussion of Spelling's settlement offer, a door that my attorneys and I assumed to be closed—at Spelling's own insistence. I was finished testifying for now but would be recalled later in the trial, close to the time of closing arguments.

Lisa Rinna was eventually hired in my stead on *Melrose Place*. A dark-haired beauty with deep liquid eyes and cushiony lips, Lisa has a tremendous magnetism and was an excellent choice for the role. I know she found herself in a difficult position testifying at my trial. What actress wants to be compared to another? She had been on the show for more than a year and would be looking at having her option picked up that next spring. She had every incentive both to maximize the importance of making the role her own and also to be a good soldier and testify strongly in Spelling's defense.

She was also now four months pregnant herself, and wouldn't want to think of her condition as something that might bring on adverse consequences—a nightmare that would have been way too close to home. As she began to testify, I knew what to expect, and never considered there to be any animosity between us. (In fact, she's sent me several nice notes since then, timed with notable events in our family's life.)

I was intrigued by how casually she dressed. She didn't wear any makeup and her little loose top and pants emphasized how the pregnancy was affecting her appearance. I wondered whether she might have been instructed to appear pregnant.

Nathan began asking Lisa questions before the day finished on November 14. He quickly established that she had as little information about the character she would be playing as I did. Then she verified for the jury that each actress develops a part differently, so that the character can be quite different depending upon the actor portraying the role. In this way, Nathan showed that the *Melrose* people could not know as clearly as they were claiming what the role would be, much less what it would require.

He went on to discuss Lisa's pregnancy with her, asking, "Has there been any discussion about whether or not they're going to write the part so that you will appear pregnant in the show?"

"My character will be pregnant on the show as well."

Nathan then showed Lisa the standard terms and conditions of her contract and asked her whether she'd ever seen it before. She'd reviewed it prior to her deposition, but not until then, in the way most of us who don't like to be bothered with legalese would.

Then Nathan asked, "Has anybody at Spelling told you that you have broken your contract in some manner by virtue of the fact that you and your husband have the blessing of expecting a child?"

"No."

Nathan had shown how changeable parts can be—that Lisa's way of playing the part would necessarily have been completely different from mine. Her pregnancy had been a surprise "gift," especially as the *Melrose* producers actually rewrote her part to make her pregnancy part of the show. Nathan was showing that, contrary to their own statements, the producers actually adapted roles for the circumstances of pregnancy. This was crucial and we had called Lisa for this purpose.

Judge Wasserman then asked for Ms. Edwards to cross-examine Lisa.

Ms. Edwards asked Lisa about the skimpy clothes the Taylor McBride character wore and her use of sexuality.

"I had to use my sexuality to the hilt," Lisa said. "I had to do love scenes like I've never done love scenes before. I had to wear less clothing than I've ever worn before. For television, the love scenes on *Melrose Place* are graphic. You are in lingerie. You're ripping each other's clothing off. The scenes I did with the character Peter Burns were almost violent. I mean, when you've got a character who's competing for Heather Locklear's man, you better blow out all the stops."

"Ms. Rinna, do you believe you could have played the role of Taylor McBride during the 1996-1997 season if you had been pregnant?"

"No. Definitely not. I wouldn't have had the stamina, or even the agility. In one scene, he throws me down on a bed and in another I straddle him. He clears off a kitchen counter and starts making love to me right there. I couldn't have done those things if I had been pregnant."

The star of *Melrose Place,* Heather Locklear, appeared several days later, on November 24. She looked great, with her shimmering blond hair and knockout figure. She wore tight black leggings and a little top that revealed her midriff—only five weeks after delivering a baby! She seemed perfectly at ease. She was, in every detail, her own woman.

Nathan Goldberg called Heather Locklear because he wanted to prove the extent to which a production can adapt itself to a performer's pregnancy. Heather had been pregnant during the past season, and the show did whatever it had to do.

Heather Locklear's testimony revealed all the tricks Hollywood uses to hide an actress's pregnancy. Heather estimated that the show had used a body double for her between five and ten times during the past season. Less drastic means, such as props—a picnic basket, tables, purses, and even a waiter—were also used. The director often chose to shoot Heather from the waist up as well.

The comparative ease with which the show hid Heather's pregnancy came through in one exchange between Nathan and Heather. After establishing that Heather chose all of her own wardrobe, Nathan asked, "In connection with the scenes when you were preg-

nant, did you change your clothing choices in view of the pregnancy?"

"No."

While Heather Locklear's testimony stressed how easily the show
adapted itself to her pregnancy, others at Spelling depicted themselves as helpless in the event of an actress's pregnancy. There was
nothing they could have done to fulfill their obligation to me.

The president of Spelling, Jonathan Levin, the tall, fashionable,
wispy-haired man I had met in the foyer of Spelling Entertainment
on the day of my appointment with the casting director, Pam Shae,
testified at length that I could not possibly have played the new
"sexy vixen" role on *Melrose Place.* What Jonathan Levin did or did
not say to my manager, Marv Dauer, about my getting an abortion
also occupied much of Mr. Levin's testimony.

The first co-counsel for the defense, Linda Edwards, elicited the
expected denials. They were talking about the call Marv made to
Jonathan Levin. "What, if anything," Linda Edwards asked, "did
you say to Mr. Dauer during that conversation on the subject of
Hunter Tylo having an abortion?"

"Nothing. I never mentioned it."

"What, if anything, did you *ever* say to Mr. Dauer at any time
about the subject of Hunter Tylo having an abortion?"

"Absolutely nothing."

"Thank you."

Nathan rose to cross-examine. He covered the same territory
and then moved on to other issues. "Now, Mr. Levin, after you
learned that Hunter Tylo was pregnant, you had discussions with
Aaron Spelling concerning the pregnancy, did you not?"

"I was party to those conversations, yes."

"You were one of the decision makers, weren't you?"

"Yes."

"And as a decision maker, wouldn't it be fair to say that the moment that Ms. Tylo became pregnant, from your vantage point,
there was nothing she could do to still be on *Melrose?*"

"I believed at that time that it made it impossible for her to be in that part, yes."

"At the point that you found out that Hunter Tylo was pregnant, do you know what she looked like at that point in time?"

"No. I had not seen her."

"Now, when you learned that she was pregnant, did you get a vision of what she would look like during the course of her pregnancy? Did you have a mental image in your mind?"

"I guess—I thought that she would gain a substantial amount of weight."

"And in your mind, what was substantial?"

"Well, in television, anything over ten pounds can be a considerable amount of weight."

"Gaining more than ten pounds, that would disqualify her from the role?"

"For this role, yes, I thought so. That was my opinion."

Jonathan Levin's testimony helped the jury see what narrow standards were applied in my case—standards based merely on supposition—and what very different judgments were made in Lisa Rinna's and Heather Locklear's cases. This not only pointed up the basic unfairness of the situation, it also gave Nathan Goldberg a means of arguing the illegality of these actions.

The laws governing pregnancy discrimination don't demand that an employer "accommodate" an employee's pregnancy by providing alternate duties. (We were careful throughout the trial never to use the word "accommodate.") Employers do not have to resort to *exceptional* means. If adapting productions to an actress's pregnancy is the *usual* or *customary* practice, though, then the production company has no right to invoke its right not to accommodate.

Hollywood has a star mentality—anything for the star. But the law, as even Mr. Waldo argued, has another mentality: the same treatment for everyone. Through Lisa Rinna's and especially Heather Locklear's testimonies, we went a long way toward proving our case. Levin's capricious judgment underlined this. Of course, the jury heard Lisa Rinna's, Heather Locklear's, and Jonathan Levin's testimonies only after learning that I was almost eight months pregnant, which the Spelling people, with all their assumptions about how pregnant women look, had completely missed.

23

In many people's minds, the trial hung on the testimony of one man, the executive producer of *Melrose Place*, Frank South. He was called both by the defense and by our side and testified over a number of days, both early and late in the month-long proceedings.

Until his deposition that previous summer, I had never met Frank South in person, although of course my telephone conversations with him prior to my hiring remained unforgettable. From those conversations, I had a mental picture of him as an older man. He was really quite young. He had wavy black hair, and a full face that dimpled when he smiled. His hazel eyes sparkled. He was fairly tall and had that L.A. producer slackened walk. He may have been a little too proud of his pearly, big-toothed smile.

Most witnesses look at their questioner, but from the first Frank played to the jury—all the way. He kept turning to them, and at one point even invited them to come by the set of *Melrose*. To my ears, his answers sounded rehearsed, but I knew how persuasive such a young, powerful man could be.

During his initial testimony, Frank South, under questioning from Nathan and Bill Waldo, gave the jury a short course on the development of plot outlines—called arcs—for a serialized show like *Melrose.*

A year's worth of scripts for *Melrose Place* were begun in the fall of the previous year, before production started in July. The process didn't begin with the writing. It started with discussions among the executive producer, Frank South—the "show runner," as he or she is called in Hollywood—the production company executives, chiefly Aaron Spelling, and the Fox network executives, especially Craig Erwich. They reviewed how the show was going. They floated preliminary ideas as to where the show should head during the next season. During these discussions, they paid particular attention to problems that threatened to drain the show of vitality.

Then Frank South met with his writing staff. (Most executive producers are the head writers on their shows and many of the other producers listed in the credits are writers as well.) They developed story arcs—plotlines spanning a number of episodes—that would take the show through the fall and spring shooting schedules. While they used notes to keep track of these rough outlines, the process was again mostly one of discussion. Gradually, the plotlines became further refined; the story of Amanda's breakup with Peter would occupy episodes one through seven, Kyle's restaurant would be planned and launched in episodes eight through thirteen, and so on.

Early in the spring, executive producer Frank South met with Aaron Spelling and presented the story arcs that he and his staff had developed and explained how they would interlace. Frank talked his way through a full year's planning. Aaron Spelling raised questions, made suggestions, and soon the two came to an understanding of the ideas they would pitch to the network. Frank South then went to Fox and pitched the story arcs for the new year. He had been on his way home from this March 29 meeting when he learned from Marv about my pregnancy.

Even after nearly six months of planning, however, none of the actual scripts had been written. Adjustments are almost always made to the show's plotlines, depending on what's working and what's not.

A classic instance of this is *I Spy.* The show began as a vehicle for its star, Robert Culp. Costar Bill Cosby proved so much more dynamic that the show quickly became his. Culp's speech patterns even began sounding like Cosby's.

To hear Frank South's telling of his studio's planning for the season of *Melrose* in which I was to be on the show, nothing could have been changed from the day he pitched the show's plotlines—its arcs—to network liaison Craig Erwich.

Frank claimed that as early as November, Aaron Spelling, the Fox network, and he had been in agreement that they needed "a new girl to come in and shake things up," a "sexy vixen," who would seduce Peter Burns away from Amanda Woodward. They liked the guest spot I had done on *Burke's Law* because it showed how I could use my body to be seductive. I was the "exact physical type" they were looking for. They knew they needed a knockout because the actress had to convince the audience she could take away a man from one of the most beautiful women on television, Heather Locklear. Even more important, they knew they were looking for someone to play a seductress and an adulterer—a woman who did nothing but scheme about how to get her way and who took the lowest possible road in that direction.

During the taking of depositions with Frank South, Craig Erwich, and Aaron Spelling himself, I had heard much the same thing. I had two feelings about this written (or spoken)-in-stone attitude toward the part. Why didn't they just tell me? It made me furious at Frank South for hemming and hawing about the matter during our phone conversations before I took the job. To hear him tell it now, if indeed he was telling the truth, they were trying to hire a Joan Collins queen-bitch type for *Melrose.* They knew this all along. I felt as though I had been tricked. I also kept wondering, though, if circumstances had led them to make absolute what were much more ambiguous ideas for the sake of justifying the actions they took. I suppose that's something I'll never know.

.   .   .

I went home after the first day of Frank South's testimony to pray and read my Bible. As I was reading, I found a passage about how King Ahab traded armor with a soldier one day to disguise himself in battle. I knew that I was in a battle, too, and I felt that a change in armor—at least for one day—was appropriate.

To court the next day I wore a leopard-print bra from Victoria's Secret. It was very sexy and because of my pregnancy, I was voluptuous to the max. That leopard bra showed some major cleavage. I wore a classy sheer silk black top over it, with a black business jacket. The sheer black top showed my midriff and created the illusion that I wasn't pregnant at all. The little guppy tummy I had looked utterly flat. The skirt I wore also had a long slit up the front. I showed the outfit to Michael the night before, and he said, "It's going to give them a frickin' heart attack." He also thought it looked classy enough not to be offensive, so I felt doubly secure in wearing the outfit.

The next day I took my seat in the chair on the outside of our table. I was extremely close to the jury, almost within arm's length in our small courtroom. I noticed, more than once, that one of the two men on the jury could not take his eyes off my cleavage. I was sure he believed that I could play a "sexy vixen" right then. The other male juror kept looking and smiling at me, too.

I wanted to show Frank South to his face that he was dead wrong, and I did. I could tell that he was affected by that outfit. He couldn't look me in the eye, but I saw him checking me out. I saw Waldo checking me out. I heard mutterings from opposing counsel about my "trick outfit." They were all checking me out that day.

As the court session began, Nathan rose to cross-examine Frank South. I felt that this might well be the decisive confrontation, and Frank South seemed to be guarding against the possibility himself: Instead of facing the jury and seeking out eye contact, as he had while being questioned by Mr. Waldo, he overlapped his arms and placed them on the witness stand as a buffer against the pressure he felt Nathan would soon bring to bear.

"You indicated yesterday that in the first episode of *Melrose Place* for the 1996-97 season, there was a scene featuring Lisa Rinna, playing the Taylor McBride character, in a police station," Nathan said.

"Yes, I did."

"And you testified that the purpose of that scene was to establish Lisa Rinna as a rival for Amanda. I think those were your words."

"Yes."

"Let me show you the scene that I think is the scene you're referring to." Nathan had set up a video monitor and he had clips prepared of all the scenes Lisa Rinna had appeared in during the time I was pregnant with Izabella—the first half of the 1996-1997 season. The scene showed Lisa Rinna fully clothed, in pants and a jacket. The only sexy shot came at the end, when the camera focused on her walking away. In that shot, the viewer couldn't help but focus on her derriere.

"And the purpose of that scene, as I understand it," Nathan asked, "was to establish her as physically attractive. It's the first time we've seen her full figure since she's been on the show, isn't it?"

"We also see her in the *Melrose Place* courtyard. We see her going up the stairs, she turns around, and we see her bottom. She also has that great way of looking at the man she wants." As Frank South testified, I made sure to try to establish direct eye contact with him.

"It is your testimony, Mr. South, that my client—the way she looks right now, in her eighth month of pregnancy—couldn't play that scene?"

He avoided my stare completely. He didn't even bother to look in my direction.

"Absolutely not," he stated for the record.

"She couldn't do it right now?" Nathan looked over at me, in my leopard bra.

"Not now, no."

Directly after this testimony, as the jury filed out for our lunch break, every man and woman on the jury turned back to check me out and I obliged by turning around to gather up some papers that were on my chair. I knew my bottom fit quite nicely into my size-four skirt and was very muscular and firm from the five sets of squats I was doing every morning before the trial.

During our lunch break, Gloria Allred cautioned me. She said, "Okay, you have proven your point, but I don't want you to dress like that in the courtroom again. I love the outfit, but I want you to dress like this is a trial and not a dinner date."

"I know, Gloria," I said. "But I couldn't resist doing this just once, when I hear them saying over and over again how pregnancy makes someone unsexy."

She eyed me up and down. "I don't think they'll be able to keep a straight face and say that today."

After lunch, Nathan put the same scene back on the video monitor. "I want to ask you again, Mr. South," Nathan said, "if Hunter Tylo were walking backward like this and you saw her from the rear . . ." Nathan stopped speaking and turned back to the TV screen. "I'll take you through the scene and I'll show you."

The video began to play.

As if Nathan Goldberg might miss the scene, Frank yelled out in a panicky tone, "Stop right there! That's a full-figure shot. You can tell that she is not . . . This is a minor thing, but look how she comes into the scene. This is a thin woman coming up to the desk."

But the jacket Lisa Rinna was wearing in the scene draped in front of her stomach much like the jacket I was wearing. There I was in person revealing my stomach—bare skin—and still looking very sexy and "unpregnant."

"I want to ask you a question about that. Mr. South, when was this shot?"

"This was shot—I have to check my production schedule. In July."

"July second through July eleventh?"

"Yeah, something like that."

"Do you know what my client looked like on July second of 1996?"

I watched as the jury turned away from Nathan to Frank South with annoyed looks on their faces. Yeah, good question, their thoughts must have run. Let's hear it, Frank.

"No, I didn't," he said.

"Do you know whether she could have played it in July of 1996?"

"She was pregnant and getting heavy."

"Are you suggesting to this jury that my client today could not credibly play that scene?"

Pausing for a moment, he then blurted out, "Absolutely."

"Are you telling this jury that my client today could not portray a sexy woman on film?"

He squinted his eyes and spoke slowly, carefully choosing each word. "She could not play this character on film from the character we had planned."

As Frank South stumbled through these denials, I could tell that my leopard bra was turning into a Miracle Bra for our side.

"Now, Mr. South," Nathan said, "you indicated, I believe, yesterday that one of the things that you try to portray in this character is a very sexy character, right? Somebody who would take her clothes off in a minute, right?"

"Yes."

"Okay. Now, as a matter of fact, isn't it true that in the first eighteen episodes, including the sex scene, the one that culminates in the affair with Peter Burns, the character Taylor McBride never takes her clothes off for Peter Burns? Isn't that true?"

"No, it's not true," he said defensively.

"When did she take her clothes off for Peter Burns?"

"Later in the season, she walks into his office, removes what she's wearing, and sits on his lap and straddles him."

"That's in episode twenty, isn't it? That's after she first seduces him. Isn't that true?"

"Yes, and then other—"

"I'm talking about the episodes leading up to the seduction."

"Yes." He curled his fingers back into his palm and inspected his cuticles as if bored. "She presents herself in bikinis to him and—"

"I'm asking you, sir, isn't it true that at no time in the first eighteen episodes, including the scene where she seduces him, does she take her clothes off in front of him?"

"She took her clothes off. She started taking her clothes off—on the golf course, episode eighteen."

"Golf course?"

"She starts taking off her top with both hands crossed to either side," he said proudly.

"What does the viewer see?"

"We cut after we see a little midriff."

"So you see a little midriff. That's it?"

"I believe."

I could see the little wheels spinning inside his head, his self-congratulation as he came up with his answers.

"As a matter of fact," Nathan asked, "isn't it true that in the first twenty episodes of *Melrose Place* for the 1996-97 season, up to and including the time that my client had her baby, there were no scenes at all, ever, where she had to be in bed with Dr. Burns; isn't that right?"

"He threw her on a couch." His tone made the scene sound so violent it couldn't help but injure a pregnant woman. "He threw her on a couch. He also put her on top of a kitchen table inside a restaurant, pushing things aside, and made love to her there. She jumped him on a chair. Their sex was of the sort that was rambunctious enough to keep them from getting into a bed. They didn't have the respectable kind of relations until later. They used other places."

"But what you're talking about happened after my client gave birth to her baby, didn't it?"

He stammered a bit. "Not all of it, no." Then he smiled at the jury, trying to regain their confidence and to rebuild his.

"As a matter of fact, at the point that the 'Great Sexpectations' episode was filmed, that was the first time they had ever made love, right, in that episode, correct?"

He turned to the jury again as if wanting to help them understand the true situation. "Yes. Yes, that's the first time they actually made love, but . . ."

"That occurs in episode eighteen, correct?"

"That's correct."

"And episode eighteen, according to my schedule, was filmed between November the eighth and November the twenty-seventh?"

"That is correct."

"My client gave birth on November the twelfth, right?"

Frank South's face turned white. "I guess so." He looked to his attorney Mr. Waldo, knowing that he had just put both feet into Nathan Goldberg's trap.

"How much of a problem would it have been to change the timing of one—or modify the timing of *one*—episode?"

Resounding objections came from the defense table.

"Sustained," said the judge.

"Okay," Nathan said, "you don't have to answer that."

The most damning testimony of all came when Nathan elicited how the actual decision to fire me had come about. "Let's go back now to the decision to fire Ms. Tylo," Nathan said. "You've testified that on March 29 you had a conversation with Marv Dauer and then Aaron Spelling and also the network representative Craig Erwich, correct?"

"Yes, correct," Frank said, trying to cover his nervousness.

"Now, you've also indicated that as a result of these conversations a decision had already been made to replace Ms. Tylo, correct?"

"That's exactly right."

"How long did the deliberations among yourselves take?"

Frank tried to sound as casual as possible—ho-hum. "The conversations took place over a period of about two hours."

"Were any of these conversations lengthy? Longer than five, ten minutes?"

"Not longer than ten."

"So as a result of three or four ten-minute conversations, Hunter Tylo was fired within the space of two hours?"

He blinked a few times. "Essentially," he said.

At that point, the trial may have been essentially over, because for all Mr. Waldo's legal reasoning and the testimony of Spelling

Entertainment's legal representatives, Frank South's testimony proved that the decision to fire me had been made without reference to anything other than Spelling Entertainment's sheer convenience.

I searched Frank South's face for any sign of remorse. After all this, he might see how unfairly I had been treated. His blank look made him appear completely indifferent. I couldn't help wondering how he would feel if this had happened to his wife.

"A few final questions, Mr. South. After Hunter Tylo became pregnant in March of 1996 . . ."

"Yes." He shifted his weight from one side to the other. You could tell he wanted this over with.

"Was there anything she could have done to keep her job at *Melrose Place?*"

His body language screamed, *Are we done yet?* "In that year?"

"Yes."

"In that year, no." He looked as if this statement absolved him of all guilt.

"Okay. What if she had had an abortion? Could she have kept her job?"

His jaw dropped as if it would hit the witness stand. "You know, that is the most obscene thing I've ever heard. That is just obscene."

Bill Waldo rose. He just stood there, silent: His look was reminiscent of a deer paralyzed by headlights.

The judge said, "Mr. Waldo is standing. Are you objecting?"

"No, not at this time."

"Move to strike the witness's response, Your Honor," Nathan said. "I don't believe I had an answer to my question."

"I believe there was, Your Honor," Bill Waldo said, alive once more. "He didn't like the answer."

"The answer will stand."

"*God,*" exclaimed Frank South, shaking his head in dramatic disbelief.

All through Nathan's cross-examination of Frank South, I was cheering. That's exactly right, I thought, that's exactly right. Afterward, the press's attitude seemed to shift in my favor. They heard how quickly the Spelling people made their judgments and how their economic interests strictly biased their treatment of people. With his virtual demolition of Frank South, Nathan seemed to have made our case that Spelling Entertainment was only fighting to retain the ability to make decisions in regard to the employment of pregnant actresses without any consideration for the woman's real-life situation. My life meant nothing to them. The "wishing you much joy" phrase in my termination letter was there only to ease their consciences for what they had done to me. It was clear to everyone in the courtroom that for the defense, this whole case was about power and control.

24

I was recalled to the stand on December 4, because the defendants were able to persuade the judge that some of Nevin Dolcefino's and my statements about Spelling's willingness to negotiate were misleading. They put Spelling counsel Sally Suchil on the stand and had her walk the jury through the April 26 settlement offer—the offer that would have left me effectively unemployed during all of the 1996-1997 season. This offer had been excluded as evidence by a prior ruling but then readmitted on the basis of "impeachment"—as a means of proving that I had lied on the stand.

Ordinarily, settlement offers cannot be introduced into evidence at a subsequent trial. When Spelling made their settlement offer to my first attorney, Paul Gleason, they swore me to secrecy before I was allowed to look at the document. My lawyers indicated to me that a settlement offer and a negotiated compromise—like a rollover deal—were two different things. A true rollover deal—an arrangement whereby we would postdate the contract from July of 1996 to January 1, 1997—would not have come with the stipulation that I give up my right to pursue legal action. So in my mind, when I said that Spelling Entertainment hadn't contacted us from the date of my firing to the time of my going-away party for *The Bold and the Beautiful*, I was telling the limited version of the truth that was allowed by law. It turned out that I could have mentioned the contact between our attorneys, and I certainly wish I had.

By bringing the settlement offer in by way of the impeachment tactic, Bill Waldo and Linda Edwards proved they were canny attorneys. I knew as I took the stand that I had been set up to look like a liar and a money-grubber.

Linda Edwards was at her most prim and proper as she interrogated me, as though she were the headmistress of a girls' school reviewing the offenses of a bobby-soxer. She pointed out that I had testified earlier that from April 10, the date of the termination letter, until the first of May, when I had my going-away party at *The Bold and the Beautiful*, I hadn't received any communications from Spelling Entertainment. "It wasn't true, was it, Ms. Tylo," Ms. Edwards asked, "that during this period of time there was no response from Spelling?"

I knew what I had meant by a response and I knew what she was now identifying as a response and the two weren't the same, so I said: "That cannot be answered with a yes or a no. It's impossible."

"Move to strike that answer as nonresponsive, Your Honor," Linda Edwards said.

From her quick request for the answer to be stricken, I could tell she expected that she'd be granted leave to badger away at me some more. But the judge said, "I'm going to let that answer stand." (Judge Wasserman rarely let Ms. Edwards box me into a corner.)

Linda Edwards went on to quiz me about my reactions to various provisions in the settlement offer. She kept comparing the original contract for the 1996-1997 season to the settlement offer, whose terms applied mostly to the 1997-1998 season. Because the latter contract included slightly higher fees for similar episode cycles, she kept trying to make me say that the settlement contract would have been an improvement over the original contract.

One question would narrow the discussion down to our two different points of view. In order to get to it, Linda Edwards took me back through the terms of the settlement offer once more. "Ms. Tylo, I believe you characterized Spelling's settlement offer as throwing you crumbs, is that right?"

"Yes."

In a well-isn't-that-special tone of voice, she said, "I would like to just take a look at those crumbs." She turned around on her half-inch heel. "Before deciding that this offer was just crumbs being thrown at you, did you add up the total amount of dollars you would receive under the eight-episode guarantee in the settlement offer and compare it to what you would have received in the eight-episode guarantee in the contract?" She pulled out two chalk-boards and wrote out the figures of the two contracts and then asked me to subtract the figures her way. She thought she had me.

I stared at her, and then pointed at the two columns that she had carefully written out and said, "I looked at the difference between the '96 contract and what the settlement would have provided me in '96, which," I paused for dramatic effect, "was nothing. Zero." I looked over at the jurors. I could see several of them shaking their heads, as if to say, that's right, that's right.

"Move to strike the answer as nonresponsive," Ms. Edwards said, her lips pursed to a thin white line.

Judge Wasserman ruled, "The answer will stand."

My lawyers had estimated that the trial would take two weeks, but it had gone on for more than a month when Bill Waldo finally began his summation on December 12. He brought his wife to the courtroom that morning, something he never did, according to my attorneys. She was a stylish, nicely turned-out woman. I wondered why he brought her, especially as his indictment of my character became ever more strident. Did he think bashing me was something his wife could be proud of?

Bill Waldo returned again and again to his original line of argument. He argued that I was a spoiled celebrity asking for special privileges and preferential treatment.

Then he started calling me a liar and worse. "On November 13, Hunter Tylo was on the witness stand, and she was testifying about her last day on *The Bold and the Beautiful,* her going-away party in early May of 1996. 'I wanted to try to work it out,' she said. 'I felt in such a false position because I couldn't tell my colleagues what was going on.' At that point she broke down and cried uncontrollably.

"There's only one thing to remember about what you saw from the witness stand. It was a lie. It was a total lie. She knew it was a lie when she said it. Because what happened on December 3? Ms. Edwards showed Hunter Tylo on the witness stand a letter dated April 26, 1996, a letter written during the very period when she claimed no one from Spelling Television would contact her. She did have a response from Spelling, and she knew it, and she lied about it from the witness stand.

"Why would she lie about it? Why? It's pretty obvious why. Because she wanted ammunition for her legal ambush of Spelling Television."

Bill Waldo turned and moved toward me, with long, heavy strides. He pointed at me. "You're not doing this on behalf of anybody but you, Hunter Tylo. You filed the lawsuit for publicity. This lawsuit is not about anything but you, about gaining publicity and leverage for you."

Mr. Waldo turned back toward the jury. "Hunter Tylo comes into this courtroom and says she is a self-styled Christian and self-styled role model. And then Hunter Tylo lies from the witness stand. If Hunter Tylo, as a self-styled Christian and a self-styled role model, gets one penny after coming into this courtroom and lying, God help us all."

As Bill Waldo's summation became bruising, I stared at him, trying to make eye contact. I was giving him a look that said, "How can you stand there and twist the truth and call me a liar!" I could feel my face burn with anger . . . but then sadness overwhelmed me. I felt as if I had let God down, particularly when Mr. Waldo closed by implying that, just as I had "lied" on the stand, my faith was a lie, too. I was trying so hard not to cry. I looked down and the tears welled up anyway and spilled out. I felt like Mr. Waldo had made me look like a failure as a Christian, which was more damaging to me than any other line of attack.

As the jury filed out for their noon recess, I tried to look at them to see if they had believed Waldo.

They all looked down. I had to wonder if I had proved an embarrassment to them. Were they so disappointed in me that they couldn't look my way? They picked up their papers and bags and purses and methodically filed out.

I thought, Oh, my God, they believed him. My legs were weak. My legs were shaking and weak and it was all I could do to stand as they left the courtroom. My fears of how the whole ordeal might be affecting my pregnancy made it seem even worse.

Dolores put her arm around me, but I pulled away from her and walked straight through the little wood swinging door that separates the participants from the public seating and I rushed right into Michael's arms. I buried my head in his coat and I said, "Michael, help me." I could hear the whole Spelling defense team snickering and laughing.

"Get me out of here," I said to Michael. We went out of the courtroom, with the Spelling defense team close behind. When they reached the hallway, they started to roar, high-fiving and back-patting and declaring Bill Waldo's summation the best they'd ever heard. I quickly walked past, trying to get to the bathroom at the end of the hall.

I was shaking and becoming more concerned all the time for my unborn child, because I was so emotional.

I completely broke down in the rest room and I could hardly breathe. My breath came in short, fast puffs, and my crying became a high-pitched wail. I had already been having Braxton-Hicks contractions—the false labor that comes on in the last trimester. I was afraid the hard-clenching cramps I was now experiencing might be much more serious. I couldn't get past the feeling that I had let God down. That I hadn't represented myself as a Christian effectively but made my faith an object of scorn.

I was in the bathroom stall when I heard the clicking of Gloria Allred's heels. I knew the sound of her steps.

"Hunter," she said, "are you okay? Are you all right?"

A fan of mine who kept coming to the trial rushed in, too. She said, "Oh, Hunter, I'm so mad. I'm so upset for you. Those people are such jerks."

Of course, her comfort, however well meant, couldn't substitute for privacy. Gloria asked her to give us some time alone together.

Gloria began asking, then begging, me to come out of the stall.

"I don't want to see anybody. I can't come out."

"Hunter, please open the door. Please open the door."

Finally, I straightened up enough to come out, and she held me for a long time and didn't say anything at first. Then she said, "Hunter, that's the way they do it. That's the way it's done. I know it was hard, but that's what their job is. That's their job. We wouldn't have expected anything less."

"I don't think I could have taken anything *more*," I said, distraught.

"Nathan's going to come back," Gloria said. "Nathan's going to come back and fix it. He will tell the truth and everyone will know it."

When Nathan Goldberg began his summation, he quickly dispatched the worst of Mr. Waldo's accusations, explaining how I had been instructed and what I had meant by "not being contacted." He also pointed out that this tactic on the defense's part showed their total desperation. "When you don't have anything else to throw," Nathan said, "you might as well throw some mud and see if any of it sticks."

Nathan then used the most compelling tactic of all, talking straight, talking true. He admitted that it might have been more difficult for *Melrose Place* to work with a pregnant actress than a nonpregnant one. "But we have values that are in competition with one another," he said. "The prerogatives of an employer versus the rights of a woman at one of the most vulnerable times in her life, when she's pregnant. The question becomes: Does our culture have a compelling interest in extending its protections—extending ourselves, our capacity to care—to a woman in that situation?"

Nathan pointed out that in deciding this question the jury would act as the conscience of the community. The moral conscience of the community needed to be informed by the situation I found myself in.

"I would like you to consider," Nathan said, "Ms. Tylo's testimony that for a very brief instant, for a very brief moment, she even considered having an abortion because she was so upset about losing her career. Every time she has to look at her child, who's now a one-year-old, and for the next I don't know how many years, she's always going to feel just a little bit of shame and humiliation. There is no reason why she or any woman should ever be put in the position of having to choose between a career on the one hand and a family on the other."

As I listened to Nathan speak, I tried to look composed and professional. But then, without warning, without any shaking or labored breathing, tears began to flow once more. No sobbing, just a silent steady stream that would not stop.

"This case is at a crossroads between the past and future," Nathan said. "The future belongs to women's rights. The future belongs to my client. It doesn't belong to Spelling and these kinds of outmoded ways of thinking about women, the stereotypes, the degradation, the insults. That's the old way. The future is about equality. And every time one person's rights are interfered with, even this much, all of our rights are interfered with.

"Choose a path in this case. Choose a path that you can respect not only for today, but for tomorrow, and for next year, and for ten and twenty years from now."

25

When the case went to the jury, I thought my part was done. I looked forward to spending time with my family—my one-year-old, Izabella, for whom I had waged much of this fight, missed her mommy. It would soon be Christmas, the first Christmas Izabella would be aware of the tree and the presents and, in her own way, the mysterious spirit that causes people to celebrate at the darkest time of the year. I had become anxious, too, about Christmas gifts for family, as I had no time left for shopping or decorating.

After the last morning of Nathan's summation, Gloria, Dolores, Nathan, Michael, and I went to lunch at Otto's, the restaurant down the street from the courthouse to which we had all walked so many times in the past two months. By now, I knew the menu by heart. I usually had the grilled salmon or a salad, but today I felt like celebrating the end of the trial—to let the reins out a bit—and I ordered a cheeseburger and fries.

"So how long do you think the jury will take?" I asked my defense team. "Should I go on home and stay dressed to come back later today?"

"They may take more than today—or tomorrow," Nathan said, trying to conceal a grin.

"Then you'll just call me when they come back in, so I can be here for the verdict?"

Gloria glanced at Nathan and Dolores. "How important is this trial to you?" she asked.

I stared back, wondering why she was asking.

"The jury is going to be at work, all day, every day, until they reach a decision. They are giving up time from their jobs and families. They'll want to see you here, too. It's human nature."

"So I should come in, just as I have been doing? I still have shows to shoot for *B&B*. It's not *over* yet?"

"Bring your scripts and any other reading material," Dolores said. "You'll be popping into the courtroom mostly at the beginning and end of however many days it takes. Otherwise, you'll be waiting in the hall. Those hours can be long ones. Come prepared."

The first two days of waiting in the courtroom hallways were as long as any I've ever spent. I kept expecting to hear that the jury had reached a verdict. As the jury began making requests to review evidence, I realized we might be in for a much longer wait. I also became concerned that the jury might not be able to reach a verdict before Christmas, and in that case it might not reach a verdict at all, because many of the jury members could not be absent from their jobs indefinitely. Dolores explained that if we lost our jury due to time constraints, we might have to start over again in a second trial. The tenuous nature of everything we had already been through threatened to send me over the edge, I was so physically exhausted.

After two days of waiting, I couldn't take being away from Izabella anymore. Between the trial and taping episodes of *The Bold and the Beautiful*, I had been away from her for nearly six weeks. I was getting home so late that I could only give her a kiss as she slept. (There were many nights during this trial that I fell asleep praying over all three of my sleeping children, full of a mother's guilt.) At that time, Bella slept in until 8:30 or 9:00 A.M., and I had to be out of the house well before then; to my baby, I realized, it was as if I had been out of town. Earlier, my child-care worker expressed concerns about regressive behavior on Bella's part that could be a symptom of her separation anxiety.

I decided I would bring her to the courthouse and we could wait together. There was a department store down the street where we could have her picture taken with Santa at the lunch break—maybe fit in some Christmas shopping as well. This was the incentive I needed to go on, something to look forward to.

I dressed her up in a beautiful outfit Dolores had given her for her first birthday, a burgundy velvet dress with a lacy collar, its small iridescent sequins twinkling. Her outfit included a matching headband. She also wore the new black ballet slippers that she was learning how to walk in, prancing around like a little fawn on her toes. With her wispy little curls, big, blue eyes, and big, puffy lips, she was one beautiful little girl. (A mommy has a right to be proud.) We brought a big diaper bag full of supplies and blankets that I could spread out for Bella to take a nap on. We were ready to make a day of it.

As I was pushing Bella toward the courthouse in her stroller, I saw several members of the press standing by the front entrance. I changed direction and cut down a side street in order to go in another entrance. I wanted to protect my child's privacy.

The defense team, Bill Waldo, Linda Edwards, Cortez Smith, and Sally Suchil, walked past where Bella was playing in the courtroom hall several times. I noticed that Cortez Smith and Sally Suchil acted as if they were tempted to play with Bella and then restrained themselves. Bill Waldo and Linda Edwards looked at us much more severely, with expressions that could only be called contemptuous.

Soon, Dolores was called into the courtroom and then Nathan. The defense attorneys were constantly bringing new motions before the judge every morning—new evidence they wanted the jury to see or new spins on old reasons for the judge to dismiss the case. So I didn't pay any attention to what Dolores and Nathan were doing.

They stayed in the courtroom a little longer than usual, though, and Gloria went in to see what was up.

When she came back into the hall, I could tell she had disturbing news by the way her chin kept twisting to one side. "Hunter," she said, "the defense is bringing a motion before the judge. There's going to be a short hearing in a few minutes."

"About?"

"They want to get Bella thrown out of the courthouse."

"*What?*"

"They're arguing that you are doing this as a plea for sympathy from the jury. That it's prejudicial."

"What?? Can they do this? I just want to be with her. Please! I can't take this! Don't let them do this!"

"The judge has extremely wide discretionary powers. Yes, they can do that."

"Well, I don't care about any of this anymore. If they throw Bella out, then I'm going home, too. I need to be with her."

"Look," Gloria said, "I think what they're trying to do is ridiculous. But that's their case, isn't it? It's what they've done all the way along. They didn't want this baby to exist eighteen months ago and they want to pretend that she doesn't exist *now*. But I bet Nathan and Dolores can get the motion quashed. Dolores is completely disgusted. Wait and see how this turns out before you make any decisions. Calm down and come into the courtroom. You'll want to hear this."

I realized as Gloria said "they didn't want this baby to exist" that she had articulated the heart of the case. She had taken up what I had said earlier on the stand and what Nathan had reiterated to the jury. It took these repetitions for me to hear another question.

You fought so hard for Izabella, why didn't you fight for me?

26

The truth was, I had resisted a flood of memories for as long as I had been engaged in this fight, ever since I heard the words, *Do you think you are the first?* For the moment when I was fired from *Melrose Place* was not the first time I had felt that everything was at risk in my life, including a child of mine.

Years before, as a young mother, struggling to make ends meet, I had become pregnant again. I considered having an abortion, since I felt I couldn't possibly cope with a second child in my circumstances. I read the pamphlets given out by the women's clinic. The abortion procedure was described in matter-of-fact terms. As I read the pamphlets, I remembered that the counselor at the clinic had been thoroughly professional, never urging me to go through with the abortion, only putting the clinic forward as being there in case I needed it. The procedure would only last a couple of hours, she assured me, and then I would be home, with my life restored. I decided to go ahead with it.

When I awoke in the recovery room, though, cold, shaking, in tremendous, throbbing pain, I knew a devastating emptiness from which I would never recover. I heard young women all around me, crying, whimpering, as if they were voicing the cries of the babies they had lost. They were crying out for their own mothers. It was so awful; so heartbreaking. I wanted my mother, too. I also wanted what had been taken from me.

In what the nurses took to be delirium, I asked what they had done with the baby. Where was it? Could I see it?

I didn't want to see that, they assured me. They removed it immediately. It was already gone.

But I did want to see it. I felt—too late—the urge to protect what had been torn from my womb.

During the days that followed my abortion, I told myself, again, that I had only lost a mass of tissue. Probably God waited to slip the soul of my child into another child's body after it came out of the womb and took its first breath. I couldn't have done otherwise, I reasoned, because I was having trouble coping with one child. I *couldn't* have handled two. The child's father would not have been interested in helping—not really. I couldn't keep on with all the things I was doing to make my life and Chris's life possible. I couldn't have done otherwise. I couldn't. Over time I convinced myself.

I convinced myself so well that in the midst of filing a lawsuit to protect myself and other women from having to choose between family and career, I thought of this child I had lost only with the greatest reluctance and kept the actual memories of that event as far away, psychologically speaking, as possible. The pressure of those memories—the weight of that flood—felt as if it would have brought catastrophic destruction otherwise. I didn't want to think about it. I didn't want to remember.

Why didn't you fight for me?

At last, I couldn't resist the question. I would be facing it now through the length of the jury's deliberations and ever afterward.

I gathered up Bella's things and we went into the courtroom to hear whether Bella would be exiled.

Bill Waldo and Linda Edwards presented their argument that I had brought Bella to the courthouse in order to win favor with the jury. They said the jurors, as they went back and forth from the room in which they were deliberating, were smiling at Bella and in other ways paying her attentions that showed she should be removed.

Dolores grew red in the face, her nostrils flaring. She stood on her feet like a fighting hen protecting her own as she argued my side in turn. She pointed straight at Bill Waldo and Linda Edwards and said, "I am sick of the defense's attitude. They tried to pretend that this baby shouldn't exist when they fired Hunter and they want to pretend that she doesn't exist now. They want the jury to assume that this child doesn't exist. She does exist and she has every right to be here."

Judge Wasserman looked at Bill Waldo and Linda Edwards in a way that revealed her own displeasure. She looked at them in disgust. She said, "I am not going to ban this baby from this courtroom. Any person has a right to be in this courthouse, especially family members of the people who come before this court. The child is another family member and she has every right to be here. Mr. Waldo, Ms. Edwards, I will instruct the jury not to play with the child on their way in and out of the jury room. But she stays." She banged down her gavel.

Members of the press heard the judge's ruling. They asked Gloria if we would come out and discuss what had happened with them. I didn't want to go out and talk to the press. Gloria insisted. (Throughout the trial, she kept pointing out that more than the jury's verdict would count. We were also fighting to correct public perceptions and we had a responsibility to take advantage of opportunities to do so.) Gloria told me she would do the talking, but I should bring Bella out and stand at her side.

Before the microphones, holding Bella in my arms, I heard Gloria repeat our argument. The child had a right to exist.

Now my thoughts were totally on the child I had denied the right to exist. She could have been among us even then, watching her little sister take her first steps. Rushing past her in the hall. Taking her by the hand to the drinking fountain. As I thought of my lost child, as I envisioned her with us, the person she would have been, the place she would have occupied in the family, I received the judge's decision, the first of many verdicts that were to come in, and I knew my overwhelming guilt. I could almost feel the presence of this other child with Bella and me. I had sinned as grievously as anyone can against a child. She had a right to exist, too, and I had denied her life itself.

Through the remaining days of waiting for the jury's verdict, the child I aborted seemed always near. I kept bringing Bella to the courthouse and it was almost as if I could turn to this lost child and say, "Look at your sister walking. Isn't it cute the way she says, 'Bell-*la*,' with that musical accent on the last syllable? I know you love her, too."

At last, on December 22, on the one day when I didn't bring Izabella to the courthouse, the clerk stepped out into the hallway and informed us that the jury had reached a verdict. They would be coming back to the courtroom in about half an hour.

The jury had to make a number of decisions—their verdict sheet listed ten questions to which they had to answer yes or no. The first judgment was the most important, as it was based on whether I had been illegally discriminated against. The other questions addressed the issues of whether Spelling Entertainment had breached their contract with me. If they decided in my favor on the discrimination and contractual issues, then they had to figure out what compensatory damages to award—what amount of money would directly compensate me for the loss. They could also award punitive damages for the distress and emotional harm I had suffered as a result of Spelling's action.

As the jury filed into their places, after more than a week of deliberation, I watched them closely to see what they might have decided. No one smiled at me or made any other reassuring gesture. They simply looked relieved to have finished their task.

Judge Fumiko Wasserman cautioned all those in the courthouse against displaying emotion as the jury read their verdicts. "I'm going to inquire of the foreperson," Judge Wasserman said. "Has the jury arrived at a verdict?"

The woman who served as the foreperson said, "Yes, we have."

"Would you please hand the verdict," the judge said, "to my liaison."

The clerk took the papers from the foreperson, turned and faced us, and began the reading.

We, the jury in the matter of Tylo versus Spelling Entertainment Group, et al., find the following special verdict on the questions submitted to us:

Question number one: Did plaintiff prove that she fully performed or had the ability to perform all of her obligations as described in the contract?

The longest of pauses in my life ensued. Finally, the answer came:

Answer: Yes.

Question number two: Did defendants prove that they terminated the contract in accordance with its terms and/or in the manner authorized by the terms of the contract?

Answer: No.

Question number three: Did plaintiff prove that defendants breached the implied covenant of good faith and fair dealing by engaging in bad-faith conduct, separate and apart from terminating her contract?

Answer: Yes.

As the first "yes" came in, I looked at each member of the jury in turn and silently mouthed, "Thank you." They would answer almost every question in my favor, and award us nearly five million dollars in damages. As I quietly thanked the jury, I heard another voice, the voice of my unborn child. She was never closer to me than at that moment. As I had begun to realize during the previous week, my fight—the battle God gave me in this—had all along been waged as a form of retribution for her, and as an act of penance for me. The jury's verdict brought me back to the moment when I decided against her life. Now my fight for other lives like her own had ended in triumph, her triumph. Without my knowing it, my journey was a means for me to confront the worst thing I have ever done and for God to bring some good out of it.

Part Seven

27

The trial barely over, Michael and I had the joy of welcoming our fourth child, Katya Ariel, on January 15, 1998. We looked forward to enjoying the security of our family, free of embattled circumstances. We would be continuing with our work lives, of course, but I envisioned spending as much time as possible holding Katya in the nook of our sectional couch, with Michael beside me, and Bella, Mickey, and Chris around us. Home at last, safe and secure.

Katya was born with tons of sandy brown hair and blue eyes. She weighed seven and one half pounds. She hardly cried, but would coo peacefully as she lay on my breast.

Then, about two weeks after she was born, her temperament seemed to change. At night, she would wake us with shrill, piercing screams. The other kids started calling her Screechy. Her poor sleeping habits soon exhausted me. I couldn't stay up all night with the baby and then walk, talk, and hit my mark on the *B&B* set the next day. Michael was kind enough to take over the night shift and walk the floor with Katya until Tylenol let her fall back asleep. (We thought tummyaches were the culprit.)

I was so tired after the trial and the birth that for the first couple of weeks I kept the Sabbath at home, listening to our church service on the radio and reading my Bible. On February 7, we all went to church again as a family. I dressed Katya up in her jammies, with a bow-decorated headband, and put her in the car seat that doubled as a carrier.

We sat in the first row of the "cry section" at Church on the Way, a set of pews toward the back. As we sang and prayed with the congregation, Katya fell asleep, her bottle falling from her lips.

Our pastor, Jack Hayford, was preaching on "Kingdom Vision." He compared kingdom vision to those 3-D pictures that at first glance seem to consist of nothing but color swirls. If the viewer concentrates on a specific point of focus, eventually an image snaps into place. Understanding our lives from God's point of view was similar; events that seem merely chaotic or purposeless come together into a unified whole when seen from God's perspective. We are called to see our lives in this perspective by the light of the Scriptures and God's conversation with us through conscience and prayer.

As Dr. Hayford spoke, the lights in the congregation were dimmed and the spotlights on the altar, the cross behind it, and the plants on either side shone brightly. It so happened that the spotlight on the cross reflected right into Katya's eyes. When she stirred and awoke, I looked down into her sweet face. I could see that the reflection from the spotlight made her right eye look red, the way the reflector on the back of a bike looks red or the way a dog's eyes look red in a photograph taken with a flashbulb.

What is that? I wondered. That wasn't right. The other eye looked normal. I wondered, of course, whether the slight difference in the angle of her face in relation to the light was creating an illusion, but I didn't think so. The red specter of her eye troubled me. I would make sure that the doctor checked her eyes at her next well-baby appointment.

At the end of February, I became ill, running a temperature of 102 degrees. All of the placenta hadn't been delivered with the afterbirth; the tissue had become infected and my cervix was still slowly hemorrhaging. I had to take horse-pill-sized antibiotics and go to bed. So I had to miss Katya's next wellness appointment in early March, but I made sure that Michael asked about Katya's eye.

Our pediatrician, Dr. Karp, wanted Katya to see a specialist in pediatric ophthalmology. He told us not to worry, but that we should keep the appointment for the first week of April. But work-related matters intervened, and the appointment was moved to April 14.

During the two weeks before the appointment, I became increasingly disturbed about Katya's eye. I noticed that it didn't follow objects moving in front of her, as her other eye did. It also appeared to bulge slightly. Katya had become even more cranky, and we would never have made it through the nights of March, 1998, if Michael's sister Teri hadn't come into town and helped out with the night shift.

In my Bible reading, I kept encountering passages about the "day of trouble" and times of distress. As much as I tried to ignore God's promises to walk with me through fire or flood—because I really had no intention of revisiting any "day of trouble" so soon after the trial—I couldn't escape the feeling that I was being warned.

Still, I tried to carry on with all the usual Easter activities and placed baskets chock-full of goodies outside the kids' doors before they awakened. I loved watching Izabella enjoy her first Easter egg hunt.

That night, I was holding Katya on the couch, Michael beside me, as we watched *The Greatest Story Ever Told*. At the climactic scene of the crucifixion, with Jesus in agony, I looked down at Katya. Even though there was a light shining behind us, her right pupil was big, dilated, while the other looked normal.

I said, "Oh, Michael, something is really wrong with the baby's eye. Look, see how the pupil's dilated. That's not right. Something is wrong."

Michael tried to keep me calm. "I see what you see. I'm just not going to think like that. I'm not going to court disaster. There's no reason to."

I couldn't help obsessing about the matter. I wondered if a muscle had become detached. They would be able to reattach the muscle, but that meant my baby would undergo surgery and I didn't want that.

I thought I would go to work for half a day before our Tuesday appointment, but Monday morning I began to feel increasingly oppressed. I decided finally that concentrating at work on Tuesday morning would be out of the question, so I called Brad Bell, Jr., to tell him I wouldn't be at work the next day. I reached his home answering machine. My message started off calmly enough, but by its end I began to cry and I confessed, "I don't know if she's blind." That's the first time I had said it, and doing so made me realize how profoundly wrong I sensed the situation might be.

That night I woke up about 2:00 A.M. with the urge to read my Bible. I found the passage in John 9 in which Jesus is asked about a man born blind from birth. Did his own sin or the sin of his parents cause this disease? "Neither this man nor his parents sinned," Jesus said, "but this happened so that the work of God might be displayed in his life."

I knew I had been directed to this passage. God was trying to comfort me. Although Katya might have been "born blind" in some sense, Michael and I were not to blame ourselves. God had allowed this unfortunate circumstance, but He would bring good out of it. The works of God would be displayed through Katya's life somehow.

My understanding of this message didn't mean I was willing to receive it. I fell to my knees and began begging God not to let Katya suffer in this way. If God cared enough to tell me about what might be happening in her life, He could certainly care enough to heal her. I didn't understand how a loving God could possibly let such an innocent child suffer. The suffering of the innocent had no place in my Christian thinking. I loved the Old Testament passages that showed how those obeying God's commandments would receive His blessings, and those who disobeyed would receive His curses. I could understand this in practical terms. As long as I had been living a life without paying attention to God, I had suffered

the consequences. Once I turned my life over to God, my life became better—my marriage was healed, and even the wrong done
to me by Spelling Entertainment had brought about a greater justice. These things made cause-and-effect sense. I didn't understand
why God would allow my child to go blind. In fact, I sometimes felt
that people who suffered from major illnesses might be responsible for their own sickness. They had probably offended God in
some way. But Katya simply couldn't have. And God was telling me
that neither Michael nor I was responsible. That was one of the
kindest, most loving things my Creator could have possibly
done—to relieve my fear of blame.

I remembered the movie from the previous evening, the scene of
the crucifixion. Jesus seemed to be saying to me, "Don't you know
that's the way I work? I am a God of suffering. I accept disaster—
even crucifixion—and bring good out of it."

I knew God was telling me this, but I didn't want to hear it. I
continued to beg that Katya be all right. I noticed that Jesus healed
the man born blind from birth, making a paste from his spittle and
dirt, applying it to his eyes, and telling the man to go wash in the
pool of Siloam. Why didn't I feel that God was going to heal Katya in
the same way? I searched the Scriptures for additional answers and
found none. I finally fell asleep, exhausted, weary, heartbroken.

The next day, however, as I began to dress Katya in a tie-dyed
shirt, jacket, and leggings, I felt much more hopeful. Chris was going to come to the appointment with us. Afterward, we would pick
up Mickey and all go out for a family dinner at a Mexican restaurant. We were going to make this a fun afternoon. I was wearing a
"God Is in Control" baseball cap. Everything would be okay.

The waiting room at the doctor's office was filled with troubled
parents and their children with vision problems. Many wore thick
eyeglasses. Through the transparent nurse's window, I could see a
dad cradling an infant who was hooked up to an IV. I wondered if
I could possibly cope with the problems they were experiencing.

When we were called and Dr. Borchert appeared at the examination room door, he reminded me immediately of Harrison Ford

in *The Raiders of the Lost Ark* film, in which Ford appears as a bow-tied professor. The doctor's hair was a shade darker, but he had the same good looks.

The doctor began the appointment by asking me a series of questions, first about what I had seen. I told him about Katya's eye flashing red.

"Did it look like there was a piece of glass under the lens?" he asked.

Then he questioned me about my pregnancy and my family history. Had the pregnancy been stressful?

"You could say that, yes," I said, thinking of the trial. "Do you think that my stress might have something to do with the baby's condition?"

He didn't. He was obliged to ask a series of basic questions, the answers to which could be used for research purposes later. A nurse was going to come in and put some drops in Katya's eyes to dilate them. He'd be back.

When he returned, Dr. Borchert used a common handheld light to look into Katya's eyes. He wasn't in the examination room more than two or three minutes. He told us he'd be back and disappeared somewhere.

He returned with a bigger handheld light box. When he looked into her eyes this time, he told us he was seeing something on the back of the retina. Then he disappeared once more.

The third time he came in, he had on a headset that made him look like a *Star Wars* warrior. His mood had changed, becoming more determined; he was now a man on a mission. He sat on a stool and looked once more into Katya's eyes through his headset contraption. He began mumbling to himself. "Mmm-hmm," he said. "Mmm-hmm. Yes. Okay. Mmm-hmm. That's it. Okay."

After looking into the baby's eyes, he gave Katya to Michael and turned to the exam room's small writing desk and began making notes. I was terrified by this time, of course. What was he seeing? Why the ever-more-sophisticated apparatus? He continued to do his paperwork for another ten minutes.

Then he wheeled around to Michael and me. He caught my eye and looked down. He looked over at Michael, saw he had his attention, and looked down. His manner said: I'm going to tell you something you don't want to hear.

Before he spoke, he reached over and gently touched Katya's forehead and traced her eyebrow and the bone around her eye. "Little Katya," he said, "has tumors in her eyes."

As I exhaled, I felt my own life rush out. It felt like every bone in my body had snapped at once. "What? What?" I asked.

"I'm sorry."

Michael's eyes welled up and he clutched Katya to him.

Chris didn't say a word. He opened his arms and let me fall into them. I tried to remember the Bible passages I had been reading, what God had been saying, but that wasn't good enough. Not at the moment.

Once I had taken the initial shock, I asked, "What about surgery? Can you fix it?"

"This has to be taken care of and soon," Dr. Borchert said. "Katya will probably be having surgery, but I'm not sure of what type yet."

"You can take the tumors out?"

"No, taking the tumors out would cause them to spread. We'll have to rely on chemotherapy."

"It's cancer?" I asked.

"I'm sorry, yes. It's cancer. It's called retinoblastoma. And it is life-threatening." He began to explain that the tumors were located around and on top of the optic nerve and that they could spread from the optic nerve into the brain.

Had they spread already?

"I don't know—she'll need an MRI immediately," Dr. Borchert said. "This is an extremely rare condition—it's the only cancer we know of that starts in the mother's womb. The tumors are worse in the eye you've noticed problems with. Eighty percent of the retina in that eye is covered and it's right on the optic nerve. She also has six tumors in her other eye."

The bad news kept coming like so many powerful blows. "We

have to start treatment, then," Michael said. "We have to save her life. That's the important thing."

The doctor nodded. "Unfortunately," he said, "the man we need, Dr. Murphree, has just had a heart attack."

Could this become more bewildering? "Well, can't you . . ."

"The good news is he has been training a fine young doctor, Dr. Tim Stout, and he'll be available to start the treatment. Dr. Murphree is expected to recover and as the treatment continues he'll probably be available to assist. I can tell you that Children's Hospital Los Angeles, where we work, is one of the finest centers in the world for this type of treatment. Katya will be given the best resources available."

Dr. Borchert asked us to wait in a private office while he went about setting up our first appointments. He was ordering an MRI for Katya tomorrow, along with a battery of other tests.

As we walked to this other office, we could see again the waiting room. I had felt so sorry for the people there; now I realized that Katya was probably the most desperately ill child of all. Once inside, we gave the baby to Chris. Michael and I fell into each other's arms.

"Mommy, Mommy, Mommy," Michael said, "I'm so sorry."

"Oh, Daddy, what are we going to do?"

"You can't lose your faith," Michael said. "Please, Hunter, don't lose faith. We're going to need all the strength we can find."

We held each other for a while longer. "I think I'd like to call Carla," I said. "Would you mind?" He thought that would be a good idea.

I offered to use my calling card, but the office manager let me have a long-distance line. Everyone had become aware of the diagnosis and how we must be feeling.

As soon as Carla answered the phone, I fell apart, crying out, "Please pray for us, Carla." I told her the doctor's diagnosis and she cried with me.

Carla said, "You have to remember that God did not do this. God is the author of life. He allows evil, but he does not create it. He is standing with you against this evil. He's there for you."

As much as I believed this, I couldn't feel its force. I asked Carla to help me pray for strength and wisdom.

She prayed for strength, for courage, for wisdom, and that Jesus would stop every evil force coming against Katya and her parents.

"You know what the Scriptures say," Carla added. "'If any of you lacks wisdom, he should ask God, who gives generously to all without finding fault, and it will be given to him' [James 1:5]. Which is a way of saying," Carla went on, "that God will get you through this. You only have to believe it. He *will*."

Dr. Borchert talked with us again and explained the hospital appointments he had set up. He told us there were going to be so many doctors' appointments over the next few days that I should buy a new appointment book to keep everything straight. The schedule would be so busy that we both would have to take off from work for the rest of the week. Or two weeks, if that was possible.

"Should I have my mom come?" I asked. "She'd have to fly in from Dallas, but I'm sure she would if we need her." I felt in asking the question that his reply would help me gauge how rough the course of treatment would likely become.

"Yes," he said, "if she's available, have her come. You should make every use of your support networks."

When we came back home, I called my mother. "Mom, can you come here? We've had some bad news."

"Oh, honey," she said, "it's not the kids, is it? It's not Michael?"

"It's Katya."

"Not the baby. Has something happened to the baby?"

"Mama, Katya has tumors in her eyes."

I heard my mother gasp and then it sounded as if she'd dropped the phone.

My stepfather came back on the line. "Honey, are you okay? Wait, here she is, here's your mom."

"Mama, I'm so scared. Please come! I don't know how to get through this!"

"I'll come right away," she said. "I'll be there before the day's through."

We spoke about two o'clock and my mother was in Los Angeles before 8:00 P.M. She stayed up with me for several hours—most of the night, really. I was tremendously afraid of Katya's being put under general anesthesia—a possibility Dr. Borchert had raised. My mother, a nurse, calmed my fears. She told me again of Children's Hospital's outstanding reputation. They put children under general anesthesia every day. I shouldn't worry. She would be there to make sure Katya had the benefit of every possible medication.

I wanted to know if cancer ran in the family somehow. I knew that my cousin's son had been diagnosed with neuroblastoma—a form of childhood cancer. The two diseases turned out to be unrelated, although I was aware of what my cousin's family had been going through, how hard it had been on them.

Even with my mother with me, I felt that I had entered into a room—a prison—in which no one could come with me. I felt locked away from the world of common happiness by my daughter's serious illness. Would she die? Would she be completely blinded? Blindness seemed one of the most difficult handicaps, more isolating than restraints on a person's mobility. She'd be walled in forever by darkness.

I didn't sleep much that night and I turned again to my Bible. I was drawn to a verse in Isaiah 42: "I will lead the blind by ways they have not known, along unfamiliar paths I will guide them; I will turn the darkness into light before them and make the rough places smooth. These are the things I will do; I will not forsake them."

All right, I said to God, but I don't want this to last more than two weeks. Please, God, okay?

Early the next morning, Michael, my mom, and I took Katya to the hospital. We hadn't been able to give the baby anything after ten o'clock. She had missed three feedings and was screaming from hunger. The bright lights of the hospital scared her, making her even more restless. As we waited for the MRI test to be performed, we kept hearing other children being treated close by. They were begging, "Stop it! Stop it! Stop it! Mommy, make them stop! Mommy!" We had descended into hell.

My mom suggested the nurse give Katya a pediatric anti-anxiety drug that could be administered orally. The nurse was happy to do so. "It's such a short test, but if you like," she said. After giving Katya the drug, which greatly calmed her, the nurse put an IV in Katya's foot. (I promised her, foolishly, that she would never have to go through that again.) I put on a lead apron and followed her into the MRI laboratory. The bed of the MRI machine rolled in and out of the central cavity a number of times during the fifteen-minute test. I read some psalms and sang lullabies to Katya while this went on.

As my mother and the doctors promised me, Katya recovered quickly from the test. She seemed largely unfazed.

At mid-morning, Michael brought Chris and Mickey from school to the hospital; the doctors wanted to perform an eye exam on each family member, especially Mickey and Izabella, since as younger children they were more vulnerable. Mickey acted up throughout the day: He was bored, he wanted to leave, he wanted to go to McDonald's, why didn't they have any videos? He couldn't voice his unease at what was happening, so he made us uneasy.

Dr. Tim Stout performed our eye exams, and then checked Katya one more time. He sat us down in his conference room. The rest of the family members were fine. We had perfectly healthy eyes, with terrific eyesight. The MRI, though, had shown that Katya's condition was as serious as Dr. Borchert feared. Dr. Stout used both a map of the eye and a 3-D model to explain the placement of the tumors.

The next day there would be more tests. Then, on Friday morning, they wanted to put Katya under general anesthesia and do a thorough eye exam. If they found the tumors in her right eye were endangering her life, they would have to perform an enucleation—removal of the eye. We should be prepared to sign permission forms.

"But then you can find a donor to give her another eye, can't you? Look," I said, pointing at the 3-D model, "you can reattach the muscles and hook the new eye up to her optic nerve." Even as I said this, I knew I was talking nonsense. I knew science was far from being able to perform eye transplants.

Dr. Stout patiently explained that more than two million nerve endings would have to be reconnected. Medicine still didn't really know how the eye worked; it was mostly a mystery, even to geniuses in the field like Dr. Borchert. For years, Dr. Borchert had been doing research on transplants, showing what an incredibly complex organ the eye is.

As Dr. Stout continued his explanations, I kept seeing Katya with her eye sewn shut, or with an open wound where her eye should be.

I found these images so horrifying that I became belligerent. "I don't know if I'll give permission. You're the first doctor we've seen. Maybe we should get a second opinion."

"We know this is difficult," Dr. Stout said. "We want you to feel as comfortable as possible. If that requires a second opinion, that's fine. But every day counts now, you understand that?"

What Michael wanted to know was, "Will she live? Is she going to be okay?"

"If we have to remove her eye," Dr. Stout said, "there's still a good chance that she'll live. And that we can maintain some of the sight in her other eye. The mortality rate from this disease is now less than twenty percent."

"Honey," Michael said, "these doctors are the best. Everyone's told us that. They wouldn't be saying these things if they weren't true. They're trying to spare her life."

I knew Michael and the doctor were right; but I still didn't know if I could *stand* them being right.

Before we left the doctor's office, his nurse told us that we had an appointment with a counselor, Nancy Mansfield, the next day at 10:30 A.M.

I didn't see why we needed counseling. We knew what was happening.

The nurse said, "Well, you don't have to go. But I know the doctor would strongly advise you to keep this appointment. Nancy works with all our retinoblastoma families. The doctor very much wants you to go."

We promised we would, but I was still thinking I might blow the appointment off, until Nancy Mansfield called us herself that evening.

When we returned home from the hospital, we saw that Marv had been calling. By Wednesday afternoon, he had received as many as fifteen phone calls from *Hard Copy, Inside Edition,* local TV news shows, and publications, asking about Katya. The TV and print tabloids put a reportorial gun to our heads. They told us they had heard Katya was dying, and they were going to run with the story whether we chose to comment or not. They only wanted to give us a chance to correct or fine-tune their information.

I didn't want any of these people interfering in what the family was going through. This wasn't any of their business. It was more than unfair; it was cruel. Marv agreed, but at the same time he let us know that the tabloids meant business. They were going to run with the story. Michael advocated putting out a press release to clear the air and make sure the facts as we knew them were reported accurately. I couldn't see telling anybody anything.

I spent most of Wednesday night in prayer. It was either prayer or a bottle of Jack Daniel's. I knew what that led to, though, and I hung on to God's promises that He would never leave us or forsake us. That nothing could separate us from God's love. I kept praying that Katya would be healed. Despite all we had been told, I kept asking God to spare my baby from any more ill effects of retinoblastoma; I prayed that the surgery would be found unnecessary; that she wouldn't have to go through chemotherapy; that as the man born blind from birth had his vision restored, so Katya would have hers restored.

On Thursday, Michael, Katya, and I went to our appointment with Nancy Mansfield. I have to admit that I was steeling myself to resist what I suspected would be her secular spin. I was praying that Katya would be healed and doing my best to believe it, and I didn't want someone who couldn't believe in miracles to steal my hope.

Nancy greeted us in her small but comfortable office. The first thing she told us was, "I want you to know that I'm a cancer survivor. I was diagnosed with breast cancer ten years ago. There's no sign of it today. People—children—can recover from cancer."

She was sharing her experience, so I would share mine. "And we want you to know that we are Christians. We are praying that God will work a miracle in Katya's life. I'm a little uncomfortable with this counseling. I mean, I don't know what to expect. I don't want anyone to be negative about what might happen here. God can heal Katya. She's going to get better."

"I'm sure Katya will get better," Nancy said. "And I respect your faith. We see faith work wonders in this hospital all the time."

I wondered how much she meant this; whether she was only trying to appease me.

"I want you to know that Katya is in the best of hands," Nancy said. "We have babies here from Rome, from France, from Indonesia. People come from all over the world with their children to this hospital."

Michael said, "Everyone's been telling us that. If this had to happen, we're glad that we live here."

"The doctor has explained to you, hasn't he, about the exam he'll perform on Friday under general anesthesia? It's important for you to be on time. The OR is always heavily booked, and staying on time is crucial."

"We understand," I said.

"If the doctors find that enucleation of one or both of Katya's eyes is necessary to save her life, they will ask you to sign a paper giving them permission to do that."

"Yes, Dr. Stout told us that yesterday."

"I know he did," she said, her voice softening. "We want you to be prepared."

"We already know what might happen," I said, snappish. "We're not going to grieve before it does, though. Isn't that okay?"

"That's fine." Nancy reached down to a stack of papers she had by her chair. "I want to share a book with you. We're going to look at this book together and then discuss it."

She handed us a book called *My Fake Eye*. It had a six-year-old girl on the cover.

"Can you guess which eye isn't real?" Nancy asked.

At first glance I knew. "Sure. The right eye. I don't want to look at this now. Why should we?"

"As I said, Hunter, we want you two to be prepared."

I sat there for probably a full minute looking at the floor. "You're telling me that Katya's eye is going to be enucleated. Why don't you come right out and say it? Why all these games?" I was becoming increasingly angry.

Nancy took a breath. "We *don't* actually know. That's why I can't say. It's still important to think about what might happen beforehand. If we have bad news, you'll be able to handle it much better."

"I'm sorry," I said. "I just refuse to do this." I gave Nancy back her book and then looked down at Katya in my arms. Her right eye was bulging unmistakably.

I felt such intense pain that I couldn't hold her anymore and gave her to Michael. I thought of Katya as a third-grader, the other kids taunting her. I thought of her as a teenager, turning to look at a boy she had a crush on and his turning quickly away, offended, frightened, repulsed. I thought of her not being with us at all. I stood up and walked away from the chair, my face in my hands, crying.

Michael came over to me. He tried to comfort me. I felt drenched in this sorrow, heavy with it.

After a while, Michael needed to go to the rest room. "Hunter, honey, can you take the baby back? I need to slip out for a moment."

"No!" I screamed. "I can't hold her now. I can't."

"I will," Nancy said. "You go on." Nancy took the baby from Michael and began walking with her around the room.

I looked over at Nancy holding my child. "You know how I feel?"

I asked. "I feel like I'm locked up in a room, on the other side of the door from everyone else who's normal. No one else wants to come into this room and they shouldn't. No one else can. You have to be put here against your will."

Nancy nodded.

"I want you to know that I'm never going to accept this. I mean, *never!*"

"You don't have to," Nancy said.

"Good," I said, in an ugly voice.

"You only have to find your own way of dealing with it."

For the next hour and a half, Nancy went on talking with us about how we might come to deal with it. I finally let her take us through the *My Fake Eye* book, and then she helped us write a press release about Katya's illness. She agreed with Michael that not saying anything would only make the media's interest spiral higher. The press release gave as many of the facts as we knew about Katya's illness and included our belief that God works all things for good for those who love God.

At that moment, I realized that even though I still believed this it didn't take away the pain. I was coming to see that my faith, however real, didn't exempt me from the common human condition and wasn't meant to—it worked on another level, changing how we deal with such adversity and how God uses such adversity to change us. Of course, right then I was only sensing these things in the midst of my anger and sorrow. I couldn't have articulated them.

By Thursday evening, Michael's parents came with his sister Terry. They were devastated. Our friends gathered in our home to pray for Katya. One of my close friends in the business, Scott Baker, was there, along with his pastor from a Baptist church in Chatsworth. Our prayers that evening brought me a comfort that extended through the night and into the next day.

The next morning, April 17, 1998, Michael, my mother, Michael's mother, father and sister and I took Katya to Children's Hospital for her 6:00 A.M. appointment. She was to be examined in the main operating room, and, as Nancy had warned us, a pool of people—parents, children, teams of doctors and nurses—gathered in the OR preparation areas, awaiting their time slots. Again we heard children crying out to be helped, to make them stop, to be taken away from there. I realized that this happens every day. Every day people are suffering like this and I had been blind to it. My prayers were with the other families, even as I prayed for my own sweet baby.

Dr. Stout came out to us and took Katya in to be examined. Michael and I went out on the lawn. Despite the impending news, I felt calm. I wasn't frantic. I knew that we were doing the right thing—the best thing for Katya.

After twenty minutes, we wandered back to the OR waiting area. Dr. Stout came out and asked Michael and me to come into a consultation room. He asked us to wait there for a moment; he needed a chart.

From his manner, Michael and I both knew what we would hear. There wouldn't be good news. This was going to go on.

When the consultation room's door opened, two little girls and a woman who must have been their mother came in. The girls, one about six, the other eight or nine, were dressed in their school clothes. Nancy Mansfield came in after them. "I have someone for you to meet," she said.

The younger girl, wearing transparent-rimmed glasses, her hair in pigtails, a mat of freckles across her cheeks and a cute upturned nose, came right up to me. "I'm Amy," she said. "Can you guess which one is my real eye?" she asked.

I looked at the girls, at their mother. They were there to comfort me, I knew. When Amy turned her eyes to the extreme right or left, her prosthetic eye didn't quite follow. Otherwise, she looked perfectly normal—and quite beautiful. The most beautiful of all the little girls in the world right then. I swallowed hard and said, "I don't know. You're so beautiful. Both of you girls are just so beautiful."

"We're here today," their mom said, "because I sat right where you are sitting six years ago. The girls wanted to come in to show you that the future can be bright."

"I can do anything," Amy said. "I go swimming, I ride my bike. We went to the beach the other day, and I got sand in my fake eye. I took it out, rinsed it, and put it back in. It's no big deal."

After initially being overwhelmed by emotion, I wanted to ask a thousand questions. Did Amy feel sad about losing her eye? Did she have trouble with her schoolwork?

She had only one problem. She had to wait for her sixteenth birthday before the doctors could align her prosthetic eye perfectly with the other. "By the time Katya is sixteen," she said, "the doctors will be even better at it. They'll be able to do even more things."

Out of the mouths of children, I thought—more truth than I had been able to grasp.

We said good-bye to Amy and her family. We thanked them. We will never forget what they did for us that day.

Dr. Stout came in. Yes, he said, they were going to remove Katya's eye. He told us that older children who had been in an accident and had gone through the same procedure remarked on how painless it was. There would be little blood. We signed paper after paper. The operation would take one hour. They would be putting in a Port-A-Cath—a hookup for IVs—near her heart, in order to facilitate her chemotherapy.

When Dr. Stout left us, Michael and I took a moment and prayed together. We accepted the course of treatment as God's decision. We knew that God often gives compensatory gifts for unjust losses, and we asked for that to be the case with Katya, that God would bring some great unexpected good out of this loss.

Michael and I walked through the hospital grounds during the hour it took for the surgery to be performed. We stopped in the gift shop, where I bought a cross. I thought to use it as a bookmark, but ended up wearing it through Katya's chemotherapy treatments. It's a simple cross, but I still wear it sometimes, because of the day when it was purchased.

When we needed to come back to the OR to stay with Katya in the recovery room, I started becoming anxious. What would she look like in the bandages? Would her whole head be swathed? Would there be blood?

She wore only a light blue compress bandage with a bottle-cap-shaped screen right over the eye socket. Her face was swollen, her lips puffy. Her hands were already searching as she struggled to come up from the anesthesia. "What have you done to me?" her gesturing hands said.

I started to give her a bottle. The nurse warned me not to feed her too much. The anesthesia might make her throw it up. My mom suggested that an anti-nausea drug called Zofran be given. As a result, Katya was able to drink the whole bottle and keep it down. Soon, she was wide awake and playing with the nurses. A tremor went through her body from time to time, showing the trauma. Otherwise, she bounced right back. The courage she demonstrated was far greater than my own.

28

The next day, Michael and I took Katya to meet with Dr. Murphree, the recent heart-attack victim who courageously returned to work to oversee Katya and other babies' treatment. Dr. Murphree is a true warrior against retinoblastoma; he loves his patients and hates the disease that afflicts them.

Dr. Murphree examined Katya's remaining eye, and then on a computer screen showed us a photograph of her retina. He pointed out the location of the six tumors. They looked like large egg whites on the medical photograph. He said they were actually only the size of a pinhead, except for one, which was the size of a lima bean.

That next week, they would begin chemotherapy treatments. First, Dr. Murphree would aim a laser beam at the tumors, not to remove them but to heat them up. The active agents in chemotherapy seek out rapidly growing cells, which is why patients' hair falls out and their stomach lining deteriorates. The chemotherapy drugs, however, have a difficult time finding such rapidly growing cells in the eye. Heating the tumors would signal the drugs to attack them.

Then Dr. Murphree asked us an unexpected question. "How did Katya sleep last night?"

We realized that she had slept soundly for the first time in months. Her "screechy" personality disappeared with the surgery. We explained to him about her formerly troubled sleep.

"That's what I expected. She had so much glaucoma—so much pressure—in her eye, she must have had tremendous headaches. The surgery relieved her of those, at least."

We would soon be meeting four new doctors, our oncologists, who, with Dr. Murphree's guidance, would be administering the chemotherapy. Katya would be receiving three courses of treatment, an IV drip given for two consecutive days every three weeks.

We were able to leave the hospital at midday. A photographer was waiting and snapped our pictures, photos that turned up in the tabloids almost immediately. From Thursday on, we had started hearing news reports about Katya—the "$4.9 million baby who is now tragically ill." Actually, of course, it was Bella who caused me to be fired from *Melrose:* She was the "$4.9 million baby." These reports nearly drove me crazy, except that I was grateful for the usual ending: "We wish Hunter and her daughter the best in their current fight."

Real friends were also rallying. Matthew Ashford from *Days of Our Lives* called to let me know that six months ago his daughter had also been diagnosed with retinoblastoma. Her eyes had been spared enucleation. But they were still going through the horrors of chemotherapy and constant eye exams. They were there for us. It meant a lot to hear from someone else locked into the prison of a child's serious illness.

The fatigue of the traumatic week finally hit me on Saturday afternoon. I took a long nap. At the end of my rest, I had an unusually vivid dream: a dream that seemed cinematic in its realism. I was in an ornate Victorian room, with carved wood columns and paintings and tapestries on the walls. A man was seated in a throne-like chair. He was wearing an elegant suit—maybe a tuxedo—and he had a white ascot around his neck and ruffled, lacy cuffs. I couldn't see his face. My attention was drawn repeatedly to his hands, gripping the ends of the chair's armrests, and his lacy cuffs. Then I did see his face. He was strikingly handsome. He snapped his fingers.

Six guards, two before and four behind, accompanied a servant into the room who was carrying a lidded silver serving dish. The servant went down on one knee and presented the tray to his master.

The elegant man lifted the lid. Within the dish rested Katya's eye. The elegant man looked at me to gauge my reaction. He smiled, mocking me, then laughed.

I woke up shaking, sweating, terrified. Why couldn't God protect me from at least this?

My mother took care of Katya that night, allowing me to sleep. I couldn't. I was thinking of all the work I had to catch up on—my stacked-up scripts. I couldn't understand why God had let such devastation come to our family after seeing us through the trial. That had been such a victory, and now we had suffered such a terrible loss. I would have much preferred to have lost out in the trial and have my family healthy. The Psalmist tells us that the Lord will never leave us ashamed, but I was feeling ashamed, as if I had been expressing beliefs that were turning out to be false. I knew not to blame God, but I was tempted. I was so depressed I couldn't turn to my Bible for answers.

I planned on skipping church the next day and catching up on my rest and perhaps looking at the looming script pile. I waited through the night, not sleeping.

Early the next day, I felt the urge to turn on the radio. I resisted at first, but the thought came back to me so strongly that I sensed this might be the Lord's suggestion. The radio was tuned to the station on which our church broadcasts its early service. I heard one of our associate pastors, Scott Bauer, saying, "We want to pray this morning for a little girl who is being afflicted by the Adversary. She's just lost her right eye and her other eye has six tumors in it. We want to pray that all the evil that's coming against this little girl be turned aside. That the fiery darts of the wicked do not prevail. That this little girl be protected by Jesus and restored to health."

Then our senior pastor, Jack Hayford, led the congregation in prayer. "Lord, you are the God of life, the one who creates all life, and with your stripes we are healed of every affliction. Be now with this little girl . . ."

We were going to church! I decided instantly. I had forgotten how much I needed the support of other believers and now I wanted nothing so much as to be surrounded by people who would pray for Katya and us.

About this time, Michael came in to tell me that Dr. Jack Hamilton had called to see if we could come in for the eleven o'clock service. They had the same thought.

During the service, about half the congregation gathered around us and held their hands up over us, covering us with a canopy of blessing and prayer. They prayed powerfully for Katya and for the peace of her parents.

I was able to spend much of the rest of the day back at home reading my Bible and praying. I knew we weren't alone; that God had seen my distress and reached out to me through my church.

On Monday, I felt strong enough to attempt work. I went in to the studio, wondering how others would treat me. The hurtful events of the past week were still too much with me for my judgments to be fair. Sympathy angered me, and the willingness of others to go on with the day-to-day work, as I was requesting, dissatisfied me as well. The one reaction I didn't anticipate and would think long and hard about was embarrassment. I felt as if a few people had concluded that my God had let me down; that I was a loser Christian, whose beliefs, in this ultimate test, had proven untrustworthy. I'm not sure, of course, whether my colleagues were really thinking this or if I was projecting.

My director, Deveney Marking Kelley, came into my dressing room to see how I was doing. I told her I felt able to do the scenes that were backing up in which I didn't have much dialogue. I didn't feel capable of memorizing speeches, but I thought I could at least do some simple scenes.

She said, "Good. I'm glad you've come in. Maybe it will be a relief to lose yourself in your character."

When she left, I found myself upset at the idea that she thought my character and I were that loosely related. I create the character, I thought, as if to chide her. If I'm wounded, the character is wounded, too. Why doesn't she know that?

That morning, a small running feud developed between my producer-director, John Zak, and me. Since I had come to work, and my scenes really had stacked up during my absence, John wanted me to try to shoot some of the more difficult scenes as well. He suggested we might use cue-cards, which we never do on our show. I told him I couldn't; not to pressure me. He sent a number of emissaries down with scripts, who once again urged that I try the scenes and see what happened.

I became belligerent, venting my frustration to my makeup artist, Donna, about how unfair the show was being by pressuring me.

She had only one question. "Are you okay?"

The first scene I attempted called for my character, Taylor, to welcome Ridge, who was coming home to our baby and me. I was tacking up a banner over the doorway that said, "Welcome Home!" He would find me there as I finished the job, I'd step down from the ladder, pick up our baby, and say, "We love you so much!" This was supposed to be the happiest moment in my character's life.

We went through a rehearsal using a doll. (We use very small children only for the actual shooting.) During the take, with the cameras rolling, I crossed to the bassinet and picked up the baby. Immediately, I thought, "She has two eyes."

I used the emotion welling up—the glistening tears—to make it seem as if this were the happiest moment in my life. My costar, Ronn, could see what was really happening. Although he wasn't supposed to, he touched my arm to steady me as the scene went on. I felt so cheated. My happiness was being stolen from me.

As soon as the scene ended, I hurriedly gave the baby to an assistant director and went over to one of the couches on the set and broke down. A flood of tears washed away my makeup and my composure. I still hadn't fathomed how profoundly I had been affected by Katya's illness; as bad as I knew it to be, it was worse.

"Honey, sweetie," Deveney said, "why don't you go home? You're not ready yet. And how could you be? You need another week. Anyone would."

"Okay," I burbled, "but do you want to do the scene again? I'd like to finish at least one scene."

"We're going to keep the scene. You did fine. Go home and we'll see you when you are ready."

By the time I arrived home, *The Bold and the Beautiful* had sent an enormous bouquet to greet me. The note on the card thanked me for trying and said that everyone understood what I was going through and that they were rooting for me. They also sent over bath salts and perfumes in a huge basket. Once again, I felt enormously grateful for the caring people I've been privileged to work with. John Zak sent over a huge dinner for our whole family from one of my favorite pasta places complete with dessert and cappuccinos.

That afternoon, John McCook, who plays Eric Forrester on the show, his wife, Laurette, and their daughter Molly—who is Mickey's age—brought over delicious soup and brownies. Laurette said to me, "You know, when I have to haul the kids around, do the grocery shopping—take care of the one thousand and one tasks of running a family—I often complain about what a hassle it all is. I feel so ashamed now. What you are going through makes me realize how grateful I am for my children. I don't know if this helps, but I wanted you to know that your pain has helped me see things in a new perspective."

What she said did help. It gave me a first glimpse of how good could come out of Katya's illness.

I went to bed early that evening, sometime between eight and nine o'clock. I had another one of those cinematic dreams. I saw a long oak dinner table, as long as twenty feet, with people around it talking. I could hear the tinkling of plates and crystal and cutlery. Large serving platters were being passed around. I realized that I was opposite the elegantly attired gentleman from my first dream—the one who sat in the throne. I couldn't see his face for all the food being passed back and forth. I knew who he was, though, by his ruffled, lacy cuffs. Finally, the serving plates passed on and I saw his face. He was holding a bowl of fruit. He picked out a cherry and held its stem above his mouth. When I focused on the cherry, I saw it was Katya's eye. He ate the eye with mocking satisfaction. He raised his eyebrows. "How good that was," his look said. He chewed as if the more he tasted it, the better it became. "Mmmm-mmmm. Is this good? You'd better believe it is."

I awoke once again in a sweating panic. I began praying, asking God what He was trying to tell me. God promises His children that they will never be defeated, but that was the way I felt. Why were these dreams coming to me?

Terry had the idea to make decorative eye patches for the baby out of children's fabrics. We made ones with lambs, balloons, hearts, and polka dots on them—like the headbands I had made for Katya earlier. Never in all my life did I think I'd be sitting down to sew cute eye patches for my child, but it did make me feel better about her condition.

It would still be a while before I became comfortable changing the bandage over Katya's eye. When we first came home with Katya after the surgery, I told Michael and my mother that I simply couldn't do this. A week went by before Katya grabbed at the bandage and tore it off while I was holding her. I looked into the red wound and screamed. Eventually, though, I became comfortable with the sight and was Katya's preferred bandage changer.

After Terry's and my sewing session, I started to change into an exercise leotard. I kept trying to restore some semblance of normality, to reestablish the old routines. I was sitting for a moment in a chair, staring straight ahead at nothing in particular, when I saw myself outside looking over a child's shoulder toward the sidewalk.

A group of children had formed around a circle of yarn, playing marbles. From the middle of the group I saw the hand of the person rolling the shooter. The ruffled, lacy cuff. The children parted enough for me to see the elegant man flash the shooter into the midst of the marbles. Instead of one or two marbles jumping, all the marbles flew out from the ring with extraordinary force. For the first time, the elegant man spoke to me. "That's what I'm going to do. I've taken Katya's eye to scatter the eyes of faith of everyone who knows about it."

I ran to Michael, screaming. I couldn't have been more shaken. I told him about all three dreams. Fortunately, he believed I wasn't making these things up. He saw how distraught I was.

"Michael," I said, "this time I wasn't sleeping or taking a nap or anything. I was sitting there, letting my thoughts wander. Why is this happening?"

Michael suggested that I call the pastor I've relied upon so much, Dr. Jack Hamilton at Church on the Way.

Explaining what he thought was happening, Dr. Hamilton cited 2 Corinthians 10:3–5:

> For though we live in the world, we do not wage war as the world does. The weapons we fight with are not the weapons of the world. On the contrary, they have divine power to demolish strongholds. We demolish arguments and every pretension that sets itself up against the knowledge of God, and we take captive every thought to make it obedient to Christ.

Dr. Hamilton explained that I was having thoughts that were setting themselves up against the knowledge of God and that I needed to pray that these thoughts would be taken captive to the authority of Christ. Whenever these thoughts came to me, I should pray that I believed in nothing but the authority of Christ and ask Christ to dispel them.

I put Dr. Hamilton's advice into practice and a real, internal healing took place. I didn't have any more of these disturbing dreams or visions and I gradually stopped feeling like a loser Christian. I knew that God would fight my battles and that He would supply the strength I needed for these battles. Despite appearances, God was still in control.

On Monday of the following week, Katya began receiving chemotherapy. The procedure took eight hours the first day and four hours the next. Although the word "chemotherapy" conjures up horrifying scenes, the actual administration of the drugs quickly becomes routine, and Katya slept through much of the day as the anti-cancer drugs flowed into her system.

To encourage one another, Michael and I sat together close to the baby, reading our Bibles to one another and praying. In those days we went to a whole new level of intimacy and loving. Imagine the fighting couple we had been—screaming at each other through the drunken nights—sitting calmly together in a hospital room reading the Bible. Only those with "kingdom vision," of which Dr. Jack Hayford spoke on the morning when I first suspected Katya's illness, could have foreseen such a possibility.

Katya went through her first course of chemotherapy with a minimum of side effects. She did become nauseated two days after each dose of chemo and these episodes became worse as the succeeding doses had their cumulative effect. The drug Zofran, which my mother made me aware of, helped a lot, though. Katya lost her bountiful brown hair, of course, but her teeth came in right on time. Our doctors anticipated that her overall physical development would be slow, but she kept up with all the usual first-year developmental markers.

The whole family did, however, suffer unexpected side effects from Katya's treatment. As the first course of chemotherapy went on from April through June, we became increasingly isolated. Because chemotherapy depresses the body's immune system, it became critical for the whole family to avoid exposure to other diseases. We hardly went out. We felt trapped and this increased our apprehensions.

Little Bella suffered from the loss of her parents' attention. After work, I wanted only to hold Katya and sit with her for as many hours as possible. I had been instructed to keep a constant watch over her, lest any blood infections or other problems caused by the chemotherapy send her into a sudden tailspin. Bella and Mickey and Chris had to adjust to Katya being the center of attention much more than in an ordinary household with a new baby, and even that shift of focus can cause enough trouble by itself, as we all know. I tried to balance things out for Bella, but I'm not sure how successful I was.

The doctors demanded vigilance for a reason. One day, Katya began running a fever and refused her late-afternoon bottle. After four hours, she had become lethargic and wasn't crying so much as whimpering. We called our doctor and he told us to come immediately to the hospital. These were the signs we had been warned about.

We arrived at the hospital that night at 10:00 P.M. The doctors ran a number of tests and came back with the report that Katya needed a blood transfusion. Fortunately, my friend Scott Baker had called the week before offering to donate his A positive blood should Katya ever need it. (Michael's father and I were the only ones in the family with A positive blood. I had lost too much weight to donate and Eddie hadn't given his donation yet, as he soon would.) We told the doctors that Scott had been in and had already left a donation for Katya.

Evidently, Scott's blood is a rare type. The doctors and nurses involved in the transfusion kept raving about the great blood our friend had.

The new procedure scared us, of course. But as the blood started transfusing into my baby, her pale gray, fishy yellow skin and purple lips turned bright pink and red within thirty seconds. Michael and I both had the same thought: There is "power in the blood." If Scott's blood had such potency to restore Katya's physical life, how much more miraculously could Jesus's blood restore spiritual life!

Within an hour, Katya was playing, slugging down a bottle, and doing everything in her coy power to attract the nurses' attention.

She still had to stay in the hospital another two days, to make sure the bacterial infection she had contracted was completely gone. By this time, I had gotten behind a full twenty shows at work and had to go in each morning. So Michael stayed with the baby for those two nights, sleeping in a none-too-comfortable chair. This man, whom the woman who had married us pronounced a "macho jerk," couldn't have been more caring with our afflicted daughter. Michael's renewed faith had brought an amazing change in his own life, too.

During the baby's illness, photographers continued to camp outside our rented North Hollywood home. We felt like we were being stalked. One time, I reached into the bushes and pulled out a photographer from his ill-concealed hiding place. "What do you want, you idiot?" I asked. "Do you want to see the baby without her eye?"

Ever since moving back to Los Angeles, we had hoped to buy an-other house. The pressure of the media gave us a final push. We found a home in a secluded location, where our family's privacy could be restored. We still have to be on guard, but we are much happier since the move.

The new home has large, wide-open rooms, which I thought would suit Katya well. I wanted her to have a maximum amount of freedom, the ability to crawl this way and that without feeling as though she was constantly going to bump into things. (As things have developed, she's never had this sort of trouble. She has enough sight in her good eye to spot her pacifier in the midst of a toy-strewn haystack. Her depth perception and long-distance sight have remained strong as well.)

Over the period of Katya's chemotherapy, I thought a lot about the Book of Job. I had never liked reading it before. In fact, nearly my whole Bible had been annotated and highlighted before I ever made a note alongside a passage from Job. Now I saw how clearly Job draws back the curtain on the suffering of the innocent. Job loved God. He had done nothing wrong. He was a righteous man. But God allowed Satan to test Job, taking away his wealth, his family, and even his own health. His wife advises Job to curse God and die; his friends advise him to repent of whatever sin has caused this calamity. Job chooses instead to ask God for a simple explanation.

God doesn't so much explain as assert His prerogatives. He is God and His ways are too high above ours to be understood. Still, His love for Job is genuine and He provides twice the blessings Job once possessed.

Reading the Book of Job, I knew that its author understood exactly what I was going through. I was comforted at the thought that God does not commission suffering—that's the work of Satan—but, like Job, I am still mystified by God's allowing it, especially in the case of an innocent like Katya or a righteous man like Job. I know that a world without the possibility of sin and evil would also be a world in which we could not return God's love. According to Genesis, humankind's free choice brought about our spiritual death and even the corruption of nature. God foresaw all this and yet went ahead with creation, because the glory of the creation's redemption, its restoration to its pure state in the days to come, will more than justify all our present sorrows.

When we are suffering, these concepts, however accurate, don't always bring much comfort. It's at these moments that we are most in need of small, personal signs that restore our faith in a master design that goes far beyond what we ourselves can fathom.

One such small sign came about in September. Children's Hospital Los Angeles and the Matthew Ashford family had begun putting together a fund-raiser for the victims of retinoblastoma. Michael and I pitched in to help. We had seen $50,000 doctor bills for two-day stays in the hospital. Our insurance covered these, but we realized that some parents had to cope with the double crisis of the disease itself and its catastrophic financial demands. The Miracles Fund-Raiser, as it came to be called, honored Rosie O'Donnell for all her good work with children and raised more than half a million dollars for the victims of retinoblastoma. I remember Leslie Nielsen bidding more than thirty thousand dollars for the simple statue we had presented to Rosie. As the Matthew Ashford family stood on the platform with their baby, alongside us and another victimized family, the Zinnemen's, we could see how real this made the devastating effects of the disease for those in the audience. A great good was beginning to emerge out of this terrible evil.

On my mother's birthday, September 20, a Monday, Katya went in for her every-three-weeks eye exam. A new tumor had begun growing on top of her optic nerve, right around the edge of an old tumor the chemo had destroyed.

I felt unwilling to go back into the intensity of grief that our first struggle gave rise to, and I resisted the whole idea of chemotherapy. I told Dr. Murphree, "We can't do this. Are you sure it's necessary? I thought the chemotherapy worked."

Michael was crying. We were both shattered.

Dr. Murphree tried to calm me down, but I persisted so much in my objections that he finally said, "Mrs. Tylo, Hunter, if that's really the way you feel, you don't have to go through it again. We can set up the operating room and remove Katya's other eye. That way she'll be safe from retinoblastoma and you won't have to worry about it anymore."

I knew he was being kind by being tough. "All right," I said. "But first, give us a chance to pray. We didn't really have time to do that before. I'd like it if we could see what God can do before we start the chemo again."

Dr. Murphree agreed to wait. We would have a week to gather our spiritual resources and do all the praying we could. Then there'd be another exam, and the chemotherapy would start once more if the tumor remained.

On the way home in the car, I called Carla. She reminded me that David had killed Goliath but then became weak later. I felt David's temptation. I knew that I could either grow stronger through this latest test or fall away from my faith completely.

Carla also reminded me that we needed our church around us.

Once again, I called Dr. Hamilton. He said that often it seems darkest just before God does something to show His brilliance. He also reminded me that God might choose to work through the doctors. I shouldn't box God into a corner, predicting how God must act.

On Tuesday, I went back into my prayer closet and lay on the floor on my side, not prostrate before the Lord but in the fetal position. I could hardly pray. I was only moaning out my hope that God would spare Katya another course of chemotherapy; that a test would show this was unnecessary.

I felt that God was telling me to pray over the baby and anoint her with oil. I was to wait and trust Him. An inexplicable hope came to me that Katya wouldn't need another course of chemo.

After I prayed, I talked with Dr. Hamilton once more. He was meeting with a group of elders. They were planning to pray together about what to do. He would call me back the next morning.

I started to do what I felt God had instructed me to do. Michael and I prayed over Katya and anointed her with oil. Every time we touched her, she screamed. We felt we were fighting a real battle against a stubborn opponent. The passage from Matthew 17:21 came to my mind: This kind does not go out but by prayer and fasting.

In the morning, when Dr. Hamilton called, he said, "We prayed yesterday and I've talked to the men this morning, and we're all agreed: We feel 'this kind does not go out but by prayer and fasting.'" He went on to tell me that the church leaders would be joining us in a vegetables-only fast for the healing of Katya. We would fast from then until the weekend, pray over Katya together on Saturday, and then break our fast together in celebration of the Lord's action. We could be certain God would answer this prayer, whatever His answer turned out to be.

I called Dr. Murphree and told him that Michael and I were praying and that others were praying with us. I had the words of James 5:14–15 in mind. "Is any one of you sick? He should call the elders of the church to pray over him and anoint him with oil in the name of the Lord. And the prayer offered in faith will make the sick person well; the Lord will raise him up." I reaffirmed to the doctor that we wanted Katya to be reexamined before she was given chemotherapy.

Dr. Murphree said once more that he respected my faith, and since we were going to reexamine Katya he would move the new course of treatment—whatever it happened to be—to Thursday.

Dr. Hamilton and the church elders kept faith with us. All of us fasted and then joined together to pray over Katya on Saturday. We felt a tremendous solidarity and hope.

Michael and I broke our fast on Saturday night, along with those praying with us. Because we had an additional few days before Katya's next exam, I asked Michael to resume fasting with me until that time. This was something we were going to do alone, without telling anyone.

We returned to fasting and a continuous immersion in prayer. I watched over Katya for as many hours as possible, continuing to pray for her, to lay hands on her, and to anoint her with oil. I played audiotapes of lullabies whose lyrics came from the Scriptures. One was from Psalm 103:

> Praise the Lord, O my soul,
> and forget not all his benefits—
> who forgives all your sins
> and heals all your diseases.

For the next several days, I would feel as if I were fighting against an enemy of titanic strength. I remember reading the account of Jesus' healing of Jairus's daughter. A servant comes out from the house and says it's too late, the girl has already died. Jesus replies, "Do not be afraid, only believe." I felt "only believe" was a message especially relevant for me, and this was reinforced when one of our friends, Sam Jones, brought by a book of teachings by the Puritan clergyman Michael Wigglesworth (1631–1705), who wrote *Meat Out of the Eater, or Meditations Concerning the Necessity, End, and Usefulness of Afflictions Unto God's Children* (1669). Throughout his writing, Wigglesworth takes as his theme the words "only believe." I couldn't help but think this was more than a coincidence, and the reinforced message of "only believe" kept me going in that direction.

I also realized from all the accounts in the Gospels of Jesus' healing that God loves to heal; it's His delight. I kept returning over and over to the accounts of miracles in the Gospels. Jesus required belief, yes, but His willingness to heal disease never varied.

Over the next few days, during the early part of the week before Thursday's eye exam, I did have times when my strength nearly failed. I was praying over Katya every night, fasting, and keeping a nearly continuous vigil by her bedside. Sometimes I wondered whether God saw all the effort I was putting in to this, whether I was simply foolish, and whether there was anyone there to notice. Then I found the story in the Gospels in which Christ is praying on a mountain while His disciples are on the Sea of Galilee, rowing hard against a storm. The disciples feel abandoned to a dismal fate when they see Jesus passing them by, walking on the water. They call out to Him for help. He stops, gets into their boat, and reassures them that He saw them even while He was praying. I was reassured once again that God was watching, even when I couldn't feel God's presence.

On Wednesday evening, our spiritual battle intensified to its greatest height. About 11:00 P.M., Katya became fitful. I prayed for the Lord to take away her fever. "Lord rebuke this fever. Let the peace of Christ and the healing of Christ come into this child's body." I put my hands on Katya's forehead as I said these words.

I took my hands off Katya and suddenly she started laughing. Great big belly laughs. Laughter as I had never heard it from my own child.

The phone rang right then, and it was Carla. It was now one o'clock in the morning my time, three o'clock in Dallas. She said, "I don't know why, but I felt I needed to call you. I have a verse for you. I tried to go back to sleep, but I couldn't. So just listen to this. It's pretty simple, but somehow I know you're meant to hear it.

'There is much joy in the presence of the Lord.' That's it. Does it mean anything to you?"

"Listen," I said, and I put the phone close to Katya, who was still giggling up a divine storm.

Carla and I wept together. She was so glad she called, and I was, too, of course. By phone, she was present as a witness at one of the most remarkable things I have ever seen or heard. I went to bed totally at peace. I knew Katya was in the Lord's hands—even if we had to go forward with the chemotherapy. I doubted we would. For the time being, I feared nothing.

The next day, while Katya was being examined by the doctors, Michael and I read the Bible to one another. We were supremely confident that God had worked a miracle and that Katya would not need chemotherapy. I remember Michael saying, "I bet the doctor is going to swallow his stethoscope." He had found a Bible verse about the Lord performing a work almost impossible to believe.

The doctor had been in the examination room for longer than normal. When he returned, he had two photographs in his hands.

"I'm sorry," he said. "I didn't mean to put you through anything unnecessary. I can't quite believe this. The tumor I was seeing last week isn't there now. We have this new fluorescent test. That's why I was gone so long. I performed the second test. We inject this dye and it causes any tumor that exists to fluoresce. Here, you see this picture from last week?"

We looked at last week's photo again, with the menacing egg-white tumor clearly visible.

"Now look at these two. This week's photo taken in the same way, and then the fluorescent one. As I said, maybe it was just a misdiagnosis, but what I saw last week or thought I saw isn't there now."

"So no chemo?" I asked.

"Certainly not. When she wakes up, you can take her home. I hope every exam goes this well. As I said, I'm more than a little surprised."

On October 4, at Katya's dedication at our church, we had an opportunity to share our joy in this miracle with the whole congregation. Dr. Hayford asked Michael to tell the story, but before Michael did, the pastor, making an important point, said, "We don't discount doctors. God uses doctors, but in this case God intervened directly."

Michael then gave an eloquent account of God's mercy on us. He quoted the passage, Acts 13:41, that he had found right before the doctor announced that the tumor was gone.

> Look, you scoffers,
> wonder and perish,
> for I am going to do something in your days
> that you would never believe,
> even if someone told you.

29

We wanted to believe the miracle signaled the end of Katya's fight, but even as we praised God for it, we knew that we'd have to keep living by faith.

Katya's next exam came only a week after her surprising healing, and the one after that came two weeks later. The doctors were so mystified by the appearance and disappearance of the tumor that they wanted to make sure their instruments weren't betraying them.

We brought Katya in for yet another exam on November 15. Dr. Murphree came out with the photograph. "You see this shape?" he said. "This milky haze way over here? It's a new tumor and it's growing fast. I could laser it, but that would take away a good percentage of her remaining sight. I'm afraid we'll have to do another course of chemotherapy. I've seen this kind before and there's no time to lose."

Once again, Michael and I were crushed. Katya's struggle with cancer had been so desperate that we wanted to believe that it couldn't return. Our need to deny the possibility set us up for huge letdowns. Besides, we had prayed before and God had taken away the last tumor. Why not now?

"But Dr. Murphree," I asked, "what about last time? You saw what happened. Let us pray. God can do it again."

"What I was trying to say," Dr. Murphree said, "was that this tumor is different. The last one was growing slowly. This one isn't. It's growing faster than any of us would like."

"But if God's ready to heal the cancer, what difference does it make if it takes an extra couple of days? If she's healed, she's healed."

"Hunter, Michael, you can pray all you like tonight, but tomorrow we ought to begin another course of chemotherapy. I'm afraid we don't have the luxury of being patient this time."

"But we have to," I said, insisting. "We just have to. You saw last time. You *saw*."

"Hunter, I did what you are asking about nine months ago for another mother. We buried that child last week. If you insist on waiting, then pick out a casket."

Once again, Dr. Murphree knew when I needed to be shocked back into reality. His strong words broke my frantic resistance. "But we can pray tonight," I finally said weakly.

"All you want. But this time, we have to keep God to a schedule or allow us to be His agents." Then he hugged me with so much empathy. "I'm so sorry I was so abrupt. I know this is hard. I know . . . I know . . ."

We went home and prayed our hearts out that night. I found the passage about King Hezekiah in 2 Kings 20, when the prophet Isaiah predicts his death. King Hezekiah then pleads the righteous life he has led, and asks the Lord that years be added to his life. Hezekiah is instructed to take a lump of figs and apply it to his boil. He is indeed healed, and God adds fifteen years to his life.

After reading this passage, I spoke again with my spiritual counselor, Dr. Hamilton, repeating what Dr. Murphree had said. I was still confused about whether to allow the chemotherapy to go forward.

Dr. Hamilton reinforced the doctor's words about physicians being God's agents. "Don't put God in a box," Dr. Hamilton said. "He often—in fact, most often—uses natural means to accomplish his purposes. He made the world a place where such means would be available."

I thought again of the lump of figs. This time, it seemed, we would have to rely on the medicines that God had given humankind the ingenuity to discover.

I can't say I was pleased to watch Katya receiving her chemo the next day. I felt beaten up by the months of anxiety and worry. I was concerned, too, that this next course of chemotherapy would have more devastating effects on her health, since the side effects of the drugs can accumulate with additional treatments.

Katya went through this next course of chemotherapy much more successfully than the first, actually. She didn't have the nausea that usually came the second day after the drugs were administered. She seemed to breeze through it.

This encouraged us, and our faith seemed to rebound more quickly after the inevitable bouts of despair. When December 22 rolled around, and Katya was due for the second dose of chemo in the three-dose cycle, we resisted the treatments only slightly. Dr. Murphree was pleased to announce that the tumor he had seen was dead. Still, he didn't know what might be there on the microscopic level; it was best to complete the three-dose course.

What a Christmas gift to give a child, I thought.

Once again, though, Katya experienced almost no side effects from the treatment. She was able to go see Santa the next day.

The third dose was scheduled for January. The doctors found that Katya's blood counts were too low to administer the drugs. They put off the treatment, thinking that her red blood cells might rebound with a little more time—or they could give Katya another blood transfusion, if necessary.

We didn't want to see Katya transfused again, because the procedure, as helpful as it had been the first time, always carries risks. We prayed that Katya's counts would come back up. And we worried about the winter flu season. For Katya to rebound from her past chemotherapy, she had to stay healthy on every other front. Throughout this time, we were praying for Katya to remain immune to the colds and flu that began swirling through schools and workplaces.

Close to Katya's first birthday, the family began to come down with the stomach flu. Bella first. She even contracted a chest infection that required antibiotics—the pink amoxicillin so familiar in households with young children. Mickey and Chris came down with it next, and finally Michael and me.

Katya never contracted the flu. She stayed healthy, and her red blood cells came back strong.

For Katya's first birthday, I ordered a two-tier cake from Hanson's that was decorated like a carousel, with toy horses, pearl-draped reins, a shiny foil canopy, and airbrushed mirror images. The cake was twelve inches in diameter and cost ninety dollars. I knew it was extravagant, but I also knew that Katya's first birthday might be the only one we celebrated. By and large, I had kept myself from thinking of her possible death, but my understanding that we might lose her had grown as the chemotherapy went on and the new tumor had appeared. So I was happy to splurge. Any parent will understand why.

Katya took the third dose of chemotherapy in stride—a literal stride, for she was starting to walk now, right on time, at age one. She could not only spot her pacifier in a crowded room, but she could see her tricycle at one end of our long driveway from the opposite end. Frankly, I kept expecting her to be much more impaired. Her eye did suffer from a constant slight shifting termed nystagmus, which results from the brain trying to focus around the scarred areas on her retina. (It has since stopped.) Dr. Murphree assured us that while we saw the eye moving, Katya was seeing a stable image. She behaved and continues to behave much as any little girl her age, laughing and playing with nonstop energy. She can point to images in books and correctly identify them. "Birdy." "Ai-pwane." "Sun."

After the chemo ended, I began praying in February of 1999 for a sign as to Katya's future. I wanted to be reassured that she'd find her way in school, in life. One evening, I prayed about this matter until I fell asleep.

The next morning, Michael woke me up. "Hunter, what kind of animal looks like a cat, but has spots, a small tail, really long, lanky legs, and tall, tufted ears? A bobcat?"

"I don't know. What do you mean?"

"Well, come look. There's one in our driveway."

"There's a wild cat in our driveway?"

"Yes. The kids have all seen him."

"The kids. Are the kids okay? Keep them away from that *cat!*"

"They're fine. You're going to miss it. Come on."

I scrambled out of bed, but not in time. The wild cat had loped across our driveway and up the side of the hill into the woods next to our house.

I went to bed that evening still thinking about the strange appearance of a wild cat in our driveway. We are located way out in the boondocks, but I didn't know we had bobcats or mountain lions around. In the middle of the night, I felt I should get up and look up "bobcat" in the encyclopedia.

I went into Bella's room to get the *Compton's Children's Encyclopedia*—our adult reference books were in the outer wing we've converted into an office. "See *Lynx*," the bobcat entry read. I looked up "lynx." The very first sentence defining the animal said that the lynx is so sharp-sighted, it is said to have the power of seeing through a stone wall. Later, I also checked in our computer's encyclopedia. It added that the bobcat is common to our area, but the lynx itself, with its tufted ears, usually appears farther north.

That night, when I found this out, I collapsed on my knees in gratitude. Of course, I don't know if what Michael and the children saw was a lynx or the more common bobcat. I also don't know if a lynx wandered far from its usual habitat to end up on our driveway. Maybe the creature escaped from some distant neighbor's private zoo. I do know that God used its appearance, telling me to look up the creature's characteristics, in order to reassure me that one day, in many respects that I'm sure I cannot imagine now, Katya will be lynx-eyed. I was also enabled to look through what often seems to be the stone wall of Katya's future and see light.

Since this roller-coaster ride we have had so many ups and downs—elations and disappointments. All I can tell you is, I wouldn't trade one of the precious moments, even the grievous ones, away. I suppose you could say I now treasure every moment with my children, even those temper-tantrum-the-house-is-a-wreck days. (A day I will forever be grateful for was August 26, 1999—Katya had her Port-A-Cath removed.) However, her life is in constant threat until she is three years old, when her retina is more mature and cell division has stopped.

Through everything that's happened with Katya, I've learned to face the ultimate question: What if I lose her?

This question, in turn, has made me face another: To whom do our lives belong? Is Katya's life mine or her own? Is my life my own?

I think of Psalm 139.

O Lord, thou hast searched me, and known me . . . thou hast covered me in my mother's womb . . . My substance was not hid from thee, when I was made in secret . . . and in thy book all my members were written, which in continuance were fashioned, when as yet there was none of them.

The Lord has fashioned us all. He created us and so our lives belong to Him. The darkness of blindness is much less a problem than the blindness of the dark and destructive illusions I lived by for many years. The Lord looks on each of our hearts and sees us aright. He determines the length of our lives—all our lives—by considerations that are too high for us to understand.

What if I lost Katya? Well, what if I lost my oldest, Chris, who is just now leaving the nest? Or Mickey or Izabella or my husband Michael? Or my own life for that matter? The irony of having once chosen against bearing a child for my own selfish convenience and then begging, praying, and believing for my youngest one to survive reminds me: I didn't give myself life. God did. He created me and everyone else and perfectly rules our days as we give them to Him. Life is not in our control, and it's not meant to be. It's in God's hands.

God loves to redeem the broken aspects of our lives as well. With everything I've been through—from the near destruction of my marriage to fighting for my baby's life—I've learned something more valuable than gold:

GOD LOVES LIFE.

My hope has come to lie not in this world, with its provisional successes and failures, but in a "sure hope" of an eternity with God. In the ultimate act of love, God sent His Son into the world to save us—we only need to receive Jesus and follow what He taught. I've found life in God's love. It's the ultimate miracle.